5.⁰⁰

Music

8/18

To Chuck—
With pleasure,

Leslie Rubinkowski

Impersonating Elvis

Impersonating Elvis

LESLIE RUBINKOWSKI

8/14/99

ff

FABER AND FABER
BOSTON   LONDON

Library of Congress Cataloging-in-Publication Data

Rubinkowski, Leslie
    Impersonating Elvis / Leslie Rubinkowski.
        p   cm.
    ISBN 0-571-19911-9 (cloth)
    1. Elvis Presley impersonators.   2. Popular culture—
    United States.   I. Title
    ML400.R85 1997
    792.7—dc21   96-51608
                                                      CIP
                                                      MN

Jacket design by Peter Blaiwas
Printed in the United States of America

For Steve

Contents

Acknowledgments

J couldn't have written this book without the help of both impersonators and the people who follow them. Many had reason to be skeptical, they told me, because journalists had made fun of them before. But that didn't stop them from sharing their stories, and I'm grateful for their faith in what I wanted to do. I interviewed dozens of impersonators during the course of my research. They were kind enough to answer my questions, and patient enough to let me into their lives. I could not include everyone I spoke to, but their opinions and emotions helped me to explain the impersonator world.

A few people were a big help. Jerome Marion, one of the first impersonators I interviewed, was an endless and generous source of information, insight, and support. In the early days of my research, Rick Marino provided advice and many names of people to talk to, not to mention enough funny stories to fill another book. Denese Dody also provided help and good humor; hearing her laugh on the phone made my day. Steve Chuke always had time to talk and enlighten, even while waiting on three customers at his jewelry store.

Dennis Stella deserves special thanks. He consented to many long visits and interviews, and he always told his story with candor and a sense of humor. Gail Wrzaskowski and her daughter, Jenna, also helped me a great deal, and, with Shelley Foeckler and Chris and Kelly Hottinger, cheerfully suffered endless questions about real life and artificial hair.

Thanks also goes to Anne Dubuisson, my first agent, who believed in this project from the start, and to my current agent, Diana Finch, who shared that same sense of possibility.

I owe a great deal to Valerie Cimino, my editor at Faber and Faber. She fielded questions and eased concerns with great patience and skill, and made editing a 600-page manuscript into a book as painless as it can ever be.

Patsy Sims urged me to undertake the book and encouraged me until I finished. She was a great teacher and friend, spending hours reading drafts and always managing to cheer me up on those days I had decided Steve Chuke was right—I had entered some sort of jungle.

My husband, Steve Urbanski, read countless drafts, offered endless advice and encouragement, and watched *Girl Happy* with me more times than anyone has a right to expect.

Impersonating Elvis

Introduction

*O*ne night I was talking long-distance to an Elvis impersonator named Steve Chuke. We were discussing the quality of his fellow Elvises when he experienced a revelation strong enough to make him change the subject.

"You know who you remind me of?" he asked.

I had to admit I didn't. I only knew who he reminded me of.

"You remind me of the lady who followed the apes, OK?" he said. "In other words, what you're doing is, you're following the Elvis performers."

It took me a moment before I realized that he was comparing me to Dian Fossey, the late animal behaviorist portrayed in the film *Gorillas in the Mist*. And I knew instantly what he meant. He was right—I followed a lot of Elvis impersonators. I spent more time with people who imitate Elvis than most productive citizens would care to contemplate, or could even imagine. And I had a blast.

First, though, I had a question. This book didn't happen because I was an Elvis obsessive. It's just that one night several years ago I saw a man on my television dressed up like Elvis. He was looking into the camera, his legs cocked into a little lunge. He looked pleased with himself. But he looked like somebody else. Somebody dead. Somebody people would ridicule and disrespect. Why, I wondered, would anyone do a thing like that to themselves—or to Elvis?

Writing about something is the best way I know to figure it out. So I wrote an article about a local guy named Arnel Pomp for the now-defunct *Pittsburgh Press*. At a Marriott one Friday night we rode the elevator to the nightclub where he would perform. Arnel meditated. He burst into song. In the lobby, his bodyguard—his bodyguard!—brushed past onlookers. I thought people would laugh. No one did. In fact, women seemed to examine the placement of his jumpsuit's studs as if they were trying to decipher some secret code meant for only them. The photographer assigned to the story looked around his camera and grinned. "Isn't this a kick?" he said. It was, but I sensed that it was also a lot more.

3

In January 1994, I began full-time work on this book. A few months later, I called Dennis Stella, an insurance salesman from outside Chicago who was singing in a show I planned to attend. The first thing he did after I told him what I was doing was to invite me to his house for a party. He promised there would be a lot of food, and he said he had just started his impersonating career, and he didn't know how things would turn out. This was exactly what I was looking for: a guy wild enough to become someone else in order to find himself, but human enough to worry about being a proper host. I told him I would come to his party. It would be two years before I left.

A few notes about reporting: I traveled all over the country researching this book, from Las Vegas, Nevada, to Oxford, Mississippi, to Erlanger, Kentucky, to Memphis, Tennessee. Along the way I accumulated about 25,000 frequent flyer miles, learned how to snap my arm the way Elvis did when he sang the refrain of "Sweet Caroline," and tried on, after much coercion, a synthetic-hair pompadour with built-in sideburns. It's less painful when I think of it as research.

I witnessed nearly all of the events in this book, which I worked on in varying degrees for about four years. Things I did not see myself—for example, the opening scene in which Dennis forgot his wig—I reconstructed through interviews with the participants and repeated visits to the locations where the actions took place. All but a handful of the impersonator performances I've described were the ones that I attended. Once I began to count how many times I'd heard Elvis impersonators sing "Polk Salad Annie" but stopped when I realized the total would number in the hundreds.

You'll no doubt notice that sometimes I surface among the impersonators. I'm not there because I find myself fascinating—it was just that in those scenes, my presence felt like the best way to show the personalities and humanity of the impersonators. Being there gave the impersonators someone to play off of or showboat to, and I hope it gives the reader a conduit into the impersonator world.

Elvis Dreams

1

Elvis Heads

*D*ennis Stella was halfway to Milwaukee before he realized he had forgotten his hair.

He woke that July morning thinking but not dreaming of Las Vegas, his mind chiming with song lyrics and the step-kick intricacies of dance moves and mild panic and the sense that if he wished to succeed he needed to remember everything, including many things he wasn't even sure he knew. The deeper he got, the more he understood how little he knew. But he did understand one truth: The only thing he could safely forsake was himself.

Yet despite his doubts, Dennis left home a happy man. He rose early and by early afternoon had packed his gear into the electric-red Corvette he had bought four months before in an attempt to make his life more exciting. When he felt ready to leave, he crossed his living room filled with black leather furniture and punched in the security alarm's four-digit code. In the driveway he eased into his Corvette's scarlet leather interior and backed out onto a narrow street that was really more of an alley, beginning his trip out of Calumet City, Illinois. He drove past elegant stone homes and smaller bungalows like his own, down wide streets shaded with elms and split by grassy medians thick with trees. Around him people went about the small transactions of their lives. They pulled into gas stations and strolled into the sandwich shops, pizza joints, and small strip plazas that line the route Dennis took. But nothing he saw made much of an impression; he found himself in a strange state of feeling anxious about what he was going to do and overjoyed that he was finally going to do it. He took the exit for Interstate 294 and aimed the Corvette for the Wisconsin state line, speeding north.

An even greater boundary stretched ahead. Dennis aimed to change his life, and to do it he needed to transform himself. He had begun two months earlier by mailing a videotape. He and 150 other people from places like Santa Cruz, California, and Cullman, Alabama, and Yonkers, New York, submitted videos of themselves wearing jumpsuits and black leather and hair of varying realities to the fifth annual Elvis Performers Showcase/Festival of the Elvis Presley Impersonators International Association. Its motto: "Continuing the Legacy of the King." Forty-eight people—forty-six men, a petite blonde from Saint Albans, England, and a thirteen-year-old boy from Brooklyn—qualified in 1994. And Dennis, on his first try, was one of them. Being chosen by the EPIIA was not only a great honor and responsibility, but it also presented a chance for major networking and media access. After all, eleven twenty-year veterans were expected to attend. The winner of the previous year's Images of Elvis Inc. international competition in Memphis, Tennessee—the Miss America of impersonator pageants—had signed up to sing two sets. In fact, so many performers applied that the organizers decided to add a third day of shows for the first time in the event's history. Enough buzz resulted that the national television station TBS agreed to fly in a camera crew from Atlanta.

What it all meant could disrupt anyone's sleep. Forty-eight contenders would converge on the Imperial Palace Hotel in Las Vegas, paying their own way and singing for free, angling to set themselves apart by trying to look, sound, and act like someone else—a man who had been dead for nearly twenty years. Dennis had performed before, but this was different. That July weekend for the first time, he planned to take the stage in a Las Vegas nightclub filled with hundreds of people sunk into plush round booths and say, in effect: Accept me as I am as somebody else. It was like stepping into a hall of mirrors where everywhere you looked you saw yourself, except that sometimes your reflection looked better.

Still, that day Dennis felt in control. He had a habit—a bad one—of running late, so he had prepared: drawn up lists, packed his bags the night before, tried to get some sleep. He had allowed himself an hour and fifteen minutes beyond the two hours it took to drive to Milwaukee, where he would pick up his girlfriend, Gail. From there they would fly to Vegas. His only worry was his voice. A cold had rubbed his throat raw and after a month had sent him to the doctor, who prescribed anti-biotics and a nasal spray that smelled, to Dennis's amusement, like roses. He was rushed enough that morning to forget about taking them.

An hour into the trip and roughly forty miles from home, he remembered. He was on the Tri-State Tollway, just past the exit for O'Hare International Airport. He glanced at the Corvette's clock and congratulated himself—right on time. He swiveled in his red leather seat to find the prescriptions and then, trying to ease his troubled mind, began to inventory every essential item shoehorned into the back of the car:

Suitcase packed with shorts, tank tops, and swim trunks; karaoke machine; case containing sixty karaoke tapes; black Spanish Flower jumpsuit with emerald glass cabochons and gold studs; matching black boots; big black belt; white Pinwheel jumpsuit with ruby glass cabochons and gold studs; matching white boots; big white belt; black pompadour with paste-on sideburns.

Black pompadour with paste-on sideburns.

Black pompadour with paste-on sideburns.

Dennis's heart seized. He clutched the wheel with one hand and flailed around the back hatch with the other, looking for the black bag that contained the hair. About twenty miles north of the O'Hare exit, there was a oasis overpass that sold necessities of modern travel—gasoline, maps, newspapers, all-beef hot dogs. Dennis pulled into its parking lot and popped the Corvette's trunk. He pawed its contents. It took him fifteen seconds to realize what he hadn't done. It would take him much longer to fully grasp what he had suddenly become: a man whose world had slammed off its axis because he forgot to pack his wig.

By year's end, Dennis Stella would question every belief he held about his dignity and resilience, about his resistance and ability to change, and, at times, he would doubt his very identity. In the months to come many would recognize the day Dennis forgot his hair as a turning point, a milestone in his evolution. But on that day, staring into the trunk, all Dennis knew was that he hated himself. He thought: *Dennis, you just can't do it. You can never do anything right. You always gotta screw up. You can never just be cool and come up on time and have everything and be prepared. You always gotta screw up—just doing things by the seat of your pants.*

It was a pleasant day for a crisis of conscience, warm and with an easy southwesterly wind. Just ahead the interstate elbowed toward Wisconsin. Dennis cooled for a while on the gum-stuck asphalt, thinking black thoughts. His appearance revealed nothing of his inner struggle. He looked exactly like what he was: a man brooding next to his car. To be precise, a thirty-seven-year-old man, six feet tall, deep tan, broad shoulders, brown eyes, wavy brown hair and an inch or so of sideburn, neatly trimmed. Nothing about his looks or his actions would arouse unusual interest or hint at fires within. Nothing about Dennis Stella would likely remind anybody of anyone. Say, maybe, Elvis Presley.

Which was precisely his problem.

Understand this: Hair means everything.

A full-bore pompadour—black with no blue sheen, long and with a shock crossing the forehead—signifies a conscious commitment to impersonating Elvis. No one looks like that by accident. Such hair reinforces the wearer's own identity by erasing it. Among impersonators and those who love them there exists a hierarchy of hair. Obviously, natural black is best. Wigs, styled right, can work. And hair that no one notices— that is, the hair that most men and women are born with—is almost always wrong. The equation balances like this: The amount of Elvis happening inside a person's head corresponds exactly to the blackness and volume of hair on top of it. That simple, that impossible.

"What people don't realize is that a lot of Elvis impersonators are very nineties—they're up to times, like with the way they're dressed, their clothes," said Irv Cass, a pompadoured impersonator from Niles, Michigan. "But if you do it for a living, to get that most natural look, you have to have your hair, without the wig, and real sideburns. I'd rather go with the real look, and when I get offstage, come across as being as real as possible. Do a good show and put up with a little guff on the side, rather than wear the wig and the sideburns. Now I'm not saying I hold it against the guys who do, because there are guys who do the wig and the sideburns and they're very good. But I've chosen to put up with the guff on the street, and it's hard for me to walk through the mall."

Sideburns punctuate the statement the hair makes like parentheses set apart a word—*I am serious about my Elvis. (Really.)* Any fool can slick back hair to hide a pompadour, but sideburns defy subterfuge. For that reason they matter even more. "You can't go out there without 'em!" said Fred Wolfe, an Elvis from Detroit who once wore a long platinum shag and sang Kiss covers in a rock band. "Otherwise, people won't believe.

"See, you can have everything but one part of the illusion and it's just not gonna work. That's the trademark: the hair and the sideburns. I mean, Elvis was always known for his sideburns—*Hey, you, sideburns, get over here!*—ever since he was a younger guy. If you don't have the sideburns, you're just—*you* know."

Ronny Craig, formerly Craig Plueger, a cattle buyer from LaCrosse, Wisconsin, wore a pompadour for two years. His hair grew so long he had to pull it into a ponytail when he played basketball. People notice Elvis hair on a man six feet four inches tall, with the face and physique of a film star and the greatest asset an impersonator can possess: a sense of humor. Anyone who saw him later in his career, his light brown hair cut short with no sideburns, would never suspect he impersonated Elvis. Which to him meant he was doing something right.

"You know," he said, "I'm the kind of guy that, if someone insults my girlfriend, I'll defend her honor. Let alone take a potshot at my hair."

The thing that changed Ronny Craig two years into his Elvis career happened in the back of a 1956 Cadillac on an Iowa summer's day. He had been hired to appear as Elvis in a parade—dress in a jumpsuit, wave and smile at the Iowans.

About seventy-five people came to see. The air was scorched and silent. The car oozed through the crowd. Ronny waved. Out of all the faces a little boy, maybe five years old, leaned forward. To this day Ronny thinks an adult put the boy up to it, but when he opened his mouth to yell it was a child's voice that cracked open the afternoon, it was pure uncut innocence that screamed: "Get a life."

"And I'll tell you what," Ronny said. "He was right. He was right. It hurt me so much. Because here I am, robbing Elvis. I'm giving him respect. How far do you want to take it? How serious do you want to take it? But that's when I knew. Either be an entertainer, and give respect to Elvis, do your own thing—or get out." Now he performs up to seven twenty-minute shows a day at the Branson Music Mall in Branson, Missouri, right in the middle of a Wal-Mart. He sings for tips and sells cassettes of himself singing Elvis and country tunes. He admits it is not glamorous. But at least he tries to succeed as himself. "I went down, rubbed shoulders with the Wayne Newtons and the Glen Campbells and like, oh, wow: I have a chance!" he said. "I got a chance to *be* something."

Some purists bemoan improper hair as an omen of decline. As Tony Grova, a twenty-year veteran from Newark, New Jersey said, "Well, everybody's got a right to perform—I mean, God bless them, you know.

But when they start throwing on a wig and fake sideburns and stuff, and they go out and put clothes together, they just get on stage because they think Elvis impersonators make a lot of money, which is not the truth. It used to be a good thing, but you know, a lot of things changed since then—there's just too many of them. And it's a joke now for people."

It is odd to think a time ever existed when Elvis impersonators were not a joke, or that impersonation is an enterprise for which people study and train. But to thousands of people, Elvis impersonation is something serious and real. It is a world all its own—a business to some, a calling to others, and a reason for living to more people, both performers and spectators, than would seem believable.

"Elvis had something that I don't think English or any other language has a word to describe—what he did to people, how he made them feel," said Dave Carlson, a veteran impersonator from Oak Forest, Illinois. "Because I've seen everyone from Tom Jones, Rod Stewart, Wayne Newton, the Beatles, all the way, the full spectrum of entertainers. And I've seen Elvis many times. And no one—*no one*—has ever made me feel in a live performance like Elvis did. Either before or since. I've never been able to feel that feeling. It was some kind of magic."

"I'm not an overly religious person," another Elvis confessed. "I believe in God, but I'm not a person who sits back and says this and that. But I believe that Elvis was a small coming of like a—I don't know, I don't want to use the word 'messiah,' but you know what I'm saying? In other words, when Jesus came down he said, 'This is how we're gonna do this, and you will feel comfort and you'll be relieved.' How many people do you know in this world, and I'm one of them, that use Elvis music to release, to relax, to just release all your frustrations and everything? I feel like his music is part of that."

The least a person can do, then, is get the hair right.

So in some ways, this is a story about surfaces. But it also goes much deeper than that. It is a story about love and ridicule, redemption and hope, and the improbable, aching weight of dreams. It is everybody's story, though sometimes this truth is hard to recognize when it arrives dressed like a dead rock star. If there is anything weird about this story, it is that there is very little weirdness in it.

"We both know that the average impersonator has a very negative stigma," Dennis Stella said, "that he thinks he's somebody that he's not, and that maybe he's living in a real dream world—and maybe to a point a lot of us are. But sometimes you look around and see the real world and the way it is, and you think, Hey, is a dream world so bad? Maybe we'd all be better off in a dream world. I see a lot of what's out there and I'm thinking, this is not that nice of a place sometimes."

If Dennis had learned any lesson from ten years of selling insurance, it was that proper presentation could make the difference between winning respect and looking, as he likes to say, like a goofy son of a gun. He could no more show up in Vegas without his wig than he could saunter into a job interview without a tie.

At the oasis, he thought about going home. But he was scheduled to walk on that Vegas stage in almost exactly twenty-four hours. He remembered he had allowed himself just over three hours for this trip—enough time to make Milwaukee, fetch his girlfriend Gail, and catch a plane heading west. And he never quite forgot that between the pompadour, the sideburns, the hair-styling products, the jumpsuits, the boots, the belts, the jewelry, the karaoke equipment, and the melody-only CDs and cassettes, he had invested more than $8,000 in pretending to be Elvis Presley.

Dennis slid back into the Corvette and gunned it. Sixty miles to Milwaukee, and he had already gone too far to turn back.

People who impersonate Elvis Presley become something less than Elvis and something more than themselves. They lose themselves to find out who they really are. People who judge impersonators only from what they can see think this is sad. To impersonators it is not. It is the whole point.

The same idea applies to people who come to watch Elvis impersonators perform. Women fill most of the audiences. Most of them remember when society considered Elvis dangerous. Many plan their lives around the next show, the next contest, and Elvis Week, held in Memphis every August to commemorate his death, chasing feeling and release. Their love has a lot to do with Elvis. But even more it is tangled with their vision of who Elvis was and how that makes them feel.

"It's really kind of weird," said Jerome Marion, an impersonator who runs his own celebrity look-alike business. "You're not Elvis, but they go up after your autograph the same way. They want your picture the same way. They want, you know, 'Kiss me, touch me,' whatever it might be. I guess just like myself, most of them never had a chance to see Elvis perform. They're viewing Elvis through me or through somebody else. And when they look at a performer on stage—you know, they've seen videos and stuff—they want to feel like they're seeing Elvis live. They want all the excitement that goes along with this, which is walking up and touching him and grabbing the scarves and all that. And that's what basically gives them that energy."

None of these men could arouse that kind of reaction from these women on their own. "When you walk out as Elvis, the girls start screaming," explained John Stuart, the producer who started the impersonator revue Legends in Concert. "Elvis has already done a lot of the work for you—if you present yourself correctly.

"However, I have been in different nightclubs or dinner clubs or whatever, and they'll introduce an Elvis, and the girls will go absolutely bonkers and scream. And the ladies, especially the over-forty-five crowd, will go crazy. And this person isn't any more like Elvis than anything you could imagine. There's nothing even close, other than the fact that the jumpsuit is white. And yet they'll still do it. In other words, people live their dreams and their fantasies through these people. So if they didn't get to experience a live Elvis concert, they will psych themselves out and hypnotically put themselves in a trance of a sixteen-year-old girl, and they will recreate that experience for themselves. It's a crackup. It's amazing."

Shelley Foeckler was just six years old when Elvis Presley died in 1977. About a year before that she had written him a letter, colored it red, white, and blue and told him that if he ever wanted to visit her house they could sit and talk and have some cookies and then maybe he could sing. Shelley grew up tall, with tumbling deep brown hair and eyes the same color. She teaches kindergarten at a Catholic school in Milwaukee called Guardian Angel, caring for children the same age she was when she found Elvis. Why she never outgrew him she could only guess.

"I think because I've never gotten to see Elvis in person," Shelley said, "it's the closest thing I can do to try to experience what it was all about. Seeing the people, how they react, and screaming. We had a local guy that we used to see all the time. And when I was six years old, I remember going to see him, and seeing him perform and getting all nervous. I mean, I remember him coming to the table, singing to me, and I knocked over a drink. I thought, This was it. This is who Elvis was."

Some people try to analyze why a woman would go crazy over a man who truly is not who he seems to be. The problem with these people is that they are applying thought to something motivated less by logic than by pure emotion. The truth is this: A lot of people want to be famous. If they can't be famous, they want to know somebody who is. Most people have no chance at either. So they take control of the situation. They create their own celebrities in a sort of grassroots hero worship. They realize they are pretending, but that doesn't mean they imagine what they feel.

Dennis Stella had worn his wig for the first time about three weeks earlier, at a nightclub in suburban Chicago called Greene's West. Actually, it was a night of firsts: Dennis would appear as a new member of the Elvis Presley International Impersonators Association at a miniconvention starring five other Chicago-area impersonators. He planned to formally debut his Pinwheel and Spanish Flower jumpsuits—floor samples, bought to save money—encrusted with hundreds of glass jewels and anchored by chunky belts hung with double rows of chains. Forty friends and relatives paid up to $13.50 a ticket just to see him sing; no one had ever done that before. And at least 200 more would come to see the other performers and, if they were lucky, something that reminded them of Elvis.

Shelley Foeckler and Dennis's girlfriend Gail Wrzaskowski—her aunt, older by eleven years—and their friends, Chris and Kelly Hottinger, roamed into the show room at Greene's West early enough to get a good seat. Gail and Shelley started attending impersonator shows in 1990, and Chris and Kelly joined them two years later. Compared to some Elvis venues they had seen, this club was elegant. The carpet was plush and green, the tablecloths spanking white, and the decor heavy on mauve and raspberry, accented by small chandeliers that gave off a lemony light. Through the door to the left wound a staircase frothed with white ribbon and netting from which the performers would descend and move through the crowd on their way to the stage.

In the corner to the left of the stage sat tables piled with Elvis Presley souvenirs and attractions: wooden guitar clocks, velvet wall hangings, silver and gold sunglasses at $12 a pair, paperweights, a sign-up sheet for the Elvis—That's the Way It Is fan club, key chains in the shape of hearts, ashtrays, and the coveted collector's plates featuring scenes from movies such as *Jailhouse Rock.* Angled alongside these tables sat others that offered some of the same merchandise, only with impersonator's faces. There were Rick Ardisano T-shirts and photos featuring Jerome Marion in nine different poses, plus two of his three-song tapes and a $10 T-shirt that depicted him wearing gold sunglasses alongside the line, "A Tribute to the King."

The four women settled at a table on the left side of the stage. They all wore evening dresses. Kelly, a smart blond with a turned-up nose, had on a large red hat that matched her dress. Dozens of women strutted around in party clothes, alongside others who favored stretch stirrup pants and T-shirts with Elvis's sullen fifties face pulled tight across their rib cages.

While the room filled, Dennis danced at home in front of a mirror. After he slid on the wig and attached the sideburns, he made his body quake to see if anything came undone. He shook his head hard. "Oh, this sucker's on," he said. "I don't have to worry about this." An hour earlier he had stopped by the club for a quick run-through with a band called the Fabulous Exspence Account, so named because its members once backed an Elvis named Johnny Spence. Dennis missed a couple of cues and muffed some lyrics. Still, he judged the rehearsal a success. He had great faith in his ability to cope with whatever the night threw at him.

After he returned to the club wearing the wig, he climbed the stairs to a changing room—its central feature a chrome rack of glittering jumpsuits—pulled on his Pinwheel and buzzed a circuit between the stairs and the lobby, nursing a Sprite. It seemed he talked to almost everyone he knew in the room—about how he couldn't sleep the night before, how his nerves felt like they were kicking in. Eventually, he made his way over to me. Like most of the people in the club that night, I had never seen Dennis perform. I didn't know what to expect. Neither did Dennis. "This is going to be interesting," he said.

The show got started around 7:25 P.M. "So we've got a lot of fun gonna happen here tonight," said Jerome Marion, who had organized this miniconvention and was serving as its master of ceremonies. He had a reputation for always doing a professional job. "All we ask is that you sit back and you enjoy the heck out of this."

He disappeared, and the Exspence Account warmed up the crowd with a couple of cover songs. Then the music trailed away, except for the pulse of a synthesizer. Charlie Parks, the lead guitarist, peered at the crowd from under his black cowboy hat. "Well, well, well," he said. The women grew quiet and faced forward. A white spotlight washed over them. The band played tendrils of a melody—Richard Strauss's "Also Sprach Zarathustra," the theme from *2001: A Space Odyssey*. It is the song that heralded the arrival of Elvis in his seventies shows.

Charlie said, "This is what you've been waiting for." Keyboards quavered. Cymbals hissed. The drummer bore down—*one-two, one-two, one-two*—and a few women whooped. Charlie's voice rose: "Ladies and gentlemen"—*one-two, one-two, one-two*—"a preview of the Elvis Presley international impersonators convention"—*one-two, one-two, one-two*—"Ladies and gentlemen, let's have a nice round of applause for JEROME! ELVIS! MARION!"

Jerome jogged through the crowd, the main feature of his Fringe jumpsuit swinging, and the women let loose one big loud sound. This is what they paid for. He started with "C.C. Rider," then swung into a cover of "Suspicious Minds" that climaxed with his arms thrashing and refracted through a strobe while the beaded fringe flew.

The women screamed *Ahhhhhh!*

"I'm gonna need a heart transplant by the time this is done," he said.

After Jerome came Rick Ardisano, a quiet man who crossed himself when he hit the foot of the stairs, then went on stage and started into "Spinout," and when he finished the first verse he whirled his pelvis and that black jumpsuit, unzipped to just below his breastbone, made his torso look like a sharp curve.

The women hooted *Whoooo!*

Then blue-eyed Bob West stalked out to "Trouble" in a two-piece black leather biker suit like the one Elvis wore in his 1968 Christmas special, "Elvis"—known in these circles as the '68 Comeback Special—while another impersonator leaned from the top of the staircase and shouted down, "Show 'em, son!" just like Elvis used to do. The women rushed to the edge of the stage and stood hip to hip, clamoring for kisses and the long skinny scarves the Elvises hung around their necks. The real Elvis gave women scarves while he sang, wiping them on his forehead and chest to soak them with sweat and the smell of his cologne. His imitators do that, too, and the women still go crazy to snare any souvenir to remind them of Elvis, or the impersonators, or that sixteen-year-old inside themselves. The women bow their heads, demure as brides, when a scarf is placed around their necks. Then they do a little victory trot back to their seats, waving their trophies above their heads.

After Bob West, Jerome returned to the stage wearing dark pants and a shining blue shirt. "We're gonna get a good friend of mine up here," he told the crowd, and then he addressed the Exspence Account: "Are you ready? Let's do it. Play it on, guys."

The band punched out the opening notes of "Patch It Up." Dennis appeared, shimmering, at the top of the stairs. "Ladies and gentlemen," Jerome shouted, "it gives me great pleasure to present: MISTER!—DENNIS!—STELLA! COME ON DOWN!"

Dennis descended. His suit shone, the white gabardine with round insets of red satin running down his chest and legs. His belt lounged around his hips. His hair gleamed black and glossy and, from a distance, looked as if it might belong on his head. He dashed down, red kick pleats flaming, so fast he almost tripped. He shook hands with a man at a front table, sprang on stage, snatched the mike and, over a large pair of gold sunglasses, sneaked a look at the crowd. Women stood, bending their knees on their mauve seat cushions, to get a better look. The jump-suit fit tightly—no one could complain about that. But the sunglasses overpowered his face and made him resemble a glamorous insect. From where the women sat, his hair called to mind melted fudge.

He started the song and tried to steady his voice. His sunglasses slid down his nose. He pushed them up. He finished the first line and jerked a look over his left shoulder. The band churned calmly on behind him: *Da-da-DA-da-da-DA . . . Da-da-DA-da-da-DA . . .* He hiked his belt and again pushed up his sunglasses. He gasped for air at the end of the next line, and the next, and every one after that. Behind him guitars pounded, cymbals crashed, and everywhere he looked, a stranger stared at him. For all his planning, he had somehow postponed realizing until this moment that 250 people would be watching his every move. And that the lights would be hot. And that the music would be fast. He dropped to his left knee and rocked his pelvis. Remember the words, he told himself. Move. Keep up with the band. *Da-da-DA-da-da-DA . . . Da-da-DA-da-da-DA . . .*

While all of this was going on inside his head, something else was happening on top of it. The wig had begun to move.

It was fascinating to watch, in a car-wreck kind of way. You could actually see his hairline recede. Time-lapse disaster! A fat muffin of hair slowly rose at the crown like the lumps cartoon characters get when someone thumps them on the skull with a skillet. Hair meant to meet the sideburns splayed atop his ears. The sharp side part slanted backward, exposing his sweating forehead. The back of his skull bulged.

Swinging into the second verse, Dennis became aware of strange sensations coming from his head. *Jeez,* he thought to himself, *the wig's moving on me.*

So he moved. Halfway through the second verse he reached up, took two fingers full of fake hair and, as if he were tipping his hat to the crowd—*thankyouverymuch, you're a fantastic audience*—he tugged. Hard. He tipped back his head, mouth open, to test whether the wig slid off. It stayed. He bent his knees toward the ground and he shook.

Da-da-DA-da-da-DA...

Oh, God, Gail prayed, please don't let the wig fall off. She watched the whole thing through the lens of her tiny burgundy video camera. Squinting at Dennis though the stamp-sized eyepiece, balancing on her high heels, she tried to form positive thoughts while at the same time trying not to bust out laughing. Shelley, Chris, and Kelly weren't making it easy—they couldn't control themselves. Knowing Dennis enhanced their sense of this drama. They dreaded every time he reached up, but every time he did it they howled all over again. Gail tried to focus on her taping. Her body felt so tight.

"Thank you," Dennis told the crowd when he finished. "I need a drink of water."

The next three songs went down pretty much the same. As he gathered strength to wail the last note of "In the Ghetto," he boosted his belt, shoved up his glasses and yanked his hair, all in time to the music. After "Let It Be Me," he left the stage. In his thirteen-minute set, Dennis had pulled down his pompadour eleven times. He had become more than who he was, and a lot less than what he had hoped to be. He walked through the audience, smiling. His head looked like a nest. The audience, wiping its eyes, smiled back.

On the day he forgot the wig, Gail had known Dennis for eleven months and dated him for two, and sometimes she wondered if she really understood him. The man she thought she knew, the one who liked to talk for hours and spend weekends at the beach, could disappear at any moment and be replaced by a stranger filled with doubts and dubious plans. The closer Gail got to Dennis, the more she shared his dreams and accepted his quest for an authentic representation of what she and her friends had dubbed the Elvis Head. Say a man has a good Elvis Head and you mean he has a thick head of hair, a clean profile, worthy sideburns. And being cute never hurt. But judging the value of an Elvis

Head, Gail now knew, was not the same as reading the thought processes of a man striving to attain one.

The day they were to leave for Vegas, Gail kept tidying her apartment to distract herself from staring out the sliding glass door in her living room, searching for the red Corvette. She lived in a suburb of Milwaukee called Greenfield, in an apartment with pale blue carpet, ivory walls, and glass-topped black lacquer tables trimmed in gold. Gail ran a cleaning service, and her apartment showed it. She had just dropped off her eight-year-old daughter, Jenna, at her mother's house a few miles away. Everything was where it belonged, except for Gail. She belonged at the airport, on a plane bound for Vegas. She had been dating Dennis just two months, not long enough to know if she should be worried or angry that he was running late. Less than an hour before their plane was due to depart, Dennis slid open her patio door and slouched into her living room. He looked sick.

"What's the matter?" she asked.

"I left the wig," he said.

The wig. She had first laid eyes on it three weeks earlier, the night before the big Saturday night show at Greene's West. To celebrate, Dennis decided to offer his closest friends a preview of his new Elvis Head by throwing a party at his house. Late that afternoon Gail, Shelley, Chris, and Kelly arrived at Dennis's house. It sat at the corner of two dead-end streets and was built of red brick and white aluminum siding, with two sand-colored stone pillars on either side of the front door. Eight yew shrubs formed a green wall across its facade. Around the side of the house near the driveway stood a tall elm. As they pulled up, Gail saw Dennis in a pink tank top and light blue denim shorts, swinging in the tree and tossing strings of lights into its branches. His voice sailed down to them on the ground: "Hellooo, guys," he called—Dennis called everybody "guys"—"how was your drive?" Gail looked up into the leaves and felt a rush of affection for Dennis. She had been engaged to a man once whom she felt she never really knew, he was so quiet. Except for the Elvis Head, she didn't have that problem with Dennis. No matter what he did, you knew exactly what he meant. She couldn't help but like him for that. She never forgot that moment late on a summer afternoon: Dennis, hanging in midair, wanting everything to work out all right.

The women got out of the car and looked around. "You didn't say it was going to be all this!" Gail cried. Around the pave-stone patio Dennis had hung plastic tiki lanterns in candy-mint pinks and yellows and greens and set up torches to scare off bugs. The grill sat ready. Next to it stood his karaoke machine.

As the first guests arrived, he jumped into his car and roared off in search of food—as always, running late. He returned after many of the guests had arrived, bearing a chilled tray of subs, plus ample beer and chips. "Come on, you guys, eat," he pleaded. The only thing Dennis liked more than eating was seeing other people eat. Then, while his guests loaded their plates, he jumped into the shower.

Before he fired up the grill, he turned on the karaoke machine and performed the fastest song in his repertoire to date, "Patch It Up." He ventured a few pelvic plunges, his eyes darting from guest to guest to monitor their reactions. The night was cool for June, and guests who straggled outside through the sliding glass door in the den hugged themselves with one arm and raised their glasses with the other.

Sometime in the hour before midnight, Dennis ducked into the house and emerged decked out in jumpsuit, sideburns, and wig. He stood before his guests. They stood before him. They studied each other for some kind of sign. Gail snapped pictures. He picked up the microphone and again began to sing and plunge. His voice sounded nice. It carried some suggestion of Elvis's softness and occasional pathos, and it hinted at a gift for ballads. But nothing he did could draw their stares from what the wig had done to his head. It had grown rounder on top and flatter in back. The hair was oily-looking and slung over his own like a saddle. The stick-on sideburns looked like stunted unshaven Alabamas, two and a half inches across and three inches deep. Dennis thought his look was honest, if a little cartoonish. Everyone seemed to be smiling at him. He got the feeling they were entertained, but for none of the reasons he had intended. In the months to come he would get this feeling a lot.

Meanwhile, Gail quickly developed her own opinions. She hated the wig—it reminded her of a hairy swimming cap. This criticism sparked a number of discussions.

"You're so critical," Dennis would tell her, "but you don't come up with any other solutions."

"Well," she would reply, "no wig, you know?"

The issue of Dennis's fledgling Elvis Head arose often in their marathon long-distance phone calls. Gail would remind Dennis that some of her closest impersonator friends dyed their hair. Even Elvis dyed his hair, for crying out loud! It was just something people did. She had wound down many nights after shows at get-togethers in someone's hotel room, socializing while the guys eyed each other's dye jobs and tilted their heads to allow for better inspection of sideburn density. It hadn't changed their personalities, as far as she could see. If anything, it showed how determined they were to get things right. You want to impersonate Elvis, you've got to have Elvis's hair. What is so hard about that? She asked Dennis this question again and again, woman to man, Milwaukee to Calumet, the question bleeding its own shades and colors over the phone lines, into the beginnings of their intimacy. Why can't you do it? Why, why a wig?

Now she tried to be sympathetic. "Oh, God," Gail said to Dennis in her apartment, "what are you doing to do?" Dennis looked at her. She was a beautiful woman, four feet ten inches tall, with wavy dark hair, tawny skin, and brown eyes that looked too big for her face when she became agitated. Like now.

"I don't *know* what I'm going to do," he said. "I gotta think. I gotta sit down."

He sat on her cream-colored sofa, which was covered with blue, pink, and black strokes, as if someone had swiped it with a paintbrush. He thought. He dreamed of being a mirror image of Elvis, he knew that much. He didn't care for the wig himself—in fact, he hated it. But it was the only plan he had. And since he had first attempted Elvis two years before, many people had complimented Dennis on his eerie resemblance to the singer Tom Jones. He put his head in his hands. All this had started with a dream, bittersweet memories of his mother, and a pair of $2.00 boots two and a half sizes too small. All he had wanted was to have some fun. And now it had all started to mean something. And no matter what decision he made, it would change the person he was. Or pretended to be.

"You've got to make a decision," Gail told him. "One way or another."

He stood. "I want to go home," he told her. "I'm gonna go home and get it, and I'm gonna fly out of Chicago."

"That's ridiculous," she said. "Let's just go." Gail had been making her own calculations, and she concluded that not only couldn't Dennis go home and make the flight, but it had been about ten years since she last visited Las Vegas, and she had no intention of staying home for any kind of hair. Besides, Shelley, who was also going on the trip, had already headed to Chris's house with her boyfriend at the time, Shawn. The plan was that he would drop the three of them at the airport, and Dennis could keep the Corvette safely in Chris's garage. But it was too late for that.

By then it was around suppertime. Chris's oldest son, Randy Hottinger, had just returned from work. He was twenty-four, had never seen an Elvis impersonator perform, and had no desire to. He could accept how women would like it, but he still considered the whole business pretty bizarre. He had flopped in the living room to watch TV when Shelley burst into the house. The next thing Randy knew, he was riding in a car with Shelley and Shawn, trailing Dennis's speeding red Corvette. They drove roughly a mile from his house to the airport. Dennis parked his car in a no-parking zone and leaped out. The Corvette's four-way lights flashed. One front wheel lurched over the curb. It looked as if it had dropped out of the sky. Everybody hopped out of the cars and ran into the terminal.

Dennis asked the ticket agent if there was any chance of him getting a last-minute flight to Chicago. During this haggling, Randy got a good look at this guy, this Elvis impersonator. His face was red, and he was sweating. To his surprise, Randy suddenly felt sorry for him.

The muscles in Gail's throat stood out the way they do when she gets upset. Her mouth had snapped into a straight line. When she flies, she prefers to arrive to the airport an hour before her plane departs. "Come on," she said to Dennis, "let's just go. We'll dye your hair—we'll figure *something* out when we get there." Randy checked the time. The plane was leaving in ten minutes.

Then Dennis got an idea. He asked Shelley's boyfriend if he could drive to Calumet City, find the wig, and put it on a plane to Vegas. He couldn't, Shawn said, he had to work. Shelley stood there smiling and nodding, ready to agree with any idea that would get them on the plane. She hated the wig, too. Randy found himself studying Dennis and Gail.

"Well, you know how she always has to look up," he said. "And her head was, like, all the way back, and she was jumping around. And Dennis just looked like a guy who was gonna go to the electric chair or something. I never really saw him before, so I didn't know what his normal look was. But it didn't look like it was normal for anybody."

He remembered how his mother, Chris, had spoken of Dennis with affection. He thought about how, if he went, he would get to drive a four-month-old, electric red Corvette.

"OK," Randy told Dennis, "I'll go."

They hurried toward the gate, plotting strategy all the way. At the gate

Dennis scribbled directions on a scrap of paper. He told Randy he would find the wig in a bag—a black duffle bag—lying on top of one of the pinball machines in his spare bedroom. He warned Randy that once he entered the house, he had about forty-five seconds to hit the four-digit code on his alarm or it would automatically dial the police. As Randy absorbed these details it dawned on him: This situation was unfolding because of a wig. His sympathies for another human being had been aroused because of a wig. And, from what he had heard, a damn ugly one. He also noticed that all of the other passengers had boarded the flight. And that the woman at the check-in desk was calling to Dennis: "Sir. *Sir.*" Gail told Dennis that they had to board. She was beginning to notice he had a tendency to think the world would wait for him.

"Gail, relax a second, OK?" he said. "This is important." He was beginning to notice she had a habit of exaggerating.

"Can *you* get him on?" the woman at the gate said to Gail.

"Maybe you can," Gail said, "but there's no way he'll listen to me."

The woman said, "Why don't you just get on? Maybe that'll hurry him."

Gail began walking, and finally Dennis followed. Then he stopped short. "My keys!" he cried. He turned and tossed them to Randy, then ran after Gail. She slowed and waited for him, and they boarded together.

"Who was that guy I just gave the keys to my house and my forty thousand dollar car to?" he asked her.

"That was Chris's son," Gail said.

"Oh," Dennis replied. He pondered this a moment. "Is he a nice guy?"

Bunch of crazy people, Randy said to himself. He walked outside, half expecting to see the Corvette attached to a tow truck. But it was still squatting cockeyed where they'd left it, lights flashing. He eased the front tire off the curb and drove home, where Chris awaited details. "You think *I'm* hyper," Randy told her when he walked in the door.

The plane lifted. Once more Dennis hung in midair, wanting everything to work out all right. He had left one ridiculous situation and prepared to give himself up to one even more ludicrous and packed with the potential for humiliation. He felt he had blown everything and he hadn't even really begun. Yet he had made his decision. He could live with that possibility. What he couldn't bear would be inching up so close to his dream, then abandoning it. That would hurt more than if he wound up looking like a fool. And besides, just because his life had come to revolve around reuniting with a swatch of synthetic hair didn't mean that was where it would end.

High above Milwaukee, the three of them relaxed. Gail and Shelley ordered drinks. Dennis ordered soda. Gail and Shelley teased Dennis again about dyeing his hair in the desert. Dennis sipped his drink, stared at the seat back in front of him and, for the first of many times, considered his destination.

August 16

*W*ithin an hour of the news that Elvis Presley was dead, people began to gather at the white wrought-iron gates of Graceland. Cars drove the stretch of Highway 51 named for the singer with his music streaming out of their windows. His shouts and whispers and moans rose and faded as the cars passed so that, over and over, it sounded like he was leaving. Overnight many more people would find their way to Graceland. In twenty-four hours, thousands would flood the highway in front of the house—so many that the world would begin to see Elvis, and the people who loved him, in a different way. But in those early limbo moments it was as quiet as it would ever be again. Outside the gates decorated with green musical notes, Elvis sang on down the road and the mourners wandered and cried and waited for something to happen.

What they didn't realize in their grief and bewilderment was that just by being there, they had set in motion a cycle of love and devotion that bordered on worship. And, as he had done for half of his forty-two years, Elvis had started something, too. Even in death, he couldn't seem to help himself.

The afternoon of Tuesday, August 16, 1977, Elvis Aaron Presley was found lying face-down on his bathroom floor clad in a pair of blue pajamas. He was pronounced dead an hour later at Baptist Memorial Hospital. No matter what they thought of him, most people would have to agree that Elvis lived an exceptional life. And one of the most amazing things about that life was that no matter how wild or unlikely its events, his fans understood every piece of it. The songs he sang, the mistakes he made, the food he ate—these were human things they knew, and this was why they loved him. They could imagine themselves living a life like his. A lot of them knew how it felt to be poor, as Elvis once was, and they dreamed how good life would be if they suddenly got rich. If they could they would buy a house big enough to share with their parents, or give away thirteen Cadillacs one Christmas—$168,000 but it's only money, honey—or drive past a furniture store, spy a display of tiki furniture in the window and buy the whole deal on the spot, just because you liked it, and move it right in, stick some green carpet on the ceiling while you're at it, why not. They recognized themselves in Elvis, saw things simple and great, impulsive and profound. They drew from his life the comfort and thrill of limitless possibility.

"I think a lot of people just felt really part of his future, you know?" said Carol Henry, who grew up in Memphis and met Elvis once when she was sixteen. "You wanted to watch. You were excited about his future. 'Well, what's this Elvis kid doing now? Making movies? Oh, good—another movie? And the next concert is when?' I don't think you feel that way about any other entertainer."

The death of Elvis Presley represented more than the loss of just a singer or movie star. For that reason, the deep feeling and cheerful excess his life had celebrated informed the mourning of his death. The millions who loved him hurt hard, suffered keenly, and didn't care who knew it. Pennsylvania, California, Texas: as soon as people heard the news, at 3:30 P.M. in Memphis and an hour later on the East Coast, they walked away from their own lives—from jobs and softball games in play and puzzled husbands and wives—and headed for Memphis. New York, Georgia, Wisconsin: they drove all night or drained savings accounts to buy plane tickets and gambled on finding a room once they hit town. Mississippi, Illinois, Tennessee: some of them had never flown on an airplane before. They didn't care. They all knew only that they needed to get to Memphis. Yet once they arrived they realized that they were, in some violent and permanent sense, lost. It showed on their faces, sweating and red and creased with grief, as they stood and stared at his house. What was left for them now? Did they ever love someone so much, or did they just dream it? What do you do when a dream dies?

By the 1970s, Memphis left Elvis alone. The *Commercial Appeal*, the city's morning newspaper, had a reporter who kept tabs on Presley's activities. But the coverage paled compared to what it was in the 1950s, when Elvis first became famous. Those times he rented the Libertyland amusement park for his friends or visited a department store after it closed so he could shop for Christmas gifts in peace, the paper would ship out a photographer to record the moment. And there was still the occasional incident. In January 1975, a freshman at Mississippi Junior College nicknamed Honeybee and a friend packed themselves into a ribbon-bedecked box and managed to get delivered to Graceland under the pretext that they were Russian wolfhounds. They hoped to be a belated birthday surprise for Elvis, who had turned forty earlier that month. It didn't work; the delivery man was told Elvis didn't need any more dogs. At the wrought-iron gates Honeybee vowed to stay until she saw Elvis, whom one story said "reportedly has gone into seclusion until such time as he loses some weight."

But for the most part, sound news judgment and common courtesy—he was, after all, a neighbor for twenty-eight years—meant Elvis had long ceased being front-page news.

"He was no longer the brash challenge to the orthodoxy [that he was] when he was a teenager or in his twenties, breaking onto the scene," said Scott Ware, a journalist who covered Elvis's death for the *Commercial Appeal*. "He was more just a citizen of the community."

Then on one steaming August afternoon, a reporter on the city desk named Shirley Downing sent over a phone call to Angus McEachran, metro editor at the *Commercial Appeal*. Another Elvis story, she told him. The caller was an ambulance driver from Wynne, Arkansas. He told McEachran he had seen a man—"a big old fat guy" was how he put it—who looked like Elvis brought into Baptist Memorial Hospital. The paper got these death calls all the time. Over the years people had called to insist that Elvis had perished in a plane crash, Elvis had wrecked his car, Elvis had smashed up his motorcycle. Still, McEachran, a burly man with a penchant for suspenders, is the kind of journalist who likes to tell the old newsroom joke that if your mother says she loves you, check it out. And he knew that whenever Elvis was sick, he went to Baptist. So he tracked down a hospital source at home and asked her if the rumor was true. Twenty minutes later, she called him back.

She said, "Well, as usual, your reporters got it half right."

He said, "Give me the half that's right."

"Well, he was in the hospital. But he's no longer there."

"They've treated and released him?"

"No. He's in the morgue."

"He's *what?*"

"He's dead."

McEachran didn't leave the office for a couple of days, but it made little difference, because the world came to him. Journalists from all over the world called the newspaper, begging to buy full-color Elvis photographs. The staff was straining mightily to finish its own work, so to shake the callers McEachran quoted them ridiculous prices for pictures, asking, say, $3,000 for a single eight-by-ten. But they paid anything he asked. And they thanked him. And McEachran knew then that not only was this story huge, but it also was a world away from normal.

The first edition of the *Commercial Appeal* rolled off the presses Tuesday night around 8:30 P.M. Enterprising types bought as many as they could carry at fifteen cents a copy and drove over to Elvis Presley Boulevard, the piece of Highway 51 in front of Graceland. Fans in the crowd rushed the overstuffed cars and trucks and bought the papers, bearing the headline "Death Captures Crown of Rock and Roll," for anywhere from $5 to $10 each. Someone with a more global view of the tragedy bought some newspapers and caught a plane to London. "We had reports," said McEachran, now the paper's editor, "never verified, but it was reported not only in our newspaper, but on the wires by other accounts, that those copies sold from one hundred to three hundred dollars.

"Then we knew the world had gone crazy."

That same afternoon, in a little leather-making and jewelry shop in Oxford, Mississippi, Mike McGregor was locking up for the day. That night he and his wife, Barbara, planned to drive the two hours north to Memphis to see a Willie Nelson concert at the Mid-South Coliseum. McGregor had worked for Elvis for nine years, living with his wife and son for most of that time in a trailer on the Graceland estate. He cared for Elvis's horses and sometimes made jewelry and leather clothes for his boss, a job made easier because they were roughly the same height and weight, and he could use himself as a model.

But fourteen months earlier he had moved back to Oxford, into a house he'd built himself a few years before on some land that belonged to his family. When he quit, the first thing Elvis wanted to know was what he had done to make him want to leave. McGregor assured him that he and Barbara were thinking only of their son, Bill. "This is crazy for him to stay up here and let him grow up on this concrete," he said, "when he can grow up on the dirt down there." Elvis had been the best boss McGregor ever had. Nine years and he had never raised his voice once, never asked him to do anything he had had to refuse.

McGregor made jewelry and saddles in a cluttered room in the back of his shop, and for some reason that day never turned on the radio, working to just the sounds of his machines and the passing traffic. Early that afternoon he left his shop, got cleaned up and was pulling shut the door of his house when the phone rang. It was about 4:30 P.M.

"I'm one of those people, the phone is ringing, I gotta answer it," he said years later. "So I opened the door and walked back in, and picked up the phone, and this friend of mine that lived here, he said, 'Hey, man, I'm sorry about your friend dyin'.'

"I said, 'Who are you talking about?' You know, I thought Leroy up the road or something. He said, 'Mr. Presley.'"

McGregor hated to hear it, but he wasn't surprised. He had visited Graceland a few times after he'd moved on to see Elvis's father, Vernon—the man he called Mr. Presley—who suffered from heart trouble. He remembered shaking Vernon's hand on a visit, seeing the suit hang loosely on the big man's frame.

"Oh, man," McGregor said on the phone. "Well, you know, he had a real bad heart anyway and two or three heart attacks. It don't really surprise me."

"You talkin' about Vernon?"

"Yeah, who you talkin' about?"

"Elvis."

"Oh, man," McGregor cried, "Elvis didn't die! Elvis is like John Wayne! Elvis don't die!"

He hung up the phone and tried to think. He flashed back to the last time he talked with Elvis, not long before he returned to Oxford. Elvis was leaving for a cross-country tour. McGregor waited on Elvis's jet, the *Lisa Marie*, to tell him he, Barbara, and Bill would be gone by the time he returned. When Elvis boarded, the two of them walked to the back of the jet together to talk. Elvis hugged McGregor and shook his hand. He told him, "If you get home and you don't like it, you got a job with us."

And McGregor told Elvis, "If you need me, you call me. You don't have to tell me why, just tell me you need me, I'll be there. And I'll call Barbara and tell her how long I'm gonna be gone after I find out what you want."

Elvis had been his employer, but he thought of him as a friend. He never thought of him as a big star; the first time Elvis strolled into the leather shop in Memphis where McGregor once worked, somebody had to tell him the name of the polite man in the sunglasses.

One day he walked into the kitchen at Graceland to pour himself a cup of coffee—they always had a pot going—and Elvis called to him from the den: "Come here. Get your coffee and come here."

McGregor walked in and saw Elvis. He was alone in what is now known as the Jungle Room, holding an album. "Look, man," he said, "I just got the lacquers on my new record and I'd like for you to listen to it, because you like country, and this is country." So they sat there, just the two of them, and listened to it on an RCA hi-fi with a walnut cabinet. McGregor liked the sound of Elvis singing country; he was never a big fan of rock 'n' roll, though he thought Carl Perkins was some kind of genius. When the last song faded McGregor stood to leave. Elvis asked him, "Where are you going?"

"Man, I got work to do," McGregor said.

"No, wait a minute," said Elvis. "Listen to it again."

It seemed impossible that he could be gone.

McGregor did the only thing that did seem possible: He picked up the phone. He got through to the house and told whoever answered that Vernon could expect him Wednesday. The next morning, he got into his pickup, headed west on Route 6 and got on Interstate 55 at Batesville. Normally he stuck to back roads, twisting a course that brought him out above Batesville clear to Sardis. But with his mind so tangled over what had happened he felt safer taking a straighter route. The drive north took the usual two hours. When he reached Memphis, he weaved through the residential streets behind Graceland. He turned onto Dolan, passing on his right a modern white house with a slanted roof where Vernon Presley lived. If you stood in its back yard and looked east, you could see Graceland's barn, which held Elvis's beloved horses.

Dolan is the first intersection with a stoplight before traffic reaches the estate's stone wall. It is close, about two-tenths of a mile. McGregor turned right onto Elvis Presley Boulevard, the stretch of Highway 51 in front of Graceland, and stared in wonder and disbelief. Everywhere he looked he saw people—standing, sitting, lying, crying in the road, staggering between the creeping cars. The bodies spread across Elvis Presley Boulevard, south toward Mississippi and north toward Memphis, spilling into the parking lot of the shopping center across the street from the house.

"The people—they were just standing in the middle of Fifty-one," he marveled. "Traffic would just move up a foot, and stop and move, wait until somebody moved. Because nobody cared. It was like, 'I don't believe that pickup that you're driving is big enough to run over me. I really don't care if you do run over me. I don't even recognize that you're there with a vehicle that can crush me.' Which just blew my mind again."

It took him an hour to reach the gate, and somebody waved him through. He drove up the gentle hill toward the house, and when he reached the top he got out of his truck and studied the crush on the road below. Funny: He and Elvis were friends, but he still wasn't sure if he ever really knew him. He wondered if you could ever really know a person. Yet those people on the boulevard had experienced Elvis only through his singing and movies—what McGregor liked to call "sound and images." And they knew, or at least thought they knew, enough about Elvis to believe that they needed to be there. Twenty years later, after McGregor became known as Elvis's jewelry maker, he would tell people that Elvis treated him better after his death than he did when he was living—and that was something, because no boss ever treated him better. By then he would know the reasons why people felt the way they did. But he still wouldn't be sure he understood.

On Wednesday, the crowd grew, and grew, until it became a story in itself. The Presley family had decided to allow fans to view Elvis's body, placed in a 900-pound, steel-lined copper coffin at the foot of the front stairs under an Italian cut-glass chandelier. By the time the gates opened at 3:00 P.M., people from all over the country jostled in rows hundreds deep against the seven-foot fieldstone wall around the fourteen-acre estate and sprawled north and south along the highway. Police estimates of the crowd expanded in the August heat, from 20,000 to 50,000 to 100,000. Police officers balanced on the wall, drawling into bullhorns, and for the most part the crowd had enough manners not to turn into a mob. Not that they would have had the room. Men and women and children, all strangers, many sobbing, squeezed without an inch of space between them in what looked like manic conga lines.

Behind the white gates, photographers hoisted their cameras above their heads and snapped. What they caught was a scene as unreal to outsiders as Elvis's death was to those in it.

It had been a dry year, but that day a light rain fell. Someone raised an umbrella decorated with white lettering that spelled "ELVIS," a little white heart dotting the i. Then the sky cleared a little, and the humidity hung down like heavy curtains. The temperature hit ninety. At the gates, where mourners crushed together and pressed their sweat into strangers' clothes, it climbed at least ten degrees more. Chests pressed into the backs of those who waited ahead. People fainted and never fell, so tightly were they sandwiched together. Women, hair wilted and makeup long sobbed away, sent up wails like flares.

"Oh, my God, my Elvis!" a reporter from the *Los Angeles Times* heard one of them cry, "God has taken my Elvis!"

Women lay in the grass inside the gates where medics had carried them, fanning themselves. Nearby a man wagged his head as someone waved smelling salts under his nose. Now and again, a policeman would turn his head and, so no one would see, wipe the tears from his eyes. An occasional fez would bob like a bottle atop this sea of bodies—one of the Shriners in town that week for a convention. All that drama, all that discomfort, all for a chance at a ten-second glimpse of a man dressed in a white silk suit, a pale blue shirt and a white tie, black hair brushed off his forehead, lying a few steps from his Music Room and the piano he loved to play. The viewing was supposed to end at 5:00 P.M. The Presleys extended it for an hour. When gates closed, people screamed. None of them could bear to think they would never see Elvis again.

Journalists covering Presley's death had a hard time believing how deep and messy emotions ran among these people who had come to be near Elvis this last time and—perhaps this amazed them most—how sincerely they shouldered their grief. "Overweight, dowdy matrons in polyester pantsuits stood for three days in the sweltering heat without a change of clothes, with little water, less food and no sleep," wrote a reporter for the *Atlanta Journal-Constitution.* "And for what?" The question made sense. After all, Elvis had passed his prime. He packed more than 200 pounds on his six-foot frame and in 1975, had split his pants on stage in Pontiac, Michigan. But people still loved him. The day he died he was scheduled to leave Memphis for Portland, Maine, to begin a sold-out, twelve-day tour. That week his song "Way Down" had hit number one on the Billboard Hot Country Singles Chart. Still, most people considered him over as a phenomenon. Though most journalists sensed that Elvis Presley's death qualified as a major story, few comprehended that it would inspire so much desperate emotion among so many.

"We knew he was popular, and he made a lot of money, and he did make several movies, but I don't think that any of us dreamed of the international reaction to his death," said McEachran. "We had gone through the death of Martin Luther King, the assassination in Memphis. And as far as measuring impact on the public, there's no comparison. Elvis's death reverberated around the world."

They buried him the next day, August 18, in the shadow of even more tragedy. Around 3:30 A.M. two teenage girls who had driven to Graceland from Monroe, Louisiana, were killed and another critically injured when a drunk driver crashed into the crowd in front of the gates.

But after the sun rose the people came again, toting babies and box lunches and wearing T-shirts freshly printed with the dates of Elvis's birth and death. They lined up three and four deep from the gates of Graceland north to Forest Hill Cemetery. The crowd was smaller than it had been the day before, maybe about 10,000 people, and quieter. Women still sobbed, hugging their purses and touching tissues to their faces. Streets around Forest Hill were jammed, and cars collided. From everywhere along the route rose the purr and click of cameras.

You could watch these scenes on TV, and a lot of people did. For every person who traveled to Graceland, hundreds grieved at home— too young or broke or tied down to make the trip. Their absence never meant the news hurt them less. The death of Elvis Presley meant the end of their way of life. But for those thousands of fans who would go on to become or follow Elvis impersonators, something else would evolve. They didn't know it then, but the death of Elvis meant the birth of something else.

The day Elvis was buried, Rick Marino, a singer from Jacksonville, Florida, finished packing for a gig to Gainesville and went outside to check his mail. When he reached into the box he came up with a fistful of sympathy cards. He considered this kind of funny. In fact, he prided himself on how he'd behaved since Tuesday. Two days since Elvis, his hero and inspiration, had died, and he hadn't cried once. So he decided to commemorate the burial in a way he thought would honor the man. He put on an album of Elvis singing gospel. And as Elvis crooned "In the Garden," something happened that made Rick's voice shake to tell it.

"I just closed my eyes," he said, "and I actually saw Elvis's spirit ascend to heaven. I saw him walking in the garden of heaven, and I saw

Jesus coming and taking him on home. And I just could not stop crying. I just couldn't stop crying. I can't explain it to you. And I remember my mom called me right about then, and I just told her, I said, 'Mom, I just can't talk to you right now.' And I hung up the phone, took my phone off the hook, and I just had me a good cry for about an hour."

Not everyone experienced such a transcendental moment. But people who love Elvis Presley, the ones who call themselves "the true Elvis fans," recall exactly where they were and how they felt when they heard the news. His death was not just a big news story. It changed their lives.

"That was something, like I can always remember about Kennedy, when he got shot," said Louise Rozek, an Elvis fan since the fifties. "It's just something that lives in your mind."

Robert Washington, who grew up in Cape Girardeau, Missouri, heard about it at Marine boot camp the day he turned nineteen. Having his favorite singer die on the day of his own birth wrecked him; he never could enjoy August 16 in the same way again.

He admired Elvis from the time he was ten, after he caught one of his movies on TV. It amazed him to hear one man sing so many kinds of songs in so many styles. Robert decided that no matter who you were, you could find something about Elvis to like. It thrilled him that one man could bring all different kinds of people together. Women liked his looks, people of all races grooved on the way he sang. "His love for his family," Robert said, "his family came first. And his mother—he *loved* his mother, you know. And God." He laughed, a little sheepishly, and he shook his head. "You're gonna make me cry."

The first time he toured Graceland, he snapped four rolls of film. It wasn't until he got the pictures developed that he realized he hadn't really seen the house because he'd been so busy trying to remember it.

"It's something that you can't describe. You just *feel* it," he said. "You can't say it's a bunch of fanatics, because how can you be fanatic about somebody you never even had an opportunity to see in real life? How many people in Japan had a chance to see him in real life? He never toured overseas. He touched people that he never even came close to. How can you touch a person when you can't even speak the same language? That Elvis phenomenon, that'll never come back. There's no other entertainer in the world that had the impact Elvis had on that many people."

After he left the Marines he got a job building Navy ships in Auburn,

Maine. He married and had two children. But Elvis followed him always. On his birthday people would wish him well, then offer their sympathies. Robert behaved the way Elvis did in this sort of social situation—polite, quiet, humble. He smiled until his dimples showed, then looked toward the floor, shaking his textbook pompadour. As the years passed, Elvis became one of the things that could always make him feel good.

In 1987, on the night before he turned twenty-nine, Robert went to Graceland to observe the tenth anniversary of Elvis Presley's death. Elvis Week—or Death Week, to the less reverent—draws thousands of fans. Some of them love Elvis; others are in love with the idea of an Elvis phenomenon. They come to Graceland from all over the world, and they hold candles as they silently file past his grave. That night, in the shopping plaza across the street from the house, Robert shinnied up a telephone pole, stood on a circuit box at the top, and marveled at the sight below him. From one end of Elvis Presley Boulevard to the other wound a frayed and brilliant ribbon of people waiting to file through the gates decorated with musical notes.

Robert arrived at 9:00 P.M.and didn't leave until 3:30 the next morning, staying until he reached the grave. "I had like fourteen candles melted all over me," he said. "I'm walking through, going, What the hell am I doing?" He clasped his hands as if they held a single taper. "Oh, yeah, wake you up. Oooh-oohp, ow! This one's burned down, gotta get another one. You watch those people coming back out, people crying and stuff, and little kids, and you look and see the front of Graceland there all lit up, and it is something." He laughed, and then he wiped his eyes with the side of one of his broad shipbuilder's hands.

Cookie Mignogno had just stretched out on her couch when the phone rang. That Tuesday was her day off from the bar where she worked, and she wondered who would have the nerve to bother her. She pulled herself up and grabbed the receiver. It was her son, Frederick.

"Mom," he said, "guess what."

"Come on, buddy," she said, "don't pull my leg." Her family always teased her about loving Elvis. "I don't want to hear this kind of stuff."

"Turn on your TV," he said.

She kept her TV on, all day and into the night. Cookie was three years younger than Elvis and had loved him long before she met her husband. And she had never found a reason to stop. She and Elvis had grown up together, and he became something she could count on, no matter what else happened in life. He had one of the most beautiful voices she had ever heard. She swooned over his blue eyes, his dark hair. But his appeal went beyond the obvious—she also adored the way he moved, the way he made the songs mean something beyond the words. She said, "He was just being different, doing what he wanted to do." She had seen him at the Spectrum in Philadelphia on May 28, 1977, less than three months before he died, and it hurt her to see how heavy he had become. But he still sounded good, better than the first two times she had seen him, when he was young. When she was young.

"For him to walk out—it was a feeling," she said. "You had to be there to know exactly what I'm saying. The whole room, all you see are flash-bulbs going off, and screaming and hollering. I was one of the more quiet fans. I would rather have heard him sing than to listen to all the screaming."

Cookie mourned him quietly, too. The only thing deeper than her love for Elvis was the hole in her life his absence made. She kept a vigil of her own. Every day she cried. Late at night she stood at her bedroom window and stared up at the sky and sobbed:

"Why, God? Why did you take him?"

In Bellevue, Kentucky, another woman, a simpler question:

"Guess who died?"

Steve Chuke heard it from his workbench in a jewelry store his buddy David owned, filing a ring. The woman—his buddy's wife, Peggy—sat up front. She had a good view of Sixth Street from where she sat; if she swung to the right, she could see Steve in the back room working, his bench against the wall near the door. And from where she sat, she could hear the radio.

Steve barely looked up at her from beneath the overhang of his pom-padour. He hated his job. A day spent squinting at scraps of gold sucked all the soul and freedom out of him.

"I don't know," he said.

"A famous singer."

"Who's that?"

"Guess."

He said the first name that came to mind: "Elvis Presley."

"I'll be darned," Peggy said. "How did you know?"

Right then the news didn't wound him. Then he went home and turned on the television, and the words on all those special reports beat on his brain like the words of a song he couldn't push out of his head: *Elvis died. Elvis died. Elvis died.* There had been a time when Steve sang and danced, when he won a dance contest in Cincinnati, Ohio, in the presence of Conway Twitty, before the motorcycle accident that broke him apart and reshaped him into a man. Once he was a little boy who had dreamed of being famous, and his main playground conspirator was his friend Wayne Walls, better known as Butch.

"Butch! Oh, God, yeah, that's all we did!" he recalled. "Yeah, that's the guy I sang on the street corners with, him and I. Yeah, we would swing till the middle of the night—yeah, *yeah* we would! We'd sing! People used to say, 'Shut up!' Yeah. We walked down the street—nineteen fifty-eight, or fifty-seven, I think it was, walking down the street and I was singing 'Teddy Bear,'—just goofing around. And people on the porch said, 'Hey, you guys are good!' And we laughed and giggled, and took off running.

"We were just kids—God, let's see, I would have been ten, eleven years old. I always thought, he always thought, that you had to be God to stand up on the stage, you know? We never knew any better. We were just from little Hicktown. I knew I had the talent, but I didn't know it, you know what I'm saying?"

When Elvis died he realized how little he had changed and how much he had never become. It was less a blinding revelation than a quick flash he caught out of the corner of his eye. He intended to figure out why he felt so strange. But first he felt like he needed to sing. He went out and bought some Elvis tapes and sang alone in his car. He had the crazy idea that if he found Elvis again, he might find the thing in himself that he had lost.

In Brooklyn, New York, the afternoon of August 16, a chubby thirteen-year-old named Michael Lepore hung out in his bedroom. He was close enough to the kitchen that he could hear his mother when she made a single sound of pity: "Awwww."

"You know what I mean?" said Lepore, who goes these days by the name Mike Memphis. "It was like one of her somebody died awwwws. I came out in the kitchen and I said, 'Ma?' She said, 'Elvis Presley died.' I was like, 'Whaaa?!' I was taken aback: 'Are you *sure?*'"

Not long before that, Mike had shown his mother a tabloid that featured Elvis on the front, looking heavy. This impressed him. This famous person, this man he watched every week on the Sunday afternoon movie, looked like someone he knew. "Oh, look at this," he asked his mother, "doesn't this look like me?"

After he convinced himself that his mother was right, he stepped onto his front porch. "My father and my twin sister were sitting out there," he said. "And I told my sister and she refused to believe me. And then I wanted to tell everybody on the block—everybody that passed by, so they could remember where they heard it from first. And they'll remember me for the rest of their lives. But I didn't, because I figured, my sister don't even believe me. Nobody else is gonna believe me.

"The thing is, everybody remembers where they were when Elvis died—whether you're an Elvis fan or not. Because it affected the world."

Midafternoon at the Memphis insurance office where Carol Henry worked went down easy. She had returned from lunch and was standing with some of her coworkers, chatting and looking out the windows at traffic on the busy street below. That was when she spotted her boss's car wheeling into the parking lot, looking ready to smash into the first person who got in his way.

He burst out of the elevator and the expression on his face frightened her. When he blurted that Elvis was dead, her first reaction was that he'd heard wrong. Carol had always pictured Elvis as the kind of person she could call if her car broke down and he would drive right over to pick her up and take her home. A person filled with that much kindness couldn't just disappear.

The phones began to ring. Friends and relatives were on the line, hungry to trade information or to talk themselves out of the truth. "Everybody's going, 'This is what I heard,' and it was almost like they were doubting it," Carol remembered, "I don't mean doubting it, but they were like, 'Hey, I *thought* I heard. This can't be right.' Because nobody wanted to give Elvis up. Nobody."

Carol had minor surgery the next day and stayed home to recuperate while her two brothers went to Graceland for the funeral. She later decided it took her longer to recover because she couldn't be there. She remembered when she met Elvis—she was just sixteen then and struck speechless. She felt the same way that August day. What could anyone say? In the aerial pictures they showed on TV, the people surrounding the house looked like a field of bright and restless weeds blowing in a weird wind. She cried with them.

"I remember going to see *Love Me Tender* over and over," she said.

"And I felt that I was watching someone that I loved and he loved me. Not as a sick kind of a love, but just maybe a friend, a brother. There's never even been another movie star with that kind of impact!

"And I can remember sitting here at home, just grieving! Grieving! It was . . . just strange, you know? It was like family. Elvis was like family."

It took Carol a long time to recover from Elvis's death. "In fact, I still don't feel like I'm over it," she said not long ago. "I still can be riding down the street, and a song will play, and tears just fill my eyes. And sometimes, quite frankly, I will be hearing a song, and I'll think, Maybe I'm not in the frame of mind to really be able to listen to this. Because my heart's broken. Why did he have to die? And I start asking all those questions, which you do with someone you really love—why? Why did this have to happen? Why him? A lot of people—and I include myself—it's almost like when he died, part of them did. I mean, I hate to sound real morbid. But I really do—I feel that a lot of people just died. Part of them died when Elvis did."

What do you do when a dream dies? Certainly, you change. You adapt. And if you possess a certain kind of passion, you transform your grief so that it assumes the shape of the thing you have lost. So it was that Elvis Presley's death gave birth to impersonators. It wasn't that impersonators didn't exist before Elvis died. But there were just a few; most fans had never felt the need for an imitation with the real one around. People didn't wake the morning after the funeral, their hair tumbled high from dreamless sleep, and decide to imitate Elvis Presley. But so many missed him so much. All that love and hope had to find an outlet.

With Elvis gone, people feared they would lose part of their reason to be, or what they had hoped to be. They saw themselves, the best part of themselves, in a man most of them had never met. Sound and images, as Mike McGregor would say, but it all connected to emotion and real lives.

When Elvis died, he left behind, among other things, a nine-year-old daughter, a grieving fiancée, a twenty-three-room mansion, $1.3 million in tickets to concerts that he would never perform, two airplanes, fifteen guitars, two Stutz Blackhawks, and thousands upon thousands of people who came to absorb the shock of his death but balked at accepting its consequences. None of them could deny that things had changed. But as soon as they pulled themselves together, they began to think of a way to change them back.

3

Memphis and Beyond

Six days before Christmas in 1976, police were called to Graceland to investigate a report of a trespasser who had pushed past a guard and onto the grounds. The man identified himself as Elvis Presley and insisted he had every right to enter his own home. When the front gate guard tried to stop him, the man said, "You're fired."

According to the *Commercial Appeal*, two patrolmen made a quick search of the estate and found the trespasser sitting in a lawn chair next to Presley's kidney-shaped swimming pool. The situation escalated.

> The officers said the man was dressed in "very mod clothes and was wearing a Santa Claus hat with Presley's name on it." They said he was singing "Hound Dog" as loud as he could.
>
> When the officers told the man he would have to leave, he inquired, "Who invited you fuzzies on my property?" Then he ordered them to "get away from my pool."
>
> Police said the officers attempted to grab the man by the arm, but he lashed out at them with a kung fu-like kick and warned them that he had a black belt in karate.
>
> After a brief struggle, however, Elvis' impersonator was handcuffed and taken to police headquarters.

Even before Elvis Presley died, there were Elvis impersonators. And even then, people thought they were weird.

Of course, some people wondered about Elvis in the years before his death—skulking top-heavy with big tinted sunglasses on the covers of supermarket tabloids. But Elvis impersonators are worse, even the ones who don't get themselves arrested. They have acquired a reputation for being freaks of their own creation, cast in the image of another. Like the man in the mod clothes, they trespass where they don't belong.

Though their numbers were small, some men impersonated Elvis even before he died. Wade Cummins, an impersonator who lived in Memphis, began in 1968, the year of the Comeback Special. Dave Ehlert, an Elvis from Chicago, says he got started a year earlier. The practice got widespread exposure in the mid-seventies, when Andy Kaufman imitated Elvis on "Saturday Night Live," wearing tight jumpsuits and sneering, "There's somethin' wrong with mah lip." Elvis, the story goes, found Kaufman very amusing.

The love and grief Elvis's death provoked sought an outlet. Ronnie McDowell, a country singer who sounds a good bit like Elvis, wrote and recorded the song "The King Is Gone" two days after his death. A week after it was released, it sold a million copies. "It's sad that the greatest singer in the world had to die for me to get my start," McDowell said at the time. "I guess it was just meant to be that way."

And it probably was inevitable that, if Elvis fans could never again see the object of their love and grief, the ambitious would sell a substitute. Seven months after Elvis Presley died, one hundred impersonators were reported hard at work playing everything from Las Vegas floor shows to tiny nightclub gigs. Some impersonators commanded real money. Alan Meyer, who worked up a Las Vegas lounge act, claimed he earned $1.2 million in 1977. Rick Saucedo performed in a Broadway show, "Elvis: The Legend Lives," with former members of Presley's own bands; he said he earned up to $10,000 a week.

"Back in the seventies after Elvis died, you could actually do pretty big, large-scale concerts," said Dave Carlson, a twenty-year veteran from the Chicago suburbs. "Which I even did myself. And have people react to you like you were Elvis, and you could work supper clubs all over the country—nice, beautiful supper clubs that people like Frank Sinatra would work. You could go in there and draw just as good a crowd, because you were doing Elvis and everyone knew what they were buying a ticket for. And people were so curious, especially after Elvis died, they would buy a ticket, and come and see you.

"There was this quote in this book, and it was so true: You could be an Elvis impersonator, put on a white jumpsuit, start at the top, and work your way down."

Some impersonators got their start on a different level altogether. In one of the more publicized cases, Dennis Wise, a car salesman from Joplin, Missouri, underwent $15,000 worth of plastic surgery so he could resemble Elvis. The idea occurred to Wise when he was a teenager that if he could have plastic surgery to make himself look like Elvis, his own life would be transformed. Nine years later, he hooked up with a manager named Dennis O'Day who thought Wise sounded like Elvis over the telephone. O'Day bankrolled the six-hour chain of operations, in which surgeons recast Wise's nose, cheeks, and chin. They also lifted the upper left-hand corner of his lip to enhance his sneer. "I saw *Elvis Presley* lying in that bed," O'Day reported when the operation was complete. What the world saw, if it could stand to look, was a more ambiguous image. Wise was photographed after the surgery dressed in a jacket with wide scroll-trimmed lapels, swathed in bandages, brandishing a picture of Elvis in a studded jumpsuit.

It is one thing to want to portray Elvis Presley. It is something else altogether to reshape your flesh into his image and then call a press conference to show it off. This kind of activity compares to declaring yourself Elvis just because you write his name on your Santa hat and insult the fuzzies—at best pathetic, at worst the work of a crazy fool.

Such stories did little to enhance the credibility of those who considered imitating Elvis a higher calling. As the number of impersonators grew, competition for jobs grew stiff; stunts flourished—more surgery, a father-and-son team, a woman who claimed Elvis burned his image into her screen door in Exeter, Nebraska. Impersonators appeared, as if out of a parallel universe, who did not look like Elvis and could not sing. It turned out to be a very crowded universe.

Many of the originals, burned out or embarrassed, faded away. Ten years after Presley's death, Wade Cummins announced that he was quitting his profession because what had happened to it shamed him. When he made this pronouncement, he owned four homes.

Sometimes Elvis impersonators are fools, just like people in general. But often they are not. They do what they do because they like it, and almost always because they love Elvis. It helps to remember, upon entering their world, the difference between unusual and weird. Just because someone behaves in a way most people consider strange doesn't mean he is oblivious to its implications. And it doesn't mean he doesn't know, or care, what people think.

And even when he knows, it doesn't mean he won't go ahead and do it anyway.

Mike Memphis emerged from his Olds 88 one July night while Times Square exploded behind him. He wore black bell-bottoms, a blue Hawaiian shirt open to the third button and slathered with large pink and purple tropical flowers, electric blue snakeskin boots with skinny heels, a black Gibraltar of a pompadour, and a thin layer of makeup, tastefully applied. This being New York, no one noticed him. To Mike Memphis this is success: Control how and when people pay attention to you and you're doing OK.

Mike Memphis has built a career providing what he has determined the people want: a little attention and a direct line to celebrity. The fact that he hungers for the same things himself only makes his job easier. He has performed as Elvis for much of his life. Once he even portrayed Elvis as dead, sprawled and slack-jawed on a bathroom floor. He appeared on a national talk show with a caption beneath his talking head that read "Mike Memphis—Had Face Reconstructed to Look More Like Elvis." But what he really has reconstructed is his whole self, nearly symmetrical, and payable by the hour.

Mike fits the stereotype of the impersonator everyone laughs at—he has big hair, bigger ambitions, and seemingly no shame. Some impersonators and fans consider people like Memphis an affront to Elvis's memory, to every decent quality he ever represented. "It's a joke, it's a mockery," said Jerome Marion, an established Elvis and officer in the EPIIA. "He's the kind of guy that goes and buys a pink Cadillac so he can look like Elvis, and drives around and wears his sideburns like they're landing strips for a seven-forty-seven. And they're the guys that the media jumps on."

Memphis sees things differently. He is a dreamer, sure, but he has learned that people don't just make out checks to dreamers. Besides, a guy calls himself Mike Memphis, he needs to be realistic about something.

"Every once in a while," he said, "I'll have people holler out their car windows: 'Hey, look at Elvis, look at that sick bastard'—excuse my language, but this is Brooklyn. But they're the ones that are the sick people, because they're the ones hollering out the window. People are looking at *them*. I'm minding my business and I made eighty grand last year and they're collecting their unemployment checks and you can laugh at me all you want. Because I'm laughing all the way to the bank."

We got into his Olds and steered down Broadway bound for Staten Island, the July skyline giving over to dusk. This summer night, love provoked our trip. Memphis was being paid to perform a couple songs at the wedding reception of a couple named Vincent and Melissa. Mike had been hired to witness the engagement, so the couple felt it only proper he attend their wedding.

As he drove he provided a tour of the city. He pointed out Madison Square Garden, where Elvis recorded a live album in 1972, and a store where he buys cheap karaoke cassettes. We whipped past the Ed Sullivan Theater, where David Letterman tapes his talk show. Mike slowed to honk and wave at Sirajul and Mujibur, the sometime Letterman sidekicks who work at a gift shop a couple of doors down. They waved back as if they knew him. Satisfied, Memphis gunned the car toward Cortlandt Street, past the World Trade Center, on course to the Brooklyn-Battery Tunnel.

He mentioned one of his associates in the world of professional wrestling, gesturing so much it became impossible to ignore his arms, which are black and blue with tattoos. Headlights from oncoming traffic played across his face, smooth yet still swollen from reconstructive work.

"A friend of mine," he was saying, "Bret Hart—Bret 'Hitman' Hart, who's the current World Wrestling Federation champion, and has sat in the same seat that you are sitting in now—has said to me, 'Mike, when they stop talking about you is when you gotta worry. When they talk about you, whether it's good or bad, you're still on their mind, and that's what counts.' "

If the Hitman is right, Mike Memphis need never worry.

"But ask away," he said. "I won't interrupt you no more."

"Tell me when you got the tattoos," I said.

"I started when I was sixteen with the bird over here, this cardinal on my left forearm." He pointed with his right arm, glancing at the road. "And I graduated from that."

"Tell me about the Elvis one."

"OK, the Elvis one is Elvis with the Pinwheel jumpsuit. The latter-day Vegas years, with 'I'll Remember You' with the music staff and the words 'I'll Remember You' on my shoulder. And on my bicep, 'Elvis 1935-1977.' Done only in black and gray, not colored like my other tattoos, because I wanted it to stand out from the other ones. As opposed to, like, you, see this cowgirl, you know, it's more or less a cartoon."

"Why the cowgirl?"

"Well, I wanted a girl on my arm, but I didn't want to get a geisha girl, because that's, you know, not right. I didn't want to get the *Playboy* bunny because it's sexist and all that stuff. And I wanted a woman on my arm. I mean, what's more innocent than a cowgirl, a country girl, you know? So I figured it's not provocative, it's not indecent, it's not the *Playboy* bunny, it's not detrimental to women. So it's something that's nice. And eventually I want to get 'Memphis Belle' written on top of it." We enter the Brooklyn-Battery Tunnel. "This is sort of like a ritual of us Italian boys in Brooklyn that we do growing up. It's part of our growing-up process that we do."

Born Michael Anthony Lepore, a chubby boy from Bensonhurst, Mike Memphis always sensed he was different from other kids. When he was seven, he discovered Elvis and began to plot the form and shape those differences would take.

"Everybody else was listening to the Partridge Family and Kiss and all that stuff," he said. "I have a twin sister also. I'm a twin also, just like Elvis, he was a twin. And she used to listen to that kind of stuff—David Cassidy, Kiss, Elton John. And I was listening to B. J. Thomas, Elvis, Tom Jones. I was, like, really weird."

But even then, young Michael understood that the weirdness he coveted took dedication and effort. At fourteen he carried a stack of books filled with Elvis pictures to a hairstylist, who dyed and sculpted his hair and baby sideburns. Then he ran around the corner to the drugstore for film so his sister could take pictures.

"I still have those pictures," he said. "There's this one picture that really looks terrific. I mean, it really looks great. My first publicity shot, so to speak. And I wish I could get back down to that weight, I tell ya."

Impressionists fascinated him—Rich Little, Frank Gorshin. "Fred Travalena," he said, "was my inspiration to get into show business." As a teenager he tried standup comedy, riding the subway to gigs. More and more his act included celebrity impressions, starting with Peter Lorre and culminating in Elvis. After Elvis died, he felt a little lost. When he realized some people felt even more lost than he did, he settled on a career.

"You know, I'm the first to admit, I'm not the greatest singer out there," Mike said. "There are a lot of Elvises out there that have terrific voices."

And as a singer, how would he rate himself?

Pause.

"Average."

Long pause.

"Average."

Besides, to him it was the entire package that mattered. He rechristened himself Memphis, for obvious reasons, and took the name legally. As he told Rolonda Watts on her television talk show, "When these people go home, a month from now they'll remember that before they'll remember Michael Anthony Lepore."

"You're right!" she replied.

And for reasons less apparent, he refuses to be labeled an impersonator. "It's because I am an actor," he explained. "I'm a gifted, natural actor. And by saying I'm an Elvis impersonator, it puts me in a group with Elvis impersonators which are black, white, women, men, children, Orientals. Nothing wrong with people doing that. I am an actor, because I not only do the Elvis shtick, but I also act as well. I've acted because I'm on commercials, I've been on television shows where I've acted, like 'Loving.' So therefore I consider myself an actor who just so happens to do a lot of the Elvis stuff."

A lot of the Elvis stuff. If you watch any television at all, especially if you watch a certain kind of television, you may have encountered Mike Memphis. He sought advice from James Earl Jones on how to use the Yellow Pages. (The Christmas cards Memphis mailed that year featured a picture of himself with the actor.) He spread his cape on "Geraldo." He helped Joan Rivers hawk Elvis watches on her now-defunct TV shopping show, speaking in a voice mystically free of its usual Brooklyn accent, his hair a flawless blue-black souffle. "I'm glad you are alive," Rivers told him.

As long as he has work, he figures he is doing something right. The thing that ticks him off are guys he believes take the Elvis gig too far— talking in a drawl all the time, sporting sunglasses after dark.

"I think that's sick," he said. "That gives me a bad reputation. People look at me and say, 'Oh, he's another nut-job Elvis.' And I get people who say to me, 'Didn't I see you in the mall, didn't I see you here?' No, you didn't, darling, *you did not.* Because I don't walk around in leather pants or a satin shirt. *I don't do that.* Those are the people looking for attention, looking for an ego boost. I don't need the attention, I don't need the boost to my ego.

"And so therefore I downplay it when I'm in public and how I keep it separate is just because I'm sane. I know this is a business—*this is a business.* I love Elvis, I love what I'm doing. But I also realize it is a business. And people said, 'Well, you shouldn't be in it to make money.' Well, then what are you in it for?"

When the television tabloid program "A Current Affair" wanted to re-enact "Elvis: The Final 24 Hours," Memphis was their man. He crawled out of a bed and told an actress playing Elvis's girlfriend Ginger Alden, "I'm gonna go to the bathroom and go read for a while." Gulped down pills. Accepted a manila envelope full of drugs with a doped-up, beaten down look on his face. Flopped over on a bathroom floor, face slack and mouth wide open, while an actor administered mouth-to-mouth resuscitation. It is hard to watch this performance without wondering how the chubby boy who still owns his first Elvis forty-fives had come, and gone, so far.

It must feel strange to play your childhood hero as a corpse on a bathroom floor.

"It was just a job," Mike said. "I didn't give it much thought. I was just listening to the director, taking his cues. It didn't give me a chance to think about Elvis, just to think about the job I'm doing."

So Elvis didn't go through his mind at all?

"What was going through my mind was, When are they gonna finish this? I'm bored. Really. And also going through my mind was, I hope this guy doesn't put his lips on mine when he's doing mouth to mouth. That kind of stuff, rather than thinking about Elvis. If I'd be thinking about Elvis, I wouldn't be doing my job. Know what I mean? I'm a professional. I'm thinking about my job, not about Elvis.

"Some guys would think it's scary and tell the director, 'You've gotta wait, I gotta get my composure, get me a beer, get me a drink.' Get the hell outta here! Stop acting like Elvis—who you trying to impress, a half dozen people in the room with you? Who you trying to impress? They're just thinking, you're wasting their time. They gotta get back to the studio. They want a guy who can pull it off. They don't want Elvis."

Among the first batch of pictures Mike Memphis mailed to me were photographs of himself posing with a Bette Davis impersonator, real celebrities such as Gene Simmons of Kiss and Brooke Shields, and color shots a nurse took of him while he was having roughly $12,000 worth of plastic surgery to make him look more like Elvis.

The operation was a success—not because it made him Elvis's twin, but because it got him on TV. Mike, who acted as his own press agent, mailed copies of these photos and his story to talk shows nationwide. Two of them, Jerry Springer and Rolonda Watts, invited him on for a chat.

To Rolonda he explained he had pec implants—purely for vanity reasons, not to enhance his Elvisness—liposuction, with some of that fat injected into his lips, his cheeks hollowed, his chin and neck thinned, his lower lip thickened, and his jawline and chin balanced with implants.

Mike was pleased with the media attention, but puzzled over why people considered his surgery unusual. "I just decided I wanted to do something to my face," he said. "I didn't like my double chin, I didn't like my cheeks, my neck. Although people would say, 'Oh, Mike, you're cute, you're cute, you're cute,' I don't want to be cute. I want to be handsome. That's the difference. You know, Lou Costello was not an ugly man, but he wasn't the rugged Rock Hudson or Engelbert Humperdinck type. You know what I mean."

He underwent the surgery on January 8, Elvis's birthday. "And because I'm in show business and I did it, I obviously marketed myself: 'Man Has Surgery to Look Like Elvis'—for publicity. That goes to show you I'm a businessman," he said.

It drives impersonators like Jerome Marion out of their minds that such a businessman can sell such a product. Jerome said that after Mike Memphis performed at the first EPIIA convention in Las Vegas and showed his tattoos to members of the media, he was thrown out of the organization.

"He was pulled off the stage, just basically because he was atrocious," Jerome explained. "There's no other word for it. He couldn't find a note if it was marked in a bag named Note. . . . And he was yelling and screaming, yelling in the back, and I'm like, 'Mike, you were not even close to keys. You were burying notes. People were getting up, walking out of the audience.' I mean, come on!"

Mike allowed that he did display his tattoos, but denied that he was thrown out or told that he stunk. "The only thing that was said to me by him and Ron Bessette (the EPIIA founder) was 'Mike, take the earrings out of your ear.'"

Mike can produce certificates and cancelled checks that indicate he paid dues as a member of the association for two years after the first Las Vegas convention. But video of that performance confirms that at times he did sing off-key. And he never attended another convention, saying that he would rather work in his home territory and get paid then spend money on a trip across the country. Though he counts many impersonators among his friends, he does not travel in the usual circuit of contests and shows, preferring to make his own way.

Jerome hastens to say that he doesn't mean to insult Mike Memphis, who is obviously an Elvis fan. "It's just basically saying that he really gets the wrong kind of attention that we're looking for," he said, "and that's the kind of attention that can really bury the association just quicker than shit."

Mike said, "Tell him, don't ever get off a plane in New York. I will make sure the cab driver will take him to the Bronx and leave him there."

Is there anything Mike Memphis wouldn't do?

He thought. "God, like what—a video of Elvis shooting heroin? Yeah, I wouldn't do that. Like Elvis doing a photo shoot out in the ghetto, buying drugs? Yeah, I wouldn't do that. For one thing, I wouldn't want to be in the ghetto dressed like Elvis."

So far, however—and for this he was grateful—no one has ever offered him a job that he found offensive.

"Look," he said, "I'm hurting nobody, I'm not bothering anybody. You could laugh, but look at me. I always dressed, my parents always dressed me very nice when I went to school. I never once wore jeans to high school or sneakers to high school. Never once. If I'm lying to you, I should die right now as I'm speaking to you. That's the God's honest truth. I was always immaculate. You could do whatever you want, say whatever you want, make fun of me, whatever, because the people that are my friends, they accept me for how I am or whatever. Because people look at you, they say, 'Look at this psychopath.' But I'm not. See?"

Speeding down the expressway toward the Verrazano Bridge in his Eighty-Eight toward the South Shore Country Club, he explained the lure of professional wrestling. Mike wrestled professionally for a short while, just shows in school gyms, and he has appeared on World Wrestling Federation (WWF) shows as Elvis. In one spot he did with Jerry "The King" Lawler, he drove up in the 1959 pink Cadillac he owned and said: "I've seen people impersonate me all my life and it's not right. I don't think they're doing me justice. And I know a lot about impersonators. I was just having lunch with my good friend JFK the other day. You know, we were talkin' about the girl we were dating—Marilyn, you know what I mean? And they were both tellin' me they don't like it when they see their impostors around. And I don't like it when I see mine."

"Were you a good guy or a bad guy?" I asked.

He shot me a look like I was nuts. "I was a good guy. Of course."

"You were Mike Memphis, good guy."

"Good guy. Although when I did the stint with Jerry Lawler, I was a bad guy because he's a bad guy. But I was basically the kind who won and lost a little."

"What made you not do it anymore?"

"Well,"—he deepened his voice—"I'm allergic to pain, to be honest with you." He paused to laugh at his own joke. "That's a good one. It's a tough business, it's a very tough business. Sometimes I regret I didn't stick with it, though. I really do. I just wish I would have stuck with it."

"You would give up Elvis to do that?"

"I would give up a lot of things, I would give up a lot of my freedom and my time. For that shot again, man. My dream came true and I did WWF television. And that was like the highlight of my career for me."

"You're kidding."

"If my career ended tomorrow, I'm very, very happy. I am extremely happy."

"That was the highlight."

"The highlight of my career."

Mike paid the toll at the bridge, grew contemplative. "I am very happy in my career, where I've gone up until now. I hope to continue doing as well as I'm doing. If my career ended tomorrow, I've done everything I wanted to do. I've done television, I've done film, I've done commercials, I've done modeling, I've been in newspapers, magazines, centerfolds of *Women's Wear Daily*, centerfold of the *Examiner, National Examiner,* all the talk shows, commercials, like I've said, and soap operas. I had a part on 'Loving,' a brief part, but it was a speaking role, and out of all the Elvises, I got it. I anchored 'ABC World News Now' with Boyd Matson, and that was a highlight for me, and out of all of the Elvises, twenty Elvises they auditioned, I got the role."

Mike decided his ad-lib skills must have been impressed them. "And the reason why they took me is because first of all, they said my look was good and my hair was excellent! My whole look is excellent."

"They said your hair was excellent."

He looked at me like I was blind. "Yes! Everybody does. They say, 'Is that a wig?' And I say, 'No, it's real.'"

"You mean they specifically said they liked . . . ?"

"I swear to God, I should die if I'm lying. Everybody. The girl asked, 'Is that your real hair?' I says, 'Yes.' 'Oh, it looks great.' I said, 'Well, thank you.'"

Headlight glare rolled off it as he drove. There was a small spit curl in the front and three separate strands falling across his forehead, sprayed to a high gloss. It was indeed some kind of excellent.

He focused on the road and said if he chose to end his career tomorrow, he would be satisfied with what he had done.

"You can only go but so far in this business," he said. "I know that. I accept that. I know for me to go further with my career, it would have to be in another field—maybe play the wacky neighbor on a sitcom. Or doing comedy or being a legitimate actor or doing country music or doing something. But I know that as far as what I've done, how much further can I go? I can continue getting good gigs, getting commercials, getting acting parts, maybe getting Legends or getting some role like that—yeah, my career can continue getting good jobs like I've been getting. But you could never get to me the point where I'm going to be hosting my own late-night show, giving, you know, David Letterman competition. Not as Mike Memphis. Not as an Elvis performer, I should say. Because Mike Memphis is not only an Elvis performer, he's a—he's a renaissance man."

Then he broke into "Born Free," then began to impersonate Walter Cronkite.

After showcasing his versions of Sylvester Stallone, Burgess Meredith, and Charles Bronson, Mike turned into the South Shore Country Club and heaved the Olds up onto the grass, where valets were parking cars. Fireflies glowed around us. Across the lawn, party sounds—bass beat, loud voices, clapping. A sign out front said, "Fine Dining/Elegant Banquet Facilities." Mike spotted a valet, a short-haired, smiling young man, and yelled out the window, impersonating a very friendly man: "Hi there, young fella!" In a low voice he said, "Now I have to take the key off of here. This way these hooligans don't make copies of my house keys."

He pulled a black duffle bag out of the back seat. Neatly folded inside was his jumpsuit, the popular white-and-blue Phoenix.

The South Shore Country Club is a colonial-style building with cut-glass doors and a chandelier in the small lobby that looked like it was dripping with icicles. The moment Mike Memphis entered, a woman in a flashy green dress shouted over the Frankie Valli song blaring behind the reception hall doors: "They're waiting for you!"

"What, everybody knows I'm here?" Mike asked. He thought he was supposed to be a surprise for the guests.

"I do," the woman replied, giggling. She introduced herself and said she worked with Vincent.

Mike introduced himself, then pointed to me. "This is one of my agents," he said. "No, really. She's a powerful person."

The woman ignored this. "I told my husband there's gonna be a big surprise here tonight," she said.

"Don't tell them that!" Mike said, teasing her. "They'll see me, they'll be disappointed!"

She walked away, shooting him a glance over her shoulder. "No, they won't."

"See what I mean?" he said after she had gone. "Most Elvises are like"—he slurred his voice Southern-style—"mfaumflbfbigsurpriseno-verybigsurprise. I do take my act seriously, but I don't mind joking around a little bit. Because, you know, it makes the world go 'round." He spotted a mirror. "Let me check out my hair."

Most of his jobs were like this one, private or corporate affairs. On TV he could talk nonstop, but here he behaved himself. He was the soul of restraint.

"Excuse me," he said to a man walking across the hall. "At your convenience, can you tell them that Elvis is outside?"

He looked Mike over. He nodded. "I'll tell them right now."

Mike settled on a green sofa to wait. Over the throb of "Shout," he insisted he wasn't nervous. "The only thing that I worry about—I don't get nervous, but I do worry—is if I'm working with a band or a DJ. Like tonight it's a DJ here. The thing I worry about is I've encountered a lot of uncooperative DJs. They won't press pause in between the songs. Just let it keep going and going. No time to speak in between songs. They don't put my microphone up loud enough, or they don't put the music up loud enough, or I get so much feedback it's impossible to work."

About ten minutes later, the couple appeared. Vincent wore a simple black tuxedo, patent leather shoes, and an earring in his left ear. Melissa's gown had a hoop skirt and pearl strands that trailed down her arms. Her bright blond hair poufed from an opening in her veil's head-piece. They beamed at Mike.

"Congratulations," he said to them.

"You look great!" Melissa said. "Did you lose weight?"

He smiled coyly. "I don't know," he said.

He promised them they would love his blue Phoenix. He informed them, "I'm not the wacko who walks around the mall. I'm a different wacko." He explained his routine: "I'll come with my stomach out like I'm pregnant and do it slow. If people are coming out expecting the rockabilly Elvis, they're going to be disappointed." He added, "If people want to take pictures of me, that's all right." They laughed, thanked Mike and started back into the hall. Vincent shook his hand.

Mike sat down again and showed me his teeth. He wanted to have them redone, not so much so he would resemble Elvis, but so he could look better. As he spoke the DJ approached, a young guy with blond hair cut very short and a wide open face.

"How you doing," the DJ said, "I'm Mike."

"I thought you were the maitre d'!" Mike Memphis said.

"No, no."

"OK, what time do I go on?"

"Probably in about fifteen minutes."

"OK. So then I'll get dressed in about five minutes. It takes me ten minutes to get dressed, and I'll just wait out here."

"Great. Great. You got that tape for me to cue up?"

"You said you didn't have any reverb or echo?" The guests were clink-ing knives against glasses in the hall.

"Yes. Nothing at all."

Out of his bag Mike Memphis extracted a cassette. "It says, 'Elvis music,'" he said to me. "This way he knows it's Elvis music."

"OK, here you go," Memphis said, handing over the tape.

The DJ promised to play the theme from *2001: A Space Odyssey.*

"OK. And then when I come in I'll get the mike. Now I'm not going to get feedback or anything, right?"

"Not at all."

"OK, you got a good system? Because I worked with this DJ last week—the worst uncooperative man. Are you Italian?"

"No, I'm Irish. I'm American, actually."

"I'm Irish, too. My real name is—is—is Mike . . . Sullivan. Now that's my real name." Memphis leaned in close. "And the God's honest truth is that I'm Catholic, so we gotta take care of each other."

Mike the DJ laughed. "That's all right. I'd do it no matter what. It's not my show, it's your show."

They talked bass and reverb and parted smiling. To me, Memphis said: "Didn't you like that? See, this is New York City, and you gotta be one of their own in this city. I can pass for Irish, Italian, I could pass for Jewish, I could pass for—no, I couldn't pass for Jewish, I got all these tattoos. Though people have asked me, 'Are you Jewish or Italian?' Well, it's almost the same thing, anyway. I can if I want to maybe pass for Latin— what do you think?" He sighed. "This is turning into a very long night."

After about fifteen minutes, the DJ returned again. "It's gonna be another twenty-five to thirty minutes."

"Oh, man, that long?"

"Yeah."

"Man. Aw, I wish you could start sooner. I had somewhere to go tonight."

"I do what they tell me," the DJ said.

"No! It's not your fault! No, it's the fault of the bride and groom to tell me to get here this early."

After he left, Memphis said, "I don't have nothing to do tonight. But I'll tell 'em that. Make 'em feel bad for me. Maybe they'll voluntarily throw me another hundred without me having to say I want it."

Around us the party blazed on. The guests inside had almost finished their dinners, and a crew of men from the kitchen were unfolding tables for dessert.

Through the reception hall doors burst a short man with a mustache on his friendly face and short brown hair gelled up and coaxed to the left. His brown snakeskin slip-on shoes matched his suit. The man introduced himself as Anthony, a high school classmate of Memphis's.

"You doing an act? You singing?" he asked.

Memphis filled him in, and they caught up on classmates. Anthony mentioned that he married a girl from their school.

"Oh, by the way," Memphis said, "I just want to confirm. I'm not the wacko. Two people asked me, 'Do you walk around the mall with sunglasses?'" This made Anthony laugh, a high-pitched, happy sound. "That's not me. I mean, maybe in high school I used to do that."

"In high school, everybody used to call you Elvis," Anthony said.

"Yeah. But now as an adult, I don't want the attention. I only blow my hair out like this and wear makeup when I'm doing a gig. Otherwise, it's a baseball cap, my hair is slicked back, you know?"

Anthony could not stop laughing.

"Elvis has been very good to me. I've become extremely, multi, multi-rich," Memphis went on. "I own a 1959 hot pink Cadillac."

"Do you really?" Anthony asked.

"The one that was in *Wise Guys* with Danny DeVito. I did a WWF with Jerry Lawler last year. I've been on 'Loving,' the soap opera. I was an actor for ABC News. Yeah, let me just show you, one second if you got a second." He unzipped his black bag, pulled out a piece of the jumpsuit, snowy white with blue embroidery the color of his boots. "And all my suits are made by Elvis's designer. And do I look different from high school?"

"Yeah," Anthony said.

"I've had a lot of plastic surgery on my face. And that's no shit. That's the honest truth."

"You do look different," Anthony said. "You do."

He zipped the bag. "I've done six commercials, I own the car, the fifty-nine Caddy. As a matter fact, Mr. Blobby was in from England, that costume character, they rented it out for six days. It's been on 'General Hospital.' I make more money renting that car out. A car nobody wanted to buy—fifteen thousand dollars. Jay Leno called me up, wanted to buy it. A hundred grand. Because I was on the cover of the *National Examiner,* the tabloid? And it had a whole nine-color picture centerfold there, me on the operating table, me before the surgery, me after, pictures with the car and all that stuff. And he saw it, told me he wanted it. He collects cars."

They talked about former teachers for a while, then Anthony headed back inside. "You notice I introduced myself as 'I used to be Michael Lepore,'" Mike Memphis said.

In the center of the lobby, kitchen staff assembled a dessert table—tiny kiwi-topped cheesecakes, finger-sized eclairs, sweet baby croissants. Near the cloakroom a knot of guys with slicked-back hair stood, snickering. One of them said something in a exaggerated southern accent. They cracked up. Mike grimaced. "See, I get that all the time!" he said. "Why don't you come up to me and go, 'Hey, guy, you look like Elvis?' But they gotta be dicks about it. Don't print that. Say they gotta be jerks about it. But I ignore it."

"Does it feel weird, that everybody who walks by—"

"Looks at me? Well, I'm used to it. Some guys will be standing there, standing like Elvis, like this, doing this, you know"—he started to shake his legs—"with the leg like this, and trying to be Elvis with the stance, and with the glasses. I mean, I'm standing here incognito, playing low key, you know? That's how I do it, because I've been doing it for so long. And I don't need a boost to my ego. I'm confident in myself." He studied the dessert table again. "After this maybe we'll stop at the Carnegie Deli or something," he said. "I'm starving."

Mike the DJ announced in a deep voice: "And now, we have a very special cake ceremony . . ." Mike Memphis looked up sharply, then down at himself, tropical and inappropriate. "The CAKE? Aw, man, they don't even tell me to get dressed. That's nice." He grabbed his bag and jogged over to the cloakroom. "Gonna get dressed in here. If somebody tries to get in here, just tell 'em Elvis is in here, I'll be out in two minutes." Through the hall doors Vincent and Melissa stood before a three-tiered cake ringed with pink, little white flowers trimmed with green leaves spraying across the top. They fed each other with forks while the guests sang a cake-cutting song to the tune of "The Farmer in the Dell."

The bride and her brother were dancing to "Bridge Over Troubled Water" when Mike popped out of the closet in his Phoenix jumpsuit and his blue boots and ducked into the restroom. When he emerged, he offered his hand to a little boy standing nearby. The boy hid his face in his hands.

Mike swung his arms and circled around the dessert table, his eyes fixed far away. He softly sang the first two lines of "The Wonder of You." He ducked into the restroom again. Just after Vincent tossed the garter, the DJ cued up "C.C. Rider" and introduced the night's surprise: "From the nineteen fifties, please welcome—Elvis Presley!"

Mike rolled his eyes: "Nineteen *seventies*," he said, and burst through the white doors.

Vincent and Melissa stood in the darkness near the cake table, holding hands and looking pleased with their surprise. The crowd roared. Men put their fingers in their mouths and whistled. Women squealed. One skinny guy near the door lowered his head and shook it gravely. Mike took a few steps. He lunged dramatically, arms flung wide. The embroidered bird on his back flickered under the lights.

"All right," the DJ said, "let's hear it for Elvis, everybody."

"This is especially for you," Mike told the newlyweds over the string introduction of "The Wonder of You." Mike spoke half the lyrics, and he threw in an *oh, baby* when things got rough. A few people looked at each other and raised their eyebrows. If they said anything, the screams drowned them out. The majority left little doubt: They loved him.

Mike strode over to a screeching woman in a strapless dress, kissed her and handed her a scarf from around his neck. He finessed a small pirouette. A guy with a beer belly and rumpled blue necktie tipped his face to the ceiling and howled like a dog. The song ended and Mike looked around, laughing and taking in the applause. His face glowed pink under the lights. "This audience, man," he said, "this is the first time I think I've really been entertained." Mike Memphis calls himself an actor, and maybe he is. For the first time all night, he didn't seem to be acting. The crowd howled some more, and he turned to the newlyweds. "Vinnie and Melissa, you guys, I want to wish you good luck in your life together, man."

"Thank you!" Vincent said. "*Thankyouverymuch!*"

"He waited four hundred days to say that," someone yelled.

Mike said: "It took me three hours to get here tonight." (Actually, it took a little over an hour.) "You guys made it worthwhile. You really did. It was really worth the drive coming out here."

"All the way from Memphis?" someone yelled.

"From Brooklyn," Mike said.

He performed "Teddy Bear" because they begged him to, then bowed deeply when they threw pink carnations on the floor at his blue-booted feet. As he left, he bent to kiss a little girl. He burst out of the room, cheers rushing behind him, only to find his path blocked by the dessert table. He smiled and sidled past. Vincent and Melissa followed him out to pose for a photo. Mike the DJ strolled over. "How did it sound, all right?" Memphis asked him.

The DJ paused a moment. His face looked pinched. "Yeah," he said, "you know."

"Nobody's Elvis," Mike said.

"Absolutely not," the DJ replied.

A raspy-voiced woman appeared, eyeing his jumpsuit. "I didn't know Elvis was available for weddings."

Mike turned to her, eyes bright. "Weddings, bar mitzvahs, grand openings, proms—just about everything and anything."

"Do you have a business card?"

"I certainly do."

He changed into his incognito clothes and strolled into the humid night. His hair had begun to curl around his ears; his makeup shone. As he unlocked his car, five girls in a silver Nissan leaned out the windows to their waists and ogled, grinning and showing big, even teeth. They looked like refugees from a float in a homecoming parade. Mike didn't notice.

He punched my arm. "See what I mean by work the crowd?" he asked. We shot onto the expressway, bound for Manhattan. For two hours on a Friday night—eight minutes of that spent actually perform-ing—Mike Memphis had earned $250. And they liked him. He pulled out his cellular phone to check his messages for last-minute weekend gigs. The Eighty-Eight laid down a noise like a train, and the lights along the road glowed with champagne halos. Half an hour to midnight and ahead of us the night shone on, jet black and lousy with possibility.

Living an Image

*E*lvis has become so much more than just a white singer," said El Vez, the famous Mexican Elvis. "He's an emblem of power and empowerment, and musical history and American dreams—an icon that can be held by anybody, or should be able to be held by anybody. Even if you thought the people don't have talent, stuff like that, I think it's the empowerment thing, to say, 'I am somebody, and I can be somebody.' Like Elvis, coming from hillbilly tradition. He was, for all intents and purposes, a white nigger, and people didn't like him. He was shunned, he was outcast, he was hillbilly white trash. And he had these feelings of no self-worth, as maybe Latinos do or women do. And he became Elvis, and empowered himself, via music, via being on stage and becoming Elvis. And then he got to say, 'OK, these are the things that you hated about me, my white trashness, and now I'm flaunting them. And now I'm better than you. Not in a negative way I'm better than you, but I rose above what expectations you placed on me.'"

Elvis Presley told a reporter at the press conference before his four Madison Square Garden concerts in 1972, "Well, the image is one thing, and a human being is another. It's very hard to live up to an image." If living up to Elvis's image hurt Elvis himself, an impersonator cannot expect an easy life. The fact that most of them accept a little pain as part of the job doesn't always help. Any impersonator with half a brain under all that hair knows that he or she can never be Elvis. The problem, as impersonators see it, is that everyone treats them as if they don't realize this. Even people who might be expected to understand criticize the average impersonator.

John Stuart, founder of Legends in Concert, receives an average of two tapes each week from Elvis impersonators who hope to star in his shows. Men, women, white, black, Asian, children, adults—all of them want to be Elvis. From what he has seen, Stuart estimates that at least 1,500 people worldwide impersonate Elvis Presley. And that 98 percent of them should find something else to do.

"But even if they're a waiter waiting for their shot," he said, "or a bus driver, or whatever they're doing, they're sitting there with a big belt on and the sideburns, and people say, 'Hey, do you do Elvis?' That's good enough for them.

"I think that the Elvis Presley look is similar to the shaven heads at the airports and the guys who wear the big spiked hairdos. It's a way for people to get attention. And it is a cult. It's an Elvis army. And they personally are able to be somebody instantly." He slid into a credible Elvis impression: "'Hey, man—how you doin'. Yes, ma'am.' They're going to the grocery store: 'Could I have some butter? My mama needs some butter.' They talk like him during the day. And what does that do? It sets them apart from everybody else. When they go to the grocery store, people look at them—for no other reason than that they've got a pompadour and they got sideburns, the big belt, and they raise their lip when they talk."

Ironically, Stuart has probably done more than anyone to promote Elvis Presley as a plausible alter ego. Legends in Concert, which he first staged in 1983 with $1.5 million of his own money, has become a multimillion-dollar global road show. It has its base at the Imperial Palace in Las Vegas, but has expanded to Hawaii, Atlantic City, Korea, Australia, Myrtle Beach, Toronto, Japan, and Branson, Missouri, in a theater built by the Osmonds. It has succeeded so well that Stuart planned to take his parent company, On Stage Entertainment Inc., public in early 1997. Elvis is not the only impersonator Legends in Concert features—everyone from Marilyn Monroe to Buddy Holly to Cher takes a turn—but Elvis closes 99 percent of the shows, except for a few places like Moscow, where for some reason Michael Jackson is a bigger draw.

Stuart credits the popularity of Elvis impersonators to the symbolic thrall of Elvis's image, rather than his own skills as a promoter. This is a culture—indeed, a world—where celebrities fuel every kind of fantasy.

People live their dreams through celebrities. Impersonating Elvis allows thousands to breathe life into these dreams, and to transform themselves into the very image that they admire. Stuart compares the Elvis phenomenon to the way men once wore red windbreakers and combed their hair to look like James Dean. By assuming a celebrity's appearance, the impersonator tells the world that he or she owns at least a piece of their magic.

Legends, however, does not employ seven full-time James Deans, as it does Elvis look-alikes. This attests to Presley's staying power as an entertainer. It also hints that—on the surface, anyway—Elvis Presley qualifies as arguably the world's easiest entertainer to imitate.

"Elvis Presley was so far out there from the look of the average person that you can put on a costume, you can dye your hair black, you can wear sideburns, and you take on a caricature of a mega-icon," Stuart said. "And whether your face looks exactly like it or not, you raise your lip, you add a little vibrato to your voice, you shake your hip a little bit, and you think that all at once you can make the girls scream and even the guys say, 'Hey, that guy is cool.' Because even the guys related to Elvis.

"It's so quick, to adapt yourself to a character who had strong characteristics in his theatrical presentation. It's easier for a guy to do that than to stand up and make people think you're Vic Damone. Nobody's gonna know you're Vic Damone. Nobody's gonna know you're Frank Sinatra unless you sing exactly like him. But an Elvis impersonator can play with it and can cheat and skirt around any real talent by the mere fact that he does the gyrations and wears the jumpsuit and has the sideburns and the hairpiece."

It has not helped their cause that many impersonators have behaved in ways that most people would consider unprofessional, even ignoring the fact that dressing up like a dead man strains a person's credibility. It has also become easy and cheap to conjure the image of Elvis. Black hair, sideburns, and a white jumpsuit have become a sort of shorthand for the strangeness of American culture and its obsession with celebrity. Movies such as *Honeymoon in Vegas,* in which a group of jumpsuited men leaped out of an airplane and helped Nicolas Cage win back Sarah Jessica Parker, have fed the notion that Elvises appear in public places, perform incongruous acts, then return to the planet from which they came. Real impersonators hate it when people ask them if they're one of the Flying Elvises. For one thing, Flying Elvises don't sing.

It is difficult to do justice to a profession most people consider deviant behavior. So in self-defense, impersonators cultivate standards and codes of conduct. It is easier to ignore people who don't respect you when you know in your heart that you are doing something right. Although even when you know what you're doing, sometimes it's still hard to tell.

"These guys are serious," said D. J. Fontana. "They wouldn't hurt anybody, and they're not tarnishing Elvis's name or his image at all, because that's what they do, and they want to do it right. And most of them do it right. You saw it yourself tonight. These guys are good at what they're doing! And they're very sincere. They wouldn't do anything to harm them—oh, no, God. They'd rather jump off a bridge than do that. Most of 'em are nice guys, they've got wives and families, just like everybody else." Out in the hallway a group of impersonators traded lines of "How Great Thou Art." He laughed. "They sing with each other."

D. J. Fontana played drums behind Elvis Presley from 1955 to 1968, both in the studio and on the road. He was responsible for the rapid-fire rolls in "Hound Dog" and the rock-smashing slam of "Jailhouse Rock." He said, "Had I not worked for him, I'd be like everybody else, probably working with everybody, not having a job, hardly." Instead he has become a celebrity, a piece of living history who wears very wide ties. Since Elvis's death he has messed with a couple of bands, including a group of the old Sun Studio musicians. They tour the world, letting loose on Johnny Cash and Jerry Lee Lewis classics, and sometimes a little Elvis. This boy from Shreveport, Louisiana, has traveled to the south of France and Argentina and Kuwait and Australia, where he hung out backstage with the Rolling Stones. "I get a kick out of talking to them," he said. "The only one you don't see is the singer. He's always goin' somewhere else. But Ron, and Keith, and Charlie—nice guys."

And when he can fit it into his schedule, he performs behind impersonators. D. J. Fontana is one of a small group of former Elvis Presley musicians and other employees who make money by working with imitators of their former boss. The Jordainares have sung backup for impersonators. Charlie Hodge, Elvis's onstage scarf and water man for years, does the same job for a former theology student from Dayton, Ohio, named Lou Vuto at the Memories Theater in Pigeon Forge, Tennessee. These people lend legitimacy to what impersonators do and draw crowds who want to get close to anyone who was once close to Elvis.

Fontana's playing hasn't changed since he sat behind Elvis in the movie *Jailhouse Rock* or on the deck of an aircraft carrier on "The Milton Berle Show;" he chews his gum, turns his head from side to side, then every once in a while lets loose, his mouth half open but his face otherwise relaxed. He has a prominent nose and a steel gray pompadour, and his sleepy eyes give the impression that nothing he has seen in the last forty years surprises him much anymore.

One night he came to Erlanger, Kentucky, for a weekend impersonator jam at Peel's Palace, a flat-roofed nightclub that shares a parking lot with a HoJo Inn and a Waffle House. He sat in the back with a Budweiser on an old couch in the dressing room and waited for his turn on stage. He sees no irony in working with people who dress up like his old boss, or in the ways that people treat these performers like Elvis.

"It's hard to tell what people are gonna do," he said. In the old days, after all, fans busted his drums and flung him into an orchestra pit.

"It's not Elvis," I said.

"No," he agreed, cheerfully.

"In some cases, it's not even close."

"No," Fontana replied. "But all they see is the jumpsuits. The voices are fairly close. Not close enough, but they're fairly close. Probably a lot of these people never seen Elvis before, even the local people. So all they're just trying to remember what he looked like. In the movies, in the Vegas days. That's what they're lookin' at, you know? They get caught up in the Elvis image. Because a lot of them, you know, they dream Elvis twenty-four hours a day, some of them—the true fans, you talk to 'em, that's all they know! Which is good. That's what keeps me workin' out here. Keeps these guys working."

If the impersonators represent an Elvis link to the fans, people like D. J. Fontana represent a history these men want and need to get inside of, the better to understand themselves. At shows they approach him to compliment his work and, in soft voices, ask for his opinion of their acts. "They're real respectful, they really are," he said. "I'd rather them not feel that-a-way. I'd rather just be one of the guys. Drink a beer, have a good time. No use making those guys nervous, you know. They'll ask you a million questions."

What do people ask him? "Oh, shoo, I don't know," he said. He stuck out his lower lip and stared into his Budweiser can, as if he hoped to divine an answer there. "Being with him. How did he think about this, and how was he thinking about that. Did he like that song, how did he record. Did he know what he was doing. They don't know. All they know is what they read. He knew what he was doing. Every minute, see. They say, 'Well, we thought that.' I say, 'No, he knew exactly what to do.' He knew *exactly* what he wanted to do. Every minute. People thought he was stupid."

Just then Chris Wilson, a Young Elvis from Cincinnati with a ruddy face and a low flat pompadour of reddish brown, walked into the room to see whether Fontana needed a fresh beer. He tugged at one of the silver lapels of his gold lamé jacket. It was a copy of half the famous Nudie-designed suit Elvis wore in the late fifties on the cover of his album *50,000,000 Elvis Fans Can't Be Wrong—Elvis Gold Records Vol. 2.* The suit is now on display in a glass case at Graceland.

"How do you like this jacket?" he asked.

Fontana gave him an up-and-down look. He raised his eyebrows, but his face showed no other expression. "Not bad," he said.

"Pretty cool?"

"Yeah."

Chris licked his lips, and when he spoke his voice sounded higher. "Did you ever see the one he wore? Elvis? That pretty close, or—?" He left the thought unfinished.

Fontana was silent a moment, as if trying to find the right words. On stage someone was singing "Way Down."

"Well, the gold was a little . . ."

"Thicker?"

"It was gold," Fontana said.

Chris's face flushed pinker. "It was *gold?*"

"Oh, yeah, it was real gold."

Chris looked down at himself. The shiny fabric reflected warp and beautiful illusion and, in its folds and drapes, bands of a brighter light. "Oh, damn," he said, "I didn't know that. I spent eight hundred bucks for this and I ain't got real gold?"

"His was ten grand," Fontana said. (The actual price was $2,500.)

"You hear people talking about the gold lamé," Chris said, shaking his head. "I was like, Oh, I'm in! Gold lamé."

"We used to have to carry that thing around, me and Scotty and Bill," Fontana said, referring to Scotty Moore and the late Bill Black, who played with Elvis from his Sun Records days. "We'd carry it around to the car. That sucker was heavy—it musta weighed twenty pounds. Because of the leather inside to keep it in shape. It was heavy. We were trying to throw it away a lot of times, but he wouldn't go for that. We got tired of carrying that around."

The way D. J. Fontana told this story, it was as if all he were talking about was a jacket. Chris Wilson watched him closely, with the look of a man who suddenly understands that he is woefully underdressed. "That's unreal," he said. Which sounded like what Fontana was trying to say.

Even if impersonators get the clothes right, so much can go wrong. It may be easy to dress like Elvis, but it is hard to physically resemble him. Few impersonators do, and even they rarely manage without help from things like hair dye, blue contact lenses, or eye liner. Many impersonators have decent singing voices, though few sound eerily like Elvis. The best test of an impersonator's voice is to listen without watching him—to turn the head or close the eyes so that the voice can be heard apart from visual stimulation. Even when imperfect, the illusion carries power.

It is so difficult to duplicate what Elvis did—not just the look but the voice, the moves, the sense of cool—that some impersonators don't want to be called impersonators. They are actors, they insist, inhabiting a role more than they are imitating Elvis. Besides, the term impersonator has for some acquired a bad reputation, smelling of trash talk shows, tabloids, and unwashed polyester. If there is anything a serious impersonator hates, it is when someone does something to cheapen the profession.

Of course, everyone has their idea of cheap. To John Stuart, it is the majority of the people he does not employ. Next to Elvis himself, Legends in Concert has set the standard that many impersonators try to attain: natural hair, authentic costumes, and even minor plastic surgery, but only when needed to enhance the image. There is also a no-drug policy. "Absolutely anyone caught doing any kind of drugs in our show gets a six-month dismissal, including Elvis or anybody else," Stuart said. And the Elvis must command respect. "He has to carry that respect about him that he's not an impersonator," Stuart said, "that he's an actor, that he's a performer."

Most serious impersonators follow this rule. "On my business cards and so forth," said Chris T. Young, who was living in Seattle while his girlfriend finished medical school, "I use the term 'performer.' I mean, I'm not really an actor, but previous to Elvis I used to be in bands. I'm a guitar player. Something else you'll find, that probably ninety-five percent of the Elvis impersonators—and that's very generous—do not even play guitar. But no—I mean, it doesn't offend me. What might offend me is if they link me in with some of these other guys that are just doing nothing but trashing Elvis's memory."

Talk to enough impersonators and a set of unwritten rules emerges. These standards are designed not only to honor Elvis, but also to protect the practitioner from looking like a fool.

If you want to be a good impersonator, you must avoid becoming a carbon copy of Elvis. The goal is to recreate Elvis closely enough for people to lose themselves in the illusion, but not so much that it advertises a lack of imagination and skill. When you listen to enough impersonators, study their moves and watch their faces, it becomes apparent how hard what Elvis did really was, no matter what you think of it.

"I don't want to look like I made a mistake in a certain part of the move," said Jerome Marion, a Chicago Elvis who prided himself on his professionalism. "Like where you got it choreographed—I don't like to do that. I like to feel natural. If I feel like shaking my leg, I shake my leg. If I feel like shaking my shoulders, or bending down, or doing whatever it might be. So there's no organization to it whatsoever. You just kind of feel the music and you just go along with it."

You do not dress like Elvis in your personal life. Pompadours don't count. Pompadours show you are serious about your job and unconfused about identity. In a related but crucial corollary, you do not visit Graceland wearing jumpsuits or other Elvis clothing, especially during Elvis Week. Avoiding this practice demonstrates respect for the memory of Elvis. It also shows respect for yourself. Go to Graceland in August and see men and women with sweat running down their necks and hair heavy as pound cake roaming outside the souvenir shops across Elvis Presley Boulevard from the house, waiting for someone to notice them. These people make serious impersonators squirm.

"And you'll see some of these bozos out there in front of Graceland Crossing, wearing some little jumpsuit that they put together, or their girlfriend put together for them or something," said Chris T. Young. "You know what I'm talking about. It's all cheesy looking. And they've got their little paste-on sideburns. Ahh, it just makes me cringe to see these people. It seems like there ought to be Elvis police or something." He sighed, the sound of a man who understands why he is misunderstood but is powerless to stop it.

If you are a proper impersonator, you practice historical accuracy. In other words, you do not wear the two-piece black leather suit that Elvis wore in for his Comeback Special in 1968, then sing power ballads like "Hurt" and "American Trilogy" that he performed in the concert era he launched a year later.

"I'll sing 'My Way,' 'Unchained Melody,' 'How Great Thou Art,' the ones Elvis did when he got older," explained Irv Cass, who specializes in Elvis circa 1970. "I try to keep the songs in the era that they were sung in. So it goes in sync, in order, from the younger seventies to the older Elvis. I think it puts across a better impersonation. I saw a guy, a fifties act, once. And he did a real good fifties act. Then he was in his fifties outfit and he tried singing 'Hurt.' Now everybody's got their own ideas about what Elvis impersonators do in their acts and stuff. But to me it was kind of out of place to sing it in the fifties outfit."

If you are a good Elvis, you refrain from wearing poor quality clothes. The easiest way to capture the right hint of Elvisness is to wear clothes that look like his. For this reason, impersonators take their outfits seriously. They stand around at shows and study each other's embroidery and studwork, brag about the good deals they got on floor samples, complain about the length of their pants—too-short ones are common and frowned upon by purists. Impersonators who have found a tailor or seamstress who does good work at a fair price won't divulge the name for the world, for fear of losing a competitive edge.

Some impersonators elevate their work wardrobe to a level beyond mere clothing. One Halloween an impersonator named Arnel Pomp did a show at a bar, then put his gear into his van and went back inside to have a drink. When he returned he discovered that a bag behind the seat containing his $700 hairpiece, stick-on sideburns, wristwatch, and cubic zirconia rings had been stolen. The thief, however, left untouched a white jumpsuit the impersonator had studded himself.

I asked Arnel why he thought the suit had been spared. He concentrated a while, then ran a hand through his own thinning hair. "Maybe," Arnel said, "he thought it was just a costume."

The story goes that Elvis wore jumpsuits because they made him feel like the superheroes in the comic books he read as a child. The same change occurs when an impersonator puts on a jumpsuit, or a baggy suit, or the black leather. They become superheroes, twice removed.

"My costumes are all quality, fifteen hundred, two thousand dollars," said Rick Marino from Jacksonville. "I keep them really nice, they don't have any threads torn out of them, or any seams torn out of them. When

I went and did the movie *Honeymoon in Vegas,* the costume lady even complimented me on my costumes and was very impressed and asked me to go ahead and wear my own outfits in the movie. [His scenes, unfortunately, were cut.] The thing I'm saying is that I spend the right money, and so the look is good. You have the right jewelry on. I don't wear phony rings. My rings are real and they're nice, and they're not tacky or gaudy. I don't wear one on every finger. I usually will wear a pinky and a big ring on my left hand, and usually a big ring on my right hand. Then of course I only wear the one necklace, the TCB necklace [initials for Elvis's motto, "Taking Care of Business"], and then I'll have a bracelet on my arm, and that's it. You don't get gaudy like that."

Naturally you must grow your own pompadour, if possible, and dye it. Most dye their own hair at home, though some visit salons. If you choose not to dye, you must select a wig that does not make your head look like a cupcake left out in the sun.

"It's important you don't have blue hair," Rick Marino said. "I don't know why all these guys insist on dyeing their hair jet black. It doesn't look natural."

You should not wear sunglasses the entire time you perform. For one thing, Elvis never did. And impersonators who do this are seen by the audience as having something to hide. Like, for instance, the fact that they look nothing like Elvis.

You may tell jokes, but never, under any circumstances, should you say anything to belittle the memory of the king of rock and roll. Drug jokes are frowned upon, though an occasional remark about jelly doughnuts will work, depending on the crowd. Jokes Elvis told always get a laugh.

"One of my biggest jokes," said Jerome Marion, "is when I'm performing onstage. I walk on and I'll start to sing, and about halfway through I'll introduce myself and I'll always start off: 'Yeah, I'd like to take a minute here to introduce myself. My name is Wayne Newton.' And people, they're like, 'What?'—and they start laughing. I say, 'Well, things have been tough in Vegas, you know, you get what you can get.'"

You should never strut around offstage in character. In other words, you are Elvis onstage, and yourself the minute you step off.

"You just have fun, you know?" said Jerome. "You play off of Elvis, but you live yourself—you don't talk like him the whole time. You don't try to be Elvis onstage, but you use one-liners, you know—he slurred into an Elvis voice—"like, 'Back in nineteen-twelve, I did this song on the Ed

Sullivan Show, back in nineteen-twelve, I think it was.' And you use one-liners, because people want to relate, but they don't want to be so scared of you that they're afraid to walk up and ask for an autograph."

The less serious you are about your own appeal the better. People often asked Jerome, "How come people stand in line to get your autograph? You're not Elvis Presley!"

"You know," he told them, "that's a damn good question. Because I have no idea."

Unless you are making a joke, never introduce a song by saying, "I did this number in nineteen seventy-three . . ." Because you did not. Because you are not Elvis. If you cannot remember this, you are part of the problem. After all, a serious impersonator sees himself as one part entertainer, one part historian.

"My show," said Irv Cass, "is a tribute to Elvis. I tell people, 'Ladies and gentlemen, this next song I'd like to sing for you is a song Elvis performed after serving two years in the Army. He came back, his first big performance was the Frank Sinatra show, old Blue Eyes. And this is the song that he sang. And then I'll do maybe like 'Stuck on You,' or 'Fame and Fortune.'

"I gear it, always, one hundred percent of the time, not toward me. My only thing is to do a good show and please the crowd. And along with pleasing them, I gear my whole show so it's talking about Elvis, what a great entertainer he was. It's a tribute. It's not, 'come see Irv Cass sing Elvis, song after song.'"

Most important, you maintain a sense of humor about what you do, even as you try to take it seriously. I do this, you might say, but I'm not like that. You remember you spend your life at a high-traffic crossroads of having fun and making fun of something and being made fun of. Luckily, in this line of work, people are always willing to remind you exactly where you stand.

And if professionalism fails to protect, brutal honesty can't hurt. This trait shows most in impersonators who have performed for at least five years. Performers who started impersonating before Elvis died or soon after carry the most emotional baggage. Spending twenty years being better known for being somebody else does things to a man's idea of himself. But it seldom does anything to tarnish their idealism about Elvis Presley. If anything, they can better understand why he lived and died the way he did.

There lies the pitfall of this Elvis business: If the impersonator succeeds at shrugging on a new identity, sometimes society doesn't see the person who gives the image life. Most people believe only what they see, discounting anything that might suggest more complicated motivations beneath the surface. So the thing meant to bring the performer glory also carries in it the seeds of mistaken identity. Fame can be fleeting when, technically, it belongs to someone else. If a person is not careful, Elvis can eat him alive.

When people ask Raymond Michael what he does for a living, he tells them that he is a choir teacher. This is the truth. But sometimes people will press him. They'll say they heard he is a singer—what kind of music does he sing? Nostalgic rock and roll, he will say. This is not a lie, but it is not exactly the truth. Raymond never tells anyone he is an Elvis impersonator and has been one for the last twenty years.

"I'll never admit to being Elvis," he said. "I'm embarrassed. Absolutely. Absolutely. Not embarrassed of Elvis—embarrassed I'm going to be associated with these other guys. There's a few others I'm proud to be associated with. But there's others like, whoo. And I hope that doesn't sound egotistical." He laughed. "They're there, aren't they?"

Raymond Michael Hebel awoke on a stage in 1972 and found that his subconscious had chosen his career. He was a freshman voice major at California Lutheran University with dreams of being an opera singer. But one night he attended a student assembly headlined by a hypnotist named George Sharp. Sharp brought Raymond on stage, hypnotized him, and suggested that he perform an Elvis song. He did the only one he knew, the one his roommate always sang: "Blue Suede Shoes."

After the assembly, a drama teacher named Don Haskell approached Raymond. He thought he made a good enough Elvis to put together a show and take it on the road. To Raymond, the idea didn't seem odd at all. As a singer, he saw performing as Elvis much like singing as Figaro in *The Barber of Seville*—a role to study, a character to inhabit. Over and over he listened to tapes of Elvis and pegged him a lyric baritone who could have done well at opera. And he went to see Elvis live. He had always been more of a fan of bands like Paul Revere and the Raiders, and the Beatles. But seeing Elvis changed his mind, not to mention his life's direction. He dropped his last name and became an Elvis impersonator.

"I have to say, after seeing him live, I looked at him completely differently, because he had incredible charisma," he said. "He had a super voice, but I knew that from listening to his tapes. Once I'd seen him when was he was very, very heavy, even heavier than he was when he passed away. And he still had the charisma. People in the audience, you could hear them talking: 'Oh, Elvis has gotten fat, I don't know why I'm here, I don't know why people go so crazy.' And these are the people that went nuts when he was on that stage. He still had that charisma and he just would move just a little bit, and that was all they needed."

On August 16, 1977, he was on the road doing Elvis when he got the phone call. He and Haskell decided to abandon the act because both agreed it would be tacky to proceed. But enough people asked Haskell about bookings that Raymond Michael was reborn. "That's when the big bucks were out there for Elvises," he said. Though he won't say how much he earned in the years immediately after Elvis's death, he toured with a full orchestra, playing in Las Vegas and all over California. Dick Clark featured him on a 1978 television special starring the nation's top impersonators. He remains one of the few original Elvises still working steadily—and well. He now performs every summer at Knott's Berry Farm in Buena Park, California. He did a stint in Atlanta keyed to the 1996 Summer Olympics. He jokingly calls himself "the Tony Orlando of Elvises." His shows often include a segment in which he invites men on stage, hands them a pair of sunglasses, and has them solo on the "chick-a-boom" bridge in "Polk Salad Annie." Women have been known to flash him from the audience.

"My goal when I perform is that I leave people with either reliving a memory of Elvis or letting them know what Elvis is all about," he said. "And that they have fun. I want them to laugh, I want them to have fun. Someone will say, 'They laughed at you when you were doing that.' That was the idea."

He has become so successful that he performs an annual charity show at his alma mater. The school established a performing arts scholarship in his name, quite likely making him the only Elvis impersonator in the world to boast such an honor.

He is proud of what he has done. Still, his life contains enough frustrations for him to hide his other identity. He hates being associated with most other impersonators. He worries that comes across sounding egotistical, as if he were the only Elvis worth seeing and the others inferior imitations. "I don't think there's any that aren't better than me," he said. "I think there's some really good ones out there. Unfortunately, though, I think there's a lot who have really destroyed what I've tried to do and what the other good ones have tried to do."

Remind him that the number of impersonators keeps growing, and that most impersonators say there is a demand for their talents, and he snorts. "But there's *not* a demand. If we all sent you our W-twos, you'd see how many are in demand. These guys are doing little parties—you know, 'Hey, Joe, you're having a backyard party? Well, I have a friend of mine that does Elvis, why don't you let him sing with his tapes in the back corner?' That's basically, I would say, ninety-eight to ninety-nine percent of the Elvises. And they spend all this money on jumpsuits and all that, so they can go to these conventions and strut around for three, four days and then they go back in the mothballs. I'm being very realistic, not sarcastic at all—that's really how it is for the majority of them. There's only a few of us that really, actually make a living at it. And I continue to do it, number one, for the money. But they do it, hoping that the big break is gonna happen for them, because they've seen other Elvises doing it. And number two, the glamour. I mean, for all the people that laugh at Elvis impersonators, there's a bunch of 'em that just go ooh-ahh over Elvis impersonators."

He attempts normalcy. Divorced, he spends a lot of time with his son, Raymond II, who occasionally joins him on stage for a duet. He teaches junior and senior high school chorus when his Knott's gig ends.

But Elvis has a way of taking over a person's life. Every year Raymond's fan club publishes a catalog that includes such items as nightshirts, the Raymond Michael commemorative Christmas ornament, and talking coffee mugs. Raymond sees this attention as intended for another person, someone who has little to do with who he really is. Offstage, free of his wig, sideburns, and replica jumpsuits, no one would ever mistake him for Elvis, with his thinning brown hair, slender face, and aquiline nose. But other people wish he would always be the person he is on stage.

"I dated a beautiful girl—she was in the Miss Universe contest and all that. She dumped me. She says, 'You're too much of a good old boy offstage.' She says, 'Why can't you be like you are onstage all the time?'" He laughed hard. "Thanks a lot, honey! But she basically wanted a flamboyancy offstage, and that's not me. My parents were hard-working, simple people. I wasn't brought up like that. I used to drink powdered milk, we were so poor."

But the simple days are long gone. Once Raymond went to a party at the home of one of his fans. As he walked around, he saw something hanging on the wall that seemed familiar. He got closer.

It was a picture of his own house.

Ask many impersonators to name the best veteran in the business and the name that comes up, again and again, is Rick Saucedo.

Rick began impersonating Elvis in 1972, five years before he died. It started almost as a joke, but quickly blazed into a career. Even at sixteen Rick looked the part, with sleepy eyes, pouting lips, and a complex pompadour with sides tucked and layered like the petals of a rose. Two days after Elvis died, he performed at a club in Wheaton, Illinois. When he tried to sing "Bridge Over Troubled Water," he faltered, turned his back to the audience, and wept in his white jumpsuit.

"You can do it for Elvis," the women cried. "Come on, Ricky. Do it for Elvis."

He did. Then he went to Broadway. For seventeen weeks he performed in *Elvis: The Legend Lives* at the Palace Theatre, sharing the stage with the Jordanaires and drummer D. J. Fontana, who backed Elvis at the beginning. The show then toured the country. Rick gained a reputation as one of the nation's best impersonators. *Newsweek* proclaimed him possessor of the "best lip curl." He appeared on Dick Clark's 1978 TV special featuring the country's finest Elvises.

Mention Rick Saucedo to most impersonators and they ask if you've talked to him, what he's up to, what he's really like.

"I think Rick is like, you know, the hoop-ta-da," said Tony Grova, the impersonator from New Jersey who started his Elvis act soon after Saucedo did. He saw him at least eighteen times when he played on Broadway. "Rick is Rick, and that's all there is to it," Tony said. "You know what I mean? He's good."

Once in a while after a show, Tony said, someone will tell him he is better than Rick. He laughed. "Yeah. Ha. Rick is Rick. First of all, there's only one Elvis, and Rick is Rick, OK? Rick is Rick. Nobody can touch him. As far as I'm concerned. I don't know where he is, though. I mean, I can't believe he's not in Legends in Concert or something."

Jerome Marion followed Rick Saucedo's career for about four years, long before he even decided he wanted to impersonate. "At the time," he said, "he had not only the look going for him, he had the charisma onstage, the vocal ability was very, very good."

Dennis Stella, like a lot of other impersonators, saw Rick at his peak and had been inspired to follow him. It stunned Dennis that someone could change themselves so completely. Rick could let loose that little smirk—perfect. He nailed down that little squint. He even laughed like Elvis. Before he saw Rick, it had never occurred to Dennis that an Elvis impersonator should laugh like Elvis.

Over the years he'd heard Rick had a bad attitude, that he believed he was Elvis. When he met him about a year into his own Elvis act, at a taping of a cable-access show, he hesitated to approach him. But the Michael Jackson impersonator was late, so while they waited Dennis got up the nerve. "I had heard years ago that he was kind of stuck up," he said. "When I finally got a chance to talk to him and get to know him a little bit, I found him to be very personable. And you know, he spent at least a good five to ten minutes giving me advice, what to be careful about in show business—about getting pulled in by the wrong people, being careful about drugs and women, late nights and all that, letting outside things mess up your life."

And then, Dennis said, Rick Saucedo tutored him in the finer points of Elvis.

"Oh, I was like a little kid," Dennis said, his voice rising. "First of all, I couldn't even believe the guy was talking to me. Now I realize that Rick is just an impersonator, he's not Elvis. But there was a time, nineteen seventy-eight, nineteen seventy-nine, when he sold out two shows a night, six or seven days a week, for like two years in a row. I heard he made a million dollars.

"So this was the guy that was in hot demand, and he tried in his own way to try to capture a lot of the Elvis mystique. He would never have been seen walking around in the audience afterward. He had bodyguards. He was kept away from the general public.

"So I got the guy sitting there showing me how to do the whipping motion and how to hold a microphone and he picks up the mike in front of me with my little karaoke machine, and five feet away from me, he's doing a few songs. I'm looking at this guy, thinking, All right, when you first glance at him, he doesn't look that much like Elvis. But within a second of starting a song, he kind of transforms into that illusion. And I thought, it's unbelievable. He doesn't have all the little stuff to fool you. I'm standing a few feet away from him and yet he still does a great job passing off that image."

For a while, Dennis and some of the others who followed Rick lost track of his career. He was still in the Chicago area, playing festivals, nightclubs, and classic-car shows. But twenty years after his rise he resurfaced in a big way, issuing shiny black press kits with many of those clippings from those fast months after August 16, 1977. In 1995, it was rumored he was earning between $70,000 and $100,000 a year.

Twelve days before the eighteenth anniversary of Elvis's death, Saucedo headlined a show at the Sabre Room, a club in Hickory Hills, Illinois, up the road from Greene's West. The entrance is guarded by a sign that depicts a giant man in white harem pants and a matching plumed turban. In one hand he holds a lantern; in his other he wields a sword spangled with small white lights that he buzzes up and down, up and down. Frank Sinatra, Dean Martin, Sammy Davis Jr., and Johnny Carson all performed there a long time ago; their pictures hang above the tiny lobby bar.

Thirty or so years later, the Sabre Room has Rick Saucedo recreating the 1973 concert *Elvis: Aloha from Hawaii—Via Satellite*. A half hour before showtime the place filled, as always, with an excitable, highly female crowd. His fan club had set up a table next to the stage to sell memorabilia with photos of Rick recreating various phases of Elvis's career. There were buttons, plastic key chains, laminated photos. A white T-shirt announced in red ink "The Rick Saucedo Show" and included these song lyrics: "It all started in the year of 1972, with two young brothers and a rock 'n' roll singer too. It was history-making, country-shakin'. . ." Rick wrote these lyrics. A schedule of Saucedo's appearances the club handed out outlined a busy summer. There were gigs at the Maplewood Lanes, the Michigan Fest, the Romeoville Fest, the Stardust Sports Bar, two at John's Hideout and one at a place called Knickers.

Paula Maggio, Rick's manager, kept watch in front of the stage. Maggio is an ample redhead with small gold hoops in her ears. She wore a flowing taupe sundress and darted on a path from the stage to the ticket table. She has known Rick since high school and thought that she had hit upon the ideal way to market her client.

"I have put cops on both sides of the stage," she explained. "The women swarmed the stage, like they did with Elvis. I have hidden him before the show, so that nobody sees him. After a show I wait a half hour. I have security OK a table where they are around him, where Rick can come out and sign autographs where he will not be mobbed. I keep the anxiousness. Now, if he woulda just walked around in a jumpsuit around the people, nobody would care. They get used to it. But you hide him, you keep him away, and you bring him out with a dramatic opening and they hear his voice. You throw the Jordanaires or the Stamps behind him, you've got a show and a half. And it really works for Rick. Because he can pull it off. He sings songs that other impersonators don't sing. He sings the hard songs, like 'Just Pretend.' Bootleg songs that they don't even do. He has to say sometimes, 'This is an Elvis song. It's off the lost record,' or something. You know when he does 'Trilogy' at the end, where the smoke machine goes on at the end of 'Trilogy,' when he sings 'I wish I were in Dixie'? He's in a blast of smoke—he looks like Elvis is in a cloud, like, going to heaven. And it's beautiful—at night, especially."

Around us security men wearing laminated all-access badges on cords around their necks walked between the wide round tables, evaluating the crowd. Their leader was a man with very blond, chin-length hair whose thick-soled cowboy boots announced his arrival before he came into view. He glared in our direction as he walked past. I asked if it would be possible to visit with Rick before he performed. "I can't let you back there," Maggio said, flatly. She explained that Rick performed a ritual before he took the stage that outsiders could not see. She did disclose that Rick told her, "The day that I'm not nervous before a show is the day I hang it up."

A Vegas-style crooner opened the show, Tony Ocean was his name. After he sang, he gave away copies of his cassette with a cover featuring his ponytailed likeness spliced between those of Frank Sinatra, Dean Martin, and Sammy Davis Jr., a little something called *How Did These Guys Get in My Room??* After a set from a female singer—Patsy Cline by way of Mariah Carey—J. D. Sumner and the Stamps took control. They stepped on stage as if they were the main attraction, and in a way they were—the group sang backup for Elvis Presley from 1971 until his death. Though they are a Grammy-winning gospel group, they can make decent money singing with men pretending to be their former boss. Sumner, a distinguished-looking man with a thin mustache and a swirl of silver hair, spent much of the show with his hand cupped over his ear, the better to hear himself when he hit his famed double low Cs. When he nailed a deep note, it hummed in your sternum.

The group sang for about forty-five minutes, then took a break. Around 10:30 P.M., the room grew dark. "Paradise Hawaiian Style," the song Elvis used to open the original special, flowed out of the speakers. When it faded the band cranked up the theme to *2001,* Sumner and the

Stamps kicking in a perfect *ahhhhhh*. A door on the right of the stage opened. The blond security officer inspected the room and gave clearance for the others to lead out Rick. He wore a replica of the jumpsuit Elvis showed off in front of more than a billion viewers twenty-two years earlier. It is the one now called the Aloha Eagle because of the two large birds made of blue and red stones that spread across the suit's chest and back and the smaller ones down the sides of each leg. The gold stars that covered the rest of the suit glowed under the spotlight. The audience responded with screams and whistling, twisting and thrashing arms.

The show reprised some of the songs Elvis sang in the "Aloha" concert, as the fans call it, but more than anything it recreated a mood. Rick didn't mimic Elvis so much as he conjured an illusion. His hair looked taller than Elvis's ever did. His face was a different shape. But this was the trick: After a while they came in a rush, the details that blurred the line and sent them screaming. At times the voice came close; almost always, the inflections were right on target—the way he slurred the word *hush* during "American Trilogy," the lazy chain of *well-well-well-well-well* before "I Got a Woman." He mixed things up—laughed during "Big Hunk of Love" the way Elvis did, but in a different spot. Spit out *cat* the way Elvis did in "Blue Suede Shoes," but the way he did it back in the fifties. And he laughed just like him, the same sharp little bark. At the grinding build to the finish of "Suspicious Minds," he copied the slow lunge, the karate hands, the look of concentration.

Whoo! the people shouted. *Yes!*

Rick panted, "Whoo, boy, I'll tell ya, I'm getting a workout tonight. Yessiree."

A woman screamed, "*We'll work out with ya!*"

And so they did. A man in a plaid golf shirt grabbed his date and they bumped hips; a woman in a short bob jumped on her chair and shook, just shook. And everywhere women bounced in their chairs, arms up and bent at the elbows, tilting like seesaws, saying *Yes, yes, yes.*

When Rick excused himself to change into another jumpsuit for the second half of the show, Sumner shook his head and laughed and said, "I think he sounds more like Elvis than Elvis did."

For about twenty minutes after the show J. D. Sumner and the Stamps signed autographs and sold tapes ($10 each, three for $25), photos, T-shirts, ball caps, and the two books Sumner wrote about his life. When they finished, they stood, stretched, and prepared to leave. Sumner once said that when he toured with Elvis, the operation ran so efficiently all he needed to remember was to show up on time. A plane would pick up the group in Nashville, their baggage would be loaded, carried, and deposited in their hotel rooms, their every whim would be satisfied. "I believe if I'd needed my teeth brushed," Sumner said in his book, *Elvis— His Love for Gospel Music and J. D. Sumner,* "somebody would have been assigned to brush them for me."

But time moves on. After chatting with a few fans, the Stamps set to work packing up everything in small cardboard boxes to load on the tour bus parked beneath the swinging saber. Sumner sat on the group's aging bus, smoking a cigarette and looking out into the emptying parking lot, while his bandmates worked.

Then came a scream: "Here he is!" From the door at stage left Rick walked out, surrounded by his security team. He wore a green sport shirt and dark blue Calvin Klein jeans, the left rear pocket torn. He had removed all of his rings. His pompadour winged up in the back. He said a few words to the Stamps, and the line of people that had formed on the other side of the table, which now bulged to the back of the room, leaned forward to hear. Women crowded and clucked. Maggio said, to no one in particular, "I make the money, but I don't get to sign."

Rick sat down and picked up a pen. Three security men took positions around him. One of the Stamps, Ed Hill, dropped a box of merchandise and the men spun instantly toward the sound, determined it to present no danger, then relaxed. Rick paused after a few autographs and ran a suntanned hand through his hair. "I'm getting too old for this, man," he said with a laugh. From out of nowhere, an arm appeared holding a Miller Lite and placed it on the table in front of him. A woman in line leaned forward and stroked one of his sideburns. Another vibrated so hard, just standing in front of him, her glasses dropped off her face onto the table. Rick retrieved them and eased them back onto her nose. Behind the lenses you could see only the whites of her eyes.

"Next!" he shouted, giving that little laugh. "OK, I'm not a doctor . . ."

This went on for almost an hour. After a while he leaned back, took a swig of the beer. Around him the women clicked like crickets: *Rick! Rick! Rick! Rick!*

I asked him what he would like to be called. He smiled and his lip slid back. Spooky. "Impressionist. I'm not an impersonator. I'm more of an actor. I'd rather be called an actor. For that time, I have to be him. Exactly what he thinks. So if you could do me a favor, just"—he fumbled a moment—"as an actor."

"Rick, say hello to her," Maggio broke in, giving a woman in a tight T-shirt a little shove. "She's shy."

He didn't hear. "My work means a lot to me," he said, and he squeezed his hands between his knees. He looked smaller than he did on stage. Almost delicate. He sat a moment, staring at the toes of his black sneakers.

"I have a little girl, and when she grows up I just want her to—*you* know. Kids are going to ridicule her, going to make fun of her—your dad was this, that. I have a lot of things to think of, you know? I just do my best, whatever I can do."

"Here's Rick," Maggio said, pushing a man to the edge of the table.

"Excellent show," the man said. A woman loomed behind him: "Before you leave, I wanna hug." A woman in a white T-shirt covered with sequins piped up, "That show was the best ever."

"How many more you want, Rick?" the blond security man asked. "Say we're done?" Rick did not appear to hear him, but the guard nodded as he if had secured the proper response. "OK. We're done," he said to the crowd. Rick looked at the line, shorter but still three deep. Then he picked up the pen and did one more.

"You know what?" Steve Chuke said. "I think of these things when I'm laying in bed. And I go, Why do I like Elvis so much? Why do I love what he did, what he stood for so much? And it's because he represents . . . *love*, you know? Like I said before, it's God, and then religion, Jesus, and it's Elvis. What can you say? Because when you get up onstage, you feel a piece of him in you, and you feel, my God, how could he have felt in front of thousands of people, when you're in front of hundreds of people?

"Elvis represented love and he just—everything he did or said, if you really listen, then you get the magic. And the worst part about Elvis Presley, *the worst part about Elvis Presley*, is not taking time and sitting down and listening to the different kinds of music that he had. He was so versatile—it was just unbelievable! And that's the magic and that's the power of Elvis. I mean, I listen to Elvis every day now and I never thought that I would ever do this—I thought I would get tired, because, you know, I'm a Corvette nut, and I'll drive a Corvette for six months and get tired of it. But I never get tired of Elvis's music. It is not because I want to perform, it's because I'm learning more. It seems like I learn more about life in his words, in his lyrics and everything—it's not just some crybaby story, like some country-western singer does. And it just— God almighty! I mean, every man wants to be caressed, every woman wants to be caressed, you know? And a lot of his music caresses you— it blows me away. That's why I'm like I am. That's why I'm doing what I'm doing."

Steve Chuke talks this way all the time. Because he has no time! "It is," he said, "a very, very short life. You gotta know what you wanna do." For a long time he didn't. For years he thought guys like him, country boys from northern Kentucky, could have dreams as big as Elvis but never could confess to them, let alone make them happen. Then his head went through a windshield one January night, and in time the mists lifted. Now he knows he can possess everything he ever wanted or lost but was too lazy or mean or young to understand. And all he needs to do is be like Elvis. Or to realize that, in some ways, he always was.

"When I look at Elvis and the things he did," he said, "going in the swimming holes and swimming, I just go: Man, that's apple pie. That's me. That's American. That's one hundred percent. That's what I did all my life, you know? And I was a rebel."

A rebel who watches *The Ten Commandments* on TV every Easter, but still. Contradictions make him crazy, keep him alive. He understands he can be like Elvis, if he can maintain enough drive and love and strength to abstain from fatty foods. Knowing these things, how could a man stay silent?

We live in a world where it has become harder to ridicule people. It is no longer acceptable or politically correct to make fun of people just because they are female or Italian or speak with a lisp. With this change in attitude, people who feel the need to belittle others to make themselves feel good have moved on to other targets, those who stray from what they consider the norm—usually people who have more choice over their destiny. It is easy to judge impersonators from what shows on the surface—when they pull on their jumpsuits, they literally wear their feelings and dreams on the outside, shining and hopeful and over-wrought. Impersonators know this; even they sometimes poke fun at who they are and what they do. But most people never bother to peer beyond the flash to see the person underneath.

"I'll tell you what's the worst," said Irv Cass, who wears a full pompadour at all times. "It's not that they call you Elvis. You kinda get used to that, even though it annoys you. Here's what gets you: 'Elvis is dead! Hey, man, why don't you let him rest? Oh, you must be an Elvis wannabe.' Let's see—oh, this is the one: 'He thinks he's Elvis! Look at that guy, he thinks he's Elvis!' Those are the ones that get you hot under the collar. It's like, take two steps back before I knock your teeth out, you know what I mean? Those make you mad—you get really upset about that. Not that somebody calls you Elvis. Not even that they crack a little joke, because I can laugh along with a joke as long as it's not real dirty or degrading towards Elvis.

"I tell you, man. After doing Elvis, you really get a sense of what being different is all about. And how crude and how rude people can be, and how a lot of people don't care about other people's feelings. And I'm not talking just about being Elvis. I'm talking about somebody who's got Down syndrome, somebody who's got a harelip, somebody who has got a disfigured face, something that happened, got burned in a fire. It just gives you a feeling about how it is to be different, no matter what the difference is. People have no respect for each other, man."

Steve Chuke has felt this way, too. Twice a year, he rents a nightclub—for a while it was Peel's Palace—hires a band and stages a two-night show starring six impersonators, himself included. It is at these shows that D. J. Fontana, a good friend, sits in with the guys. One raw spring morning after one of the shows he took the band, the always popular Fabulous Exspence Account, to one of his favorite restaurants, the Cracker Barrel in Erlanger, Kentucky. He ordered his usual: chicken and dumplings; a cheese home fry casserole; and two pancakes. And the waiter looked down at him and said, "Well. If that's what you want, that's what you get." Steve was shocked. He lost count long ago of all the grilled cheese sandwiches he had skipped to fit into his black leather pantsuit. Almost fifty and he's playing Elvis at thirty-three. Who is any stranger to judge? Can't a man order dinner food for breakfast without people thinking something is wrong?

Impersonators can be sensitive this way: they develop convictions, and people dismiss them as quirks. Steve knows what people think. He had doubts himself that he could pull off this Elvis gig well enough for people to view his tribute with respect and a straight face. But all his life he had been trying to figure out some way he could show the world he mattered and that his dreams carried weight. By emulating Elvis, Steve hoped to unearth a better version of himself. Was that so wrong? If people could just pay attention when he impersonated Elvis, then they would understand him as he really is. "If you stuck me with a pin, I would blow up," he said. "I mean, there are all these things inside of me."

He is six-foot-one and around 200 pounds, with a short pompadour he dyes black, a long face, and a lip that curls when he smiles. He drinks several glasses of water a day to keep his complexion clear. "If I'd have done this when I was a kid, I'd have really looked pretty!" he said. "Ha ha!" He visits a tanning salon when he can. "I look a little bit like Elvis," he said. "Not the higher cheekbones, but I got his lower jaw. I was told. If I had the higher cheekbones on any given night . . ."

On one given night, he hosted one of his impersonator shows at a club in Newport, Kentucky, called the Syndicate, a classy mock speakeasy around the corner from a White Castle. He wore a shirt and pants of black—his favorite color—with a salmon-colored sport coat and black-and-white oxfords, shined to reflect the spotlight. He wandered over, still juiced from performing, with a strange look on his face, both awake and dreaming. He leaned against a low wall by the bar, holding a scotch, and said nothing. I remarked that it looked like things were going well. "Yeah," he said. His tropical print tie splashed light up to his face. "Ha ha!" he said, and his eyes refocused. "I wanted to ask you: Did you think I did better tonight than I did last night?"

"I thought you did well last night."

He smiled, regarded his brilliant shoe caps, then looked up, troubled. "Better than tonight?"

To truly understand Steve Chuke, to comprehend the heights to which he aspires, it is necessary to seek the level of his ambition, which disrupts not only his unconscious life but also breaks into the earth and under his house, inside his basement. His basement, Steve Chuke believes, is the one place he can sing the way he imagines during his nocturnal ruminations. "I guess it's my breathing techniques," he says. "When I'm down in my basement, I breathe so easy." He returns to the subject of his basement again and again: If only people could see how he is down deep, where he can breathe, then they would understand how he feels.

"And I tell you what," he said, "it would be like day and night if you could see me. If you could see me in my basement, you'd go, 'God, Steve, if you would do this in Vegas on the stage—you would be The Top! Or Up There!' You know what I mean."

To know what he means, you must dig even deeper. Steve Chuke was born in 1946 in Oneida, Clay County, Kentucky. His family spent time there, in another little town called Sandgap and in a resort town now evaporated off the map: "It's beautiful country. You remember how Mighty Mouse's girlfriend would get stolen by the villain? And he'd ride up in his big car around through the mountains? The mountains would go round and round? That's how you get there." Most of his childhood he spent in northern Kentucky, looking at Cincinnati across the Ohio and devising ways to escape being a country boy.

His father left for good when he was nine. That parting, Steve says, killed his childhood dream of being a famous entertainer. "That part of my life was blown," he says, stretching that last word into two syllables. A little drawl slides into his voice when he grows emotional. "I always knew that I was just as talented as other kids, but I never had no father to let me know that you could do this or do that." His mother, Vilene, supported the family by waitressing. Steve would wake some mornings at 4:30 to find his mother at the kitchen table, counting her tips.

In the childhood stories Steve tells, movement always forms the core. He has always hated to stand still: He floated down the Ohio on a log. He walked through Covington to Ludlow, singing "I Want You, I Need You, I Love You." On January 6, 1957, Elvis appeared on "The Ed Sullivan Show" from the waist up. Steve's sister and one of her friends squealed at what they saw and even more at what they didn't. Steve watched them carefully. His ten-year-old mind mulled over what their mood might mean. And he started to dance, crazy legs in the living room. As soon as he could get away with it, he grew a pompadour.

Steve owns a large black-and-white photo of himself taken when he was sixteen. He keeps it leaned against the wall next to the sofa in his TV room. This room has soft green-striped furniture and carpet thick enough for children to sprawl on. Other photos decorate the room— several school pictures of his children, and a formal portrait of Steve, two of his sons and their mother, his auburn-haired wife, Kathy. In the photo Steve wears a dark suit and a hopeful expression, and he bears an eerie resemblance to Bill Clinton. He complained to the photographer about this. On the wall above these portraits hangs a picture of Jesus dressed in white robes, kicking a soccer ball to a group of laughing children.

Steve propped the picture on an ottoman one night, straddled an arm of the sofa and studied himself. The picture is black and white but Steve remembers an olive suit, a tricolor tie in black and shades of gray, a white tab-collar shirt. He owns one just like it now. He was a skinny boy, but his shoulders were broad. He looked off to the right and smiled, shyly, so his gums wouldn't show.

The drawl sneaked back: "I remember going downtown to get those taken," he said, softly. "Cost my mother two-fifty, and that was a lot back then." The other thing about the photo that has not faded from memory is Steve's hair. Time has touched his face, but it has failed to affect his hairstyle—a low-riding pompadour slathered with Vaseline that crests to the left while one piece jives right.

His hair fit the image he wanted to cultivate—James Dean, Marlon Brando, the vulnerable tough who chafed at authority. More and more, he killed nights on the street corners. He turned up his collars. He drove fast. He fell behind. He dropped out of high school at sixteen, the same year he posed for the picture. "Because my attitude was different," he said. "I didn't want to be smart to people, but I kept saying, 'Why do I gotta learn about Newfoundland? How many times am I gonna learn about Newfoundland? And why do I need to know about the common denominator? I don't like math, I don't wanna *be* this, you know?' "

Three years later he married for the first time. "The day I met her she was one month pregnant," he said. "And then two months later, she said, 'I'm pregnant.' I said, 'There's only one thing to do—let's get married.' So we got married real quick. And then three months after that, I found out it wasn't mine. That's when I got wild. And that's when I had my motorcycle accident."

It happened in Southgate, Kentucky, in early January 1966, near a Burger Chef restaurant on Route 27. Steve was riding a buddy's Triumph motorcycle, 1956 model as close as he can remember, 650cc engine, wearing a heavy wool jacket and a beret.

"A friend of mine, I was babysitting for him. 'Steve,' he said, 'don't drive the bike.' He knew I loved his motorcycle. And I said, 'OK, Freddy, I won't.' And when he walked out the door I went '*ah-ha-ha-ha-ha!*' Like I was getting over him. So anyway, I just took it out for a joy ride. And, matter of fact, you ain't gonna believe this, but this had to do with Elvis. You know the song called 'Don't?' Well, I sang that that night to a girl-friend of mine. When I left, I was singing that, I can remember—that is the only thing that I remember—nineteen sixty-six, singing that song, and then leaving. I can't remember the accident or anything.

"No, I didn't see it coming. I went through the windshield of another car, and I pulled myself out of the windshield. I busted right through—broke through the windshield with my body. And I pushed the rear-view mirror up against the ceiling with my head. No helmet. A hundred forty-five stitches in my head. My ear was hanging off down the side of my neck. All the scars are gone, did a hell of a job on me. Contusions, fractured skull, this and that. My leg was cut off and sewed back on. It was completely off except for the calf muscle and the tendon. I lost three and a half pints of blood on the ground, they said.

"Have you ever heard of a burger restaurant called Burger Chef? OK. Well, there was a Burger Chef out there at Southgate, Kentucky. And now it's called a McDonald's. But when I went by there, I had a beret on. People were saying, 'Look at that faggot,' you know, stuff like that, when I drove by, and when I came back down I gave them the finger on the way back. Ha ha! And then a half a block after that is when I wrecked. The guy hit me head on. He was in a car. Sixty-five Oldsmobile. It was a brand-new car.

"I was in a coma or something for twelve days. They expected me not to come alive at all—well, if I did, they said I'd be a vegetable."

But he did wake up, and he spent another three months in the hospital. In his bed he reflected that there was a difference between wild and stupid, and maybe he needed to figure it out. "I think God said, 'I'm gonna punish you. I'm gonna settle you down, boy.' And that's what he did."

But first, Steve needed to dance. It took time to figure out how to do it with his leg in a cast, a steel ball substituting for the sole of his shoe. Friends would snatch his crutches from under his arms and he would flail his arms and drop back onto the dance floor, like he was falling into a swimming pool. The Shing-a-ling and the Skate got him back on his feet.

Elvis's death sobered him even more. When the truth hit him, he felt as if for years he had been stumbling through a long waking dream. He had let Elvis go for a long time, but now he wanted him back, desperately. He bought a stack of Elvis eight-tracks and sang along, just like he was at the playground again. To him, it sounded like he had soul.

He worked odd jobs selling stereo equipment, clothes, and shoes. He worked in nightclubs for Larry Flynt. He got his GED. He burned through another marriage, had his oldest son. In 1978, he married Kathy, a majorette four years behind him in high school, the kind of girl he never thought would look at him twice. They have been together ever since.

"See," he said, "everybody thought I was gonna turn out to be Mr. Bad Goofy, no class at all, no money. No nothing. And I told 'em, I said, 'You're not giving me love. You give me love, and I'll do anything in the world for you. I'll make something happen.' "

In 1980, Steve opened his own store, Jewel King Jewelers, because he hated working under other people's rules. He did not consciously name the place for Elvis, but he wanted its name to sound impressive, and he decided nothing sounded loftier than the word "king." The store sits on the corner of Eighth and Monmouth Streets in Newport. Around the corner is a store that promises *Professional Shoe Repair—Complete Billiard Supplies and Accessories.* Next to that stands the Free Christian Church of God and next to that the Candlestick Fellowship. A block over is the Pepper Pod Restaurant. To the left across Eighth is Dixie Chili. The air on this block smells like onions. Mention this to Steve and he says: "Really?"

His store's exterior has a facade of weathered gray wood and a sidewalk of blue-and-white tile. The inventory, displayed in cases on swirls of silver and black velvet, includes sterling-silver rosaries, gold soccer-ball charms, diamond rings in sturdy settings. A sign on the wall reads, "Smile—It's the 2nd Best Thing You Can Do with Your Lips." Next to that a sign reads, "No checks accepted."

But mostly, the decor revolves around Elvis. There are cardboard cutouts of Elvis dancing; a black velvet portrait from the Aloha period, a pumpkin-colored scarf around his neck, a single white tear trailing down his cheek; a certificate that proclaims Steve first-place winner in the *Cincinnati Post* Elvis Look-Alike contest. Steve collects Elvis memorabilia. People often stop in the store to drop off old eight-tracks and pictures, which he takes in like stray kittens.

The more his life settled down, the more Steve thought about how Elvis shaped him. If anyone got him talking about it he found it hard to stop:

"I am, like I said, down to earth. I'm straight across the board, and I can put myself in a mode that'll blow your mind. When I say blow your mind, it would be through my years of experience with people, running nightclubs, doing this, doing that. But the problem is that, unfortunately, for me as far as Elvis goes, for me to be a performer, I have my life here. I have my store. It's like I got fifteen suspenders on and they're all pulling me back, holding me back from what I really want to do. From what I could really be. Because I tell you what, if somebody said, 'Steve, I'm gonna take care of your home, I'm gonna take care of your family, I'm gonna take care of everything for you for about a year and then boom, boy, not even one year, man, you're gonna go places. You're gonna do things that you can exploit and just have a ball and just really go out.' Because I'm not a gambler. I'm not a dope addict. But I love to entertain. And there's something out there for me. Now whether I find it when I'm sixty-nine or seventy-eight, I'll find it, believe me. But I love to entertain—I love to get out and I like to burst. And like I said, if I just could—oh, man! People would like me more as an Elvis entertainer if I could let out like I do in my basement. I can't believe that I don't. Sometimes I do, you know? But I was told that I look like a stripper sometimes. And I can't help that, but I've watched Elvis do it, and I said, Well, he did it, too, but he just didn't do much. And—if I could just let go, I would be, I would feel that I am my own Elvis, OK? You can name me Melvis, Pelvis, it doesn't make any difference. I think I could turn faces as well, you know, if I had the time. Because—don't get me wrong when I say this, OK? Please don't. I am highly talented and I am—I can do so many different things and voices and things—I mean, I could be a standup comedian. I could do all kinds of crazy things— I mean that.

"And I just, I'm in a little nutshell. Because—I just don't know how to explain myself, you know? I really, really don't. I'm left-handed. I have more gray matter on my brain, you know? At least that's what they tell me. And I think things differently—you know, I'm like the Chinese, I don't count with a calculator, I can flip them things faster than I can use a calculator. I don't know why or how I do it. And I never was that great in school, because I didn't care. I just wanted to get out and *move*. I was the last one there, and I was the first one to leave. You know? That was me. And I'm gonna be hyper the rest of my life. I might die in a year from now, I might die two months from now, I might die tomorrow, you know? But that's me."

Steve lives in Fort Thomas, Kentucky, an eight-minute drive from his store—through Newport, up a wooded lane, past a trailer park called

Shady Terrace and a road called Gunpowder Ridge, in a red-brick house with white shutters and two tiny pines out front. A basketball hoop stands in the driveway, and two thick rope swings hang from the trees in the side yard. The house sits across the street from a road called Memory Lane. This detail helps when Steve gives directions. "When you go past Memory Lane," he says, "you've gone too far."

Visitors are greeted at the front door by Steve's two Shih Tzus, Pele and Pixie, a puppy. Steve likes to pad through the house in his tube socks cradling one or both of the dogs in his arms, rubbing his nose in their fur. His babies, he calls them. The living room, to the left of the foyer, contains a black tropical-print sofa and an antique chair and desk. To the right of the fireplace, under a window, is a old hi-fi with a walnut cabinet, an RCA New Vista Victrola. When Steve walks past this room he looks at the stereo, as if he cannot believe it is there.

Across the hall from the living room is the TV room. One rainy March night Steve and two of his fellow Elvises hung out there, switching from a college basketball playoff game to a videotape of one of the EPIIA impersonator conventions in Las Vegas—try this and feel the brain pan fry—while debating whether to order pepperoni and extra cheese on their pizza.

These guys critiqued basketball and Elvis in the same way. They'd be talking speed, movement and agility, and you'd look up in time to see a guy in a jumpsuit kicking his foot over his head. Once, during an Elvis interlude, Steve smirked at the cheap cut of an impersonator's jumpsuit. Ronny Craig, his closest Elvis friend, looked up from where he lay sprawled on the couch. His tube socks pointed skyward, and one was wet from Pixie's teething. "Oh, yeah," he said. "Almost fifty years old and you're doing Young Elvis."

"Hey, Ronny," Steve said and shot to his feet. He rose up on his toes and popped his shins like scissor blades to illustrate how he would look as Elvis with no teeth and artificial knees.

"I'll be doing it when I'm seventy!" he crowed.

"Uh, that's pretty good, Stevie," Ronny said. He switched back to the contest. On the screen an impersonator lunged and flung out his hand. A ring on his index finger exploded, setting off a short white flash and a puff of breathy smoke. Chris Wilson, the young Elvis from Cincinnati, sat on the floor hugging a pillow to his chest, his mouth hanging open.

"You've never been to Vegas before, have you," I said.

"Noooo," he said. He formed the word without ever closing his mouth.

Steve had recently remodeled his kitchen to resemble a fifties diner, with a chrome kitchen table and a bar with four stools—two pink, two aqua—that he bought at Sears. On a wall hangs a print of a make-believe place called the Hollywood Diner; in it, James Dean has found work as a soda jerk who waits on Marilyn Monroe, Marlon Brando—who looks sullen at finding himself in a malt shop for all eternity—and Elvis, wearing black leather and looking eternally twenty-one. "I love this picture," Steve said. He swept his hand to touch each person. "I am every one of these people. This is my life."

From the TV room, if you took a sharp left into the hall and opened a door—not too far, the hinges are stiff—you could see a staircase painted poodle-skirt pink. It led to Steve's basement. That night he descended the stairs, paused on the gray-painted floor and entered a room on the right. "This is my slop room," he said, stepping backward into its center. "This is my thinking room."

In this room, it was impossible to think of anything but Elvis. Its floor, walls, and two long tables on either side are covered with Elvis items, including a multicolored tapestry depicting a scene from the 1973 *Elvis: Aloha from Hawaii* satellite telecast, a bronze-painted bust of Elvis circa 1965 with the left half of the nose chipped off, an album copy of *Moody Blue*, framed black-and-white stills from the movies *Kissin' Cousins* and *It Happened at the World's Fair*, a songbook called the *Elvis Presley Anthology*, framed sepia-toned publicity photos, sheet music for the song "Rock-A-Hula Baby" and, on one baby-pink wall, hung in a diamond-shaped frame, a royal blue scarf signed by Elvis Presley, a gift from the friend of a friend.

Steve stood in the center of the room. "If I did a song for you now, and you heard me do this song tomorrow night, you'll go, God, he sounded a hell of a lot better in the basement."

"Will you do something for me now?" I asked.

"What do you want?" he replied. He snatched up the microphone, suddenly full of purpose. "Let me think." He rifled his karaoke cassettes, muttered, popped in a tape. The speakers squealed and then issued the opening notes of "Are You Lonesome Tonight." He eased into the song's question. His voice echoed Elvis's huskiness, and after all the talk and drawl it was funny to hear his voice sound so soft. He turned toward two long horizontal mirrors on the wall to his right; both of them reflected him from the waist up. He wore a white tuxedo shirt, untucked, tight pale jeans greasy at the knees, tube socks puffed out at the toes. His eyes closed. As he finished the first verse his head tilted back, and his left hand opened like a fan. When he came to the spoken bridge he spun front again, recited the words from memory—*Honey, you lied*—then slid into the song's coda, looked down at his socks, sighed and said, *Ooooh yeah.*

He kept his head lowered a moment.

"Well," he said, finally, "that's a piece of my action."

And, this time, that was all he said.

5

Dennis

♩ think this is the earliest one," Dennis Stella said. "I'd like you to take a quick look."

Two days after Dennis performed at a combination Elvis concert and bridal fair, we sat at his kitchen table and reviewed his progress as an impersonator. After each show Dennis liked to dissect his act—pick apart his stage patter, measure the affection of the crowd, grieve over mistakes. This was in the first few months of his serious impersonating career, when his biggest technical problem continued to be the way he moved. "With each time that I'm performing, another two, three weeks, a month is going by, where I've got more time to fine-tune things I had already thought I was doing OK," he said. "I'm now working a lot more on not moving so much. Because a lot of my movement I thought was good before turned out to look like nervous movement."

From where we sat, we could have been talking about anything. The decor in Dennis's house would disappoint the curious who expected a candlelit shrine or a velour tapestry depicting Jesus greeting Elvis in heaven. The kitchen was spotless, with beige tile counters and white appliances. A picture of Gail smiling from someone's front porch tilted on the refrigerator door at Dennis's eye level, held fast by a magnet. Inside the refrigerator sat a half-empty pizza box and a carton of orange juice. Off the kitchen toward the back of the house was the den, probably the most cluttered room of the house. Here Dennis kept his karaoke machine and collection of sing-along cassettes. On a piece of kitchen counter that served as the divider to the den tumbled dozens of CDs that represented a survey of Elvis Presley's career—hillbilly blues, gospel ballads, love songs. Among these was a CD of songs by Engelbert Humperdinck. Many impersonators in their thirties name Engelbert Humperdinck as an influence. None of them can really explain why.

Next to the karaoke machine—big and blocky enough, actually, to call to mind a shrine—Dennis had propped a mirror close to the microphone so he could monitor his movement as he sang. "If I'm starting to look stupid," he said, "I'm seeing it firsthand."

So there we were, talking over Pepsi about nervous movement, when Dennis remembered this videotape of himself and asked if I'd like to see it.

"Yeah," I said, "I'd love to." And I meant it. And I didn't. We slid our chairs under the table and walked toward the front of the house into the living room. It began to dawn on me what was going to happen. I was going to watch Dennis pretend to be Elvis while Dennis watched himself pretend to be Elvis. And he was going to watch me watch him, and I was going to rubberneck from one Dennis to the next while not letting on that I knew Dennis, the real one, was watching me. And then—I would bet my next breath on it—he was going to ask me what I thought.

Dennis was always asking me what I thought. In the first four months I knew him, he asked my opinion of his Elvisness at least 150 times. Over the phone he played tapes of himself singing "American Trilogy"— did he nail that last note OK? In a crowded bar he unholstered the arm thrashes from "Polk Salad Annie"— did they look authentic? This I could handle. It is always possible to hit on something constructive: Your voice sounds deeper. Your wig stayed on. Accurate, and always true. Still, it's difficult to know how far to go. What if you say the wrong thing? What if the wrong thing is the truth? And then this video: Comparing a guy to Elvis is one thing, but telling him he stinks as himself is something else altogether. My options boiled down to telling Dennis the truth and hurting his feelings, or telling a lie, which was no option at all. I noticed I was having trouble walking into the next room.

Dennis, meanwhile, had practically broken into a trot. He wore a loose tank top, baggy shorts, and sneakers with sloppy socks. He was saying something about not forcing his sound, and how his television allowed him to watch seven stations at once, not that he'd want to. On the wall opposite the front door sat a forty-six-inch Sony with a black wood cabinet. He slapped through the tapes in the bottom of the VCR stand, the tank top drooping to offer a view of his lats, and pulled one out. He said, "Now I should tell you—I did capture something on this first tape. This is my second performance at the Ramada Inn. This is six months after I started to do this." He popped the tape into the VCR and fast-forwarded toward himself. "Something that I had in this—it wasn't Elvis," he explained. "It looked more like a combination of Andrew Dice Clay, Tom Jones, and the Fonz, maybe. But it was kind of . . . *interesting* to watch." I offered a smile and glanced around the room. Tasteful shades of gray, with a sofa, chaise, and love seat in black leather, plus a glass coffee table with stone pillars for support. Carpet pale gray and thick. No Elvis memorabilia in the room, other than the host.

"You're going to hear a lot of screaming," he was saying, "probably more than you ever heard for me before. But I looked more like a stripper or something. Watch."

The tape rolled. The screen filled with Dennis, shrink-wrapped in Comeback black leather, stomping around like he was trying to put out a small fire. His hair was light brown and long and very fluffy. The soundtrack consisted of a wail that sounded like extremely female banshees, accompanied by the five-note thud of "Trouble."

"Hear what I'm talking about?" Dennis shouted.

I looked at him. He was standing next to the television, retracing the steps his image made on the screen. *He was dancing with himself.* He had split in two before my eyes. He had become both the man he was and the man he wanted to be. Dennis and Trouble Dennis.

On the screen he grabbed the mike and choked it—you want Elvis, ladies, that's what the hell you're gonna get—and started to sing. Lunge. Kick. He screamed that he was trouble, and the banshees screamed *eeeeeee* right back. He warned that he was evil. The women squealed as if this was precisely their point. Dennis studied Trouble Dennis, all four knees pumping. *Eeeeeee.* He flinched a little. I suppressed a smirk.

"I sure don't look like a guy who's scared," he said.

"That's your hair?" I asked.

We seemed to be focusing on different aspects of this experience. He started a new verse. His pelvis appeared to have come unhinged. He flinched again. "Oh, look at this here," he said. This time, we laughed. "By the way," he said, "I wasn't wearing any underwear this particular night. And I did tear my pants in the next song."

Suddenly we were focusing. "Oh, really," I said.

"Thankyou. Thankyouverymuch," Trouble Dennis slurred at the

crowd. "Ladies and gentlemen, I'd like to sing a little love song. It's called 'Let Yourself Go.'"

The music intensified, and Dennis stood appraising his spasms on the tape. "Like I told you, there is some appeal here," he said. "I can't figure out what it is. Maybe it's because I really didn't know what I was doing." He laughed. I joined in.

Trouble Dennis began to dance. He moved as if he had just noticed he was standing on a snake.

"I was really trying hard, though, I swear to God," the other Dennis said. We laughed again. The synthesizers swelled, and it hit me: We were *both* laughing. He thought this was as funny as I did. I had been worried about lying, and instead got a lesson in the shifting levels of truth. The interesting thing about knowing an Elvis impersonator is that you can never anticipate what will surprise you more—the impersonator's behavior, or what you assume and expect based solely on what you see. There are, it turns out, all kinds of illusions. I watched Dennis wiggle across the screen. He was right: There was some appeal there.

"I'll turn on the lights," Dennis said, while the audience on the tape cheered. He flipped a switch, and the track lights over the fireplace beamed down on us. "Let Yourself Go" is a song of seduction, but Trouble Dennis made it sound more like something you'd hear at a rugby game. He turned to face the band and ground his backside toward the floor. A slice of his suntanned back smiled at the women below the waistband of his leather jacket. "Ohhh, this is bad," Dennis moaned.

He brightened a bit and pointed to Trouble Dennis's leather pants. "This is where I tore it—this jump: Right. There."

This would have been weird if it weren't somehow so reassuring. This would have been excruciating if we both weren't laughing so hard.

Trouble Dennis stalked off, trying to walk like his pants hadn't sprung a four-inch chasm in the crotch. The master of ceremonies passed him on his way to the stage.

"Dennis Stella!" the MC barked. "An excellent job—and congratulations for getting into those pants." The audience roared. "Later on we'll be getting the vise grips out and removing them."

He stopped the tape. "What do you think?" he asked.

We headed into the den, where he sang "Let Yourself Go" live, so I could hear his progress. He was better. "More Elvisy," I told him. He moved into another number he was still too shy to do in public, "Polk Salad Annie." At the fast part he snapped his arms like whips. After thrashing the finale he could barely breathe. "I think I sound quite a bit like Elvis in that song," he said between gasps. "What did you think? Honestly?"

"Considering you just started doing it," I said.

"Yeah, the movement's not perfected." He panted. "None of my movement's perfected."

By now we were both hungry. At a place near his house called Cafe Borgia, we split an appetizer of polenta with portabella mushrooms and ate huge salads and plates of pasta with vegetables. He brought up Greene's West, the spectacle of his levitating hair. "It was a travesty," he said.

"You were having a bad hair day," I allowed.

"That was," he said, "a very experimental day."

He asked me to pass the salt, then seasoned his salad using arm movements not nearly as dramatic as the ones in "Polk Salad Annie," but just as purposeful. "I have a death wish," he said cheerfully, digging in.

He said the secret to impersonating Elvis is to care about what you do, but not to care too much about what people think, even if they tell you truths you'd rather not hear. "I take things pretty well, though," he said. "If somebody came up to me and said, 'My perception of you is that you're a little bit of a goofy son of a gun,' I might nod my head in agreement."

I nodded and watched Dennis for a moment. To look at him, you would never know he'd just been pretending to be Elvis. Then I said it must take a certain kind of person to dress up like Elvis Presley. I said the absolute last thing a person like that must want in life is to be ignored. I asked him if I was right.

He swallowed and reached for the bread. "One hundred percent," he said. "You're one hundred percent correct."

Dennis Stella loved Elvis Presley from the first time he saw him, wearing a gold sport coat and singing about girls. But it took years for him to realize that what he loved was also what he wanted to be.

He was born June 26, 1957, in Chicago, the third of four children in a family of three boys and one girl. Both of his parents grew up in Italy. His father, Antonio, was born in the United States then sent to Italy by his father, who had prospered in mining and groceries. Antonio returned to America during the Depression, then was drafted by the U.S. Army and shipped over to Italy during World War II. While stationed in Naples, he met a young schoolteacher named Assunta. They married, had Mario, their first child, then moved to Chicago.

They settled in the Roseland section of the city's South Side. His father, an easygoing man, worked for Pullman-Standard, the train car manufacturing company. Everybody called him Tony. His mother, known as Tina, was bright and restless, a woman who never sat still. Except for a few years before Dennis and his brother Tony were born, she never worked outside the home.

"My mom was different than many women who grew up in the early part of the twentieth century," Dennis said. "She went to college in Europe back in the thirties, and that was a little different back then. And she came to this country and got her associate degree here in the United States. So my mom was a woman who had dreams and ambition, and apparently she had to forgo a lot of those for her family."

She hated it when people assumed she was uneducated because she spoke English with a thick accent. For that reason, she refused to teach Italian to her children. Dennis remembered her vowing that they would never have to endure what she did.

But Dennis felt different anyway. He was small for his age, with an inability to keep quiet around boys who were bigger. "I got beat a couple times," he said.

One day in grade school, the teacher asked everyone to stand and tell the class what they'd had for breakfast. When his turn came, Dennis stood and announced he'd had a glass of *oranja juice.* Everyone in the class began to laugh, and he looked around and wondered what he had done that was so funny. In time he figured out that it wasn't that he drank orange juice. It was that he pronounced it the way his parents did, with an Italian accent. For the first time Dennis experienced how it felt to be judged just because he did something a little differently from everyone else. He never forgot how confused and angry that made him feel.

About the same time, Dennis discovered that being different could be a great advantage. Saturday afternoons in the sixties, their father would drop Dennis and Tony off at a theater in their neighborhood; it was usually the Roseland, which showed second-run movies. Their mother—no doubt dreading a day spent with two small boys tearing through her house—would give Dennis and his younger brother, Tony, a dollar each to cover the thirty-five cents admission and enough snacks to last the afternoon.

One Saturday the movie opened with a handsome man dancing on a stage wearing a gold sport coat and skinny black pants. He played the guitar and sang in a sweet, husky voice, and on the screen young women in snug clothes looked at him like they were hungry. For the first time in his life Dennis wanted a girl to look at him like she was hungry. He had no idea why, but this man made him think he might like it.

The movie was *Girl Happy*, and seeing it was Dennis's first memory of Elvis. It premiered in 1965 with a plot common to many of the twenty-seven films Elvis made during that decade: Boy meets girl, boy sings to girl, boy—after some misunderstanding and often some race-car driving or water sport—gets girl. "I really didn't understand what all that stuff was about," Dennis said years later, "but I just remember thinking it was cool. I think my brother and I both equally thought he was cool, but it was just an unknowing thing—we'd maybe look at each other, like: 'Yeah! Yeah, that's the way! This is the guy! Check him out!' You know: He's got the sports car. He's got the girl. And he's singing like crazy."

Dennis sucked it all in, spellbound. Elvis drove a red convertible and wore a shirt to match. He sang that spring made his fever rise. He played a guitar next to a pool with an artificial palm tree floating in the center. He cocked his right eyebrow. He sunbathed in a long-sleeved dark blue shirt and tight black pants. He sneaked up behind a girl and cupped her elbows in the palms of his hands. He cocked his left eyebrow. He held another girl while he steered a sailboat against a boundless blue-white sky. He dug a hole to enter a jail filled with twenty sleeping girls. He wore a woman's gown with shoulders and sleeves made of some sheer black fabric. He fondled a blond guitar while dressed in shirt and pants of clinging black. He sprung some karate on two men in a strip club. He got the girl.

Dennis never dreamed a world or a man like this existed. He wasn't sure he understood any of it, but he knew exactly what it meant. As a boy, Elvis pored over comic books and loved superheroes for their bravery and incongruous clothes. Twenty years later, Dennis gazed into this fantasy of honey-colored sun and taut bodies dancing the Clam and claimed a role model of his own.

"You have to say, even if you weren't a big Elvis fan, he was a decent-looking guy," he said. "And he had a nice way about him. He sang well, he was always smiling, and the movies were generally upbeat.

"Here he is—he has pretty girls in bikinis chasing him around the pool, and he's singing all these cool songs and having a good time. I remember thinking, this is the coolest guy I've ever seen. I wish I was like him."

Lives can realign and pivot like the planets on moments like these, fueled by the strength of a simple wish. The transformation of Dennis Stella didn't explode in some grand cinematic flash—at nine he was too young to know who he was, let alone that he wanted to be someone else. But the dream started here. After that matinee he sheltered a memory of Elvis as handsome, dangerous, irresistible, and basically decent— the kind of guy he admired and wanted to be. The kind of guy who could be different and people would like him in spite of it, or even because of it. Years later, when his future seemed uncertain, the memory would return. His great change would begin.

But that Saturday afternoon, Dennis was nothing but a happy child. He sat surrounded by other laughing children. He ate popcorn he bought with the change from his dollar. He grinned speechless at Tony: This is the guy! Check him out! He would tell Tony later that Jerry Lewis movies were now his other favorite.

He stared up at the screen. Elvis looked down at a girl writhing on a chaise, tanned breasts trembling out of her white dress. And Elvis mumbled: "Just gimme a minute to slip out of my suntan lotion."

See something like that when you are nine and it can follow you for the rest of your life.

But even Elvis couldn't compete with teenage dramatics. As he got older, Dennis put Elvis aside. His family moved from Roseland to the suburb of Dolton just after he turned fifteen. He was growing up, but he wasn't getting much bigger. In his sophomore year of high school he stood five foot three and weighed 110 pounds. His junior year he shot up seven inches, but he put on only seven pounds. He played some sports, more out of adolescent desperation than natural skill. Girls unnerved and ignored him: "A lot of people knew me, but mostly the women my age looked at me like, 'Oh, he's cute,' kind of like you would pet your dog. I remember them petting my head a lot."

He doesn't remember watching any of Elvis's televised concerts, the Comeback Special in 1968 or "Aloha From Hawaii" in 1973. He does, however, remember seeing Foghat four times. He and his buddies attended a lot of rock concerts, everything from Elton John to Ted Nugent to the Rolling Stones. "But you know what?" he said. "I tell you, some of this stuff would not have always been my first preference. But my buddies were hugely into it, and these guys were my friends." He preferred bands whose lead singers, to his ear, controlled their voices—Paul McCartney, Paul Rodgers in Bad Company. His buddies would tease him that he liked only "control singers," guys who sang like Elvis. At the time Dennis didn't even own an Elvis record. In fact, he never had. But he found himself drawn to singers with some sense of melody.

He sang, too, though no one knew it. "I started to have a little bit of a crush on this girl," he said. "Has this ever happened to you: You listen to the radio, you would hear a love song, or some mooshy-puppy-love kind of song, and it would remind you of somebody you liked? Well, there was this song called 'Nice to Be with You' by Gallery. You remember that? And I remember being in my garage, and I don't know what I was doing, if I was working on something or playing hockey in there, doing something weird, having the radio on, singing 'Nice to Be with You.' And I was trying to figure out how I was gonna sing this song to this girl, thinking I was really gonna impress her." He laughed. "I never did it, though."

His junior year, he was assigned to a study hall supervised by a speech teacher who sometimes used the period as a practice time for his students. Dennis watched in awe as kids his own age, kids he knew, stood in front of the class and spoke easily, as if they knew some secret. He signed up for a class in dramatic arts and won his first acting role in a play, as Rapunzel's father.

If Dennis's life were a play, this part would be the turning point—the brilliant friction between wishing he could be someone else and realizing that he can. It felt almost too easy: He retreated into another person's speech and mannerisms and somehow, he became more real himself. People wanted to meet him. Girls noticed him more. Usually this just meant he got petted more on the head. Still, it was something.

Whenever he recalled his stage debut, his voice rose and turned warm. "We played to two full houses of a thousand people," he said, "and I loved it.

"And when I got done at the end of the show and went out for the applause—people were just going nuts—it was a tremendous high. I remember thinking, *I like this.*"

Real life thrilled Dennis less. He graduated from high school in 1975, a mediocre student with no clue about what he wanted to do with his life. He worked at an A & P and in two years advanced from grocery bagger to cashier. He made $4.25 an hour. After work he drove around with his friends, drinking beer and singing "Can't Get Enough of Your Love" in his imitation of a rock star's voice. Antonio Stella, worried about his son's future, got Dennis a job at the factory where he worked, a division of General Motors that made train engines. Dennis drove a forklift, ferrying parts from one part of the factory to another. The plant was smoky and filthy and loud, and the work bored him. Yet for all the motion his job entailed, he lacked the means to move himself.

"I used to see all these old men there," he said. "They were miserable. They didn't like the job, they didn't like their wife, they didn't like life. I would tell them that I'm gonna be different, and these guys would say, 'Ahhh, no—that's what we used to say thirty years ago, too. You're gonna die in here just like we are.' And that used to scare the daylights out of me."

It took a death to redirect his life. One morning he dragged in from the factory after working a night shift. Around 8:00 A.M. he fell into bed but couldn't sleep; it always bothered him to know the world zoomed on without him. In the living room the television was on—his mother, always watching soap operas—and he slumped in front of it. Then a newscaster, a flash: Elvis Presley had been pronounced dead at 3:30 P.M. Central Time.

Dennis sat still for a long while, steeped in shock—first at the news, then at his reaction. Why did he feel so terrible? Then he remembered: the Saturday matinees. The nine-year-old boy. Elvis. Himself. The station returned to its regularly scheduled program. And Dennis, to his great surprise, began to cry. He recalled going to the matinee when he was young and Elvis was cool. If someone like Elvis could die so young, anyone could. It wasn't that Dennis hadn't always known this, but he was young. No one he cared about had ever died before.

Elvis Presley's death forced Dennis to study his own life and question its direction. For two years he had coasted in low-end jobs, trading decent pay for uneasy feelings of longing and loss. Now he began to ask himself, seriously, how he wanted to live the rest of his life. Did he like his job? Not really. What did he want to do? He didn't know. But he believed he was destined for something better. And somehow all his doubt and yearning translated into a need to hear Elvis sing again. So Dennis bought a couple of Elvis cassettes—the first he had ever owned—and he started to sing along. He even tried out a couple of tunes on his rock-concert buddies. They told him to turn that shit off. And they told him that he sounded like Elvis, a little.

Late that year he heard the local community college was planning a production of *Bye Bye Birdie*. He interpreted this news as a dream in four easy steps: Dennis knew the lead role of Conrad Birdie was based on Elvis. Dennis knew how to play roles. Therefore, Dennis could be Elvis. He went to the audition, walked on stage, stood next to the piano, informed the director he would sing "One Last Kiss" and remembered, suddenly, that he had never before sung in public. He gripped the side of the piano as if it were the edge of a cliff. The director suggested that Dennis let go long enough to move to the front of the stage. He did.

"I never sang that before," he recalled. "I didn't even know if I could. It didn't matter, though. Whether I got picked or not was irrelevant. The fact was I went out there and auditioned to do this Elvis part. I thought, even if I don't get it, I don't care, I'm up here on stage, doing Elvis.

"Well, I got it."

Over the next four years he won several small roles in local productions of *Annie Get Your Gun*, *Jesus Christ Superstar*, and *Oklahoma*. It made him forget his forklift boredom, and it reminded him how much he enjoyed playing a part and hearing applause.

In November, 1981, when he was twenty-four, GM laid him off. By then he was making $11.40 an hour, good money. For months he had suspected he might lose his job, so he already had hatched a plan. All that fall, he had been driving up to DeKalb to visit his brother Tony, by then a student at Northern Illinois University. Dennis liked the campus, and he loved the idea of learning skills that did not require him to operate heavy machinery. A week after he lost his job, he registered for classes.

In college, Dennis majored in advertising and excelled in transformation. After breaking up with a girlfriend, stung that she preferred a weight lifter, he started lifting weights himself until no one could call him scrawny. He studied Italian, and the bounce he had grown up hearing in his mother's voice made him a natural speaker. He pledged a fraternity, Lambda Chi Alpha, and was elected to several offices. And at parties, he sang. "That was," he said, "a very, very good period of my life."

He would never admit to being the most eager student, but when it came to being a frat brother, Dennis applied everything he learned in class. One idea that intrigued him was how appearance could convey a message that a person lacked the words to express. So when Dennis began to help his frat refine its image, he turned to surfaces. "When I

first joined the house, we were totally scorned by any of the good sorori-
ties," he says. "We were considered dorks. Not because of me, but just
because the house was new."

Dennis considered Lambda Chi Alpha as he would a product. He
studied the popular frats. He planned mixers for which he wrote cute
poems about some of the girls on campus—"I almost got my tail beat a
couple times," he said—and designed a satin jacket in gold with green
trim, the fraternity colors, for the brothers to wear around campus. "The
gold certainly let us be seen," he said. "It's almost obnoxious, but it
served its purpose—because it let the people out there know about this
house." Enrollment rose, and the last Dennis heard, they were still wearing the jackets.

After graduation, he had trouble landing an advertising job. One
night at the health club where he lifted weights he bumped into a guy
who told him the insurance firm where he worked needed new sales-
men in Calumet City. He guaranteed Dennis that, with commission, he
would earn between $20,000 and $24,000 his first year. Dennis took the
job and earned $30,000, and $10,000 more the year after that. After
years of selling himself, the job was easy.

He worked for Allstate at the Sears in River Oaks for four and a half
years before he moved to a small office that he operated with two other
company agents. The office was across from a school and shared space
in a small strip plaza that contained a real estate office, a hair salon, a
tanning salon, a practitioner of natural medicine, and a mailing service.
Dennis worked in the first of three small offices. All had windows that
overlooked a central hall and were close enough that the three could
talk if they raised their voices. The walls, blinds, and furnishings were
oatmeal colored, a tranquilizer for the eye. Anyone who spent any time
watching Dennis work would conclude that his success as an agent
probably had less to do with his sales technique than the fact that he appeared to lack one. He talked to strangers as if they were friends, pillow-
ing his sales pitches with a mix of compliments and personal revelation.
He liked to believe that if he treated people well, this goodwill would return to him.

"Coming from an ethnic family," he told a man calling who called
one afternoon for car insurance, "I know what it's like to have people
not understanding your heritage." He tapped on the IBM computer
squatting on the right corner of his dark brown desk. On the left corner
sat a large jar of generic nondairy creamer. Rolled-up documents held

fast with rubber bands boiled over his Out basket. He slurped at a jumbo fast-food soda while he reviewed the accidents and misfortunes of people's lives, reduced to a series of letter codes.

"Twelve years?" he asked one customer. "Since you were sixteen? I wish all my customers had that kind of loyalty . . ."

People straggled in after work to pay their bills. Dennis invited them all to sit and talk a minute. He stood to greet them, his starched shirt a little wrinkled but his tie still knotted tight. Above the chairs where customers sat he had hung three plaques that proclaimed him Southern Territorial Top Retail Agent, District 43 Agent of the Month, and Chicago Metro Region, Southern Territory Agent of the Month. Down lower, in his line of vision, he kept his diploma from Northern Illinois, to remind himself he was capable of unexpected things.

"There was a period when I was scrawny," he confided to another man over the phone. "How many miles do you have on your Lincoln?"

There was nothing artificial about Dennis. He had matured into both a thoughtful man and a guy who wanted to have fun, a hopped-up combo of frat-boy pragmatist and matinee dreamer. He had many friends, and he seemed to be drawn to people from other countries. Because of his own upbringing, their experiences fascinated him, and he would question them about their lives and the places they came from. At gatherings of friends or family, he seldom stood still. He moved from group to group, embracing friends, kissing women, fetching rounds of drinks, begging people to eat, telling stories, lowering his voice at the dramatic parts—*Oh, and there is something else I should tell you*—in a way that made people feel singled out and special. At parties, it took him an hour to say goodbye. He loved to sing and dance and talk—and talk. Soon after he and Gail began dating, their phone bills totaled $200 a month.

Gail supposed that his talking was what endeared him to her. "I really liked that in him," she said. "I don't know, he just always seems able to understand or discuss everything. I guess I felt like I was engaged to somebody I didn't even know because the guy never hardly talked or expressed himself. And so I think that really attracted me to Dennis, was the fact that he had the ability to communicate his feelings and everything."

But in 1992, something was growing inside of Dennis that even he could not put into words. Loss and loneliness created something inside of him that begged expression, and he had to teach himself the means to translate his feelings into movement and action.

Dennis began the whole Elvis business in earnest out of a simple human need: He missed his mother. She had died a few months earlier at seventy-three, after years of heart trouble and diabetes. As with Elvis in 1977, he saw his own mortality through another person's death. He wasn't dating anyone, and he had mastered his job. During this time one of his insurance partners, Kim Mullen, visited his house. Just for fun, Dennis put on a tape and sang for her his version of "My Way." She told him he sounded good. He didn't believe her, though he wanted to. Soon after, she tossed on his desk an item she'd clipped from the newspaper. It was a notice for an Elvis impersonator contest.

Twice a year, in winter and autumn, the Ramada Inn in South Bend, Indiana, sponsors an Elvis contest, open to all. The hotel itself is unassuming, a simple brick building two and a half miles from the Michigan-Indiana border, just down the road from the Howdy Doody Saloon and a plant nursery called God's Green Earth. But to people in the impersonator world, the Ramada is both launching pad and pit stop. Performers use it to warm up for bigger contests and shows in places like Memphis and Vegas, and fans come to get their fix between those big-time shows. Dennis thought this contest might be the kick he needed. Since his mother's death, sadness had shadowed him. He needed relief. And, one way or another, dressing up like Elvis would make him laugh.

Still, logic told him to resist. He knew people laughed at impersonators. He didn't need anyone to laugh at him. Yet he couldn't help but imagine he would be different. As he argued with himself he realized the reason he felt so torn. It was his mother.

"You know, she didn't work too much after she got married, maybe a few years," he said. "And many times there were things that she had wished she had done. And near her death, when she thought she was probably sick and saw she was older, periodically I would see her crying, or feeling sad. I remember asking her about what was wrong, and sometimes she said that she had a lot of dreams, and she didn't pursue most of them. And that, if she had any advice for me before I got too old, to go and try some of that stuff that I wanted, because, even if you fail, you can always say you tried it.

"So I think that kinda stayed with me a little bit. I knew once I started the Elvis thing, I had a long way to go and there was a very big chance that I might fail. But it was a challenge—you know, to say, hey, it's real hard for me to do this. Can I do it? Can I pull it off?"

And even if he didn't succeed, he figured he could fail quickly. Pull on some jeans, go to this hotel, sing in front of 100 people, tops, grab a drink, and go home. How hard could it be?

The woman at the Ramada told him he needed a costume. He figured he could do the '68 Comeback look cheapest, so he bought a black leather jacket, borrowed a pair of matching motorcycle pants from a buddy and stopped at an AMVETS thrift store on his way to South Bend and paid $2.00 for a pair of black boots, size ten. He normally wore a ten and a half, but for the price he could withstand a night of pain.

Dennis owned no videotape of himself performing that night, but he kept those moments inside his head, a running loop of humiliation. He pulled into the parking lot of the Ramada and the first person he saw was Fred Wolfe, six foot three, black muttonchops to his jawbone, black leather jacket bristling with tassels and fringe. "I looked at him and I felt reassured," Dennis said, "because he looked more of my caliber—he was new and you could tell he didn't have all the stuff, and I went, OK, I'm all right." Then he turned and saw Kevin Mills, a pizza-shop owner from New Jersey and one of the top fifties-era Elvises, dressed in the hillbilly cat uniform—long, loose-fitting jacket and baggy pants. Poor guy, Dennis thought, couldn't even afford a real Elvis outfit, he had to come in his suit. Next came Mike Albert, the auctioneer and famous Vegas-era Elvis from Columbus, Ohio, jeweled jumpsuit pulsing like a galaxy. Dennis felt like he was having a heart attack. And there was more. He saw Ronny Craig from LaCrosse, Wisconsin, all honey smiles and beautiful suit. And Doug Church, a hometown boy considered by some fans to have the best true Elvis voice in the world, destined for Legends in Concert. Then he noticed there weren't 100 people in the audience—it looked more like 600, and they looked like they knew their Elvis. The Vineyard Room, where the contest took place, had high ceilings and cement-block walls painted white, carpet the color of pine needles, and a small kidney-shaped pool to the right of the stage. An hour before these shows, the room filled with loud laughing people, mostly women looking to whoop and swoon back through time, and the air acquired that sweetish party smell of hairspray, squeezed limes, and cigarettes. "It just started to dawn on me," Dennis said, "that I was in way over my head."

Things got worse. The Elvises drew numbers to set the order of performances, and Dennis chose one. A camera crew from a local TV station approached, shoveled a microphone under his chin and asked Dennis about his career as an impersonator, which struck him as funny, because he wasn't aware he had one.

His act gave little clue that he did. By midnight, his feet hurt so much he could barely walk. When he finally peeled off the boots he understood why: What he thought were a pair of size ten men's boots were actually women's size ten boots. He had paced, danced, and socialized for five hours in boots two and a half sizes too small. So not only had he pretended to be another man, he had done it in a woman's shoes. This Elvis business was proving to be much harder than he thought.

But despite his pale debut, South Bend became an incubator for Dennis's Elvis dreams. He enjoyed singing with a band, and he appreciated the fact that he could flop like a fish and the audience would applaud just because he tried. "It was my first humbling experience onstage," he said. "But although I was probably awful at best, I had many people from the crowd come up to me and tell me, 'Boy, you had one of the better voices up there. You just looked like you didn't know what you were doing.'"

So his skills were weak. College had taught him that meant he could only improve, if he refined his presentation. And if he came to South Bend twice a year, he could hang out with guys who already knew the moves and the words to songs and the best place to buy boots. He might learn something. He might even stumble upon a galaxy of his own. But first he needed new boots. He returned to the thrift store and bought a pair of men's boots in his own size. They were brown, so he dyed them black. It was his first successful attempt at disguise.

The Vineyard Room at the South Bend Ramada had a rear center door that opened into a room with a small bar and space where performers could set up card tables and sell pictures of themselves pressed into plastic key chains and stamped onto linen kitchen calendars. The doorway also offered a central spot to get a clear view of performers as they burst through the curtain and onto the stage. On her first trip to the contest Gail stood with Shelley, checking out the action. She really wasn't in the mood to be there. She almost hadn't come at all.

She had been dating a man for five years; they had gotten engaged. The relationship had ended weeks before she could admit it to herself.

After that she just wanted to stay home and keep away from men. And she did, for a while. But Shelley, Chris, and Kelly started telling her about the Elvis show in South Bend, and they begged her to stop moping at home and live a little.

"OK," she told them, "I'll come along, but I'm not gonna go to the show or anything." She thought she and her daughter, Jenna, could lounge by the pool. Once she got there they talked her into going to the show. They told her maybe she might meet someone.

"Forget it," she told them, "I'm never gonna meet anybody again unless he falls from the heavens."

Dennis did the best he could. He strode out to the opening twang of "Walk a Mile in My Shoes," stepped in a puddle of spilled drink, flew into the air and crashed to the floor, nearly taking a speaker with him. Gail and Shelley looked at each other. They shrugged, their code for expressing what would sound mean out loud. Gail didn't even bother to turn on her video camera.

But after the show one of the Elvises set up a karaoke machine in his room, and Gail and her friends wandered over to watch. She noticed Dennis there, singing. It struck her how friendly and nice he was, and how he talked to everyone in the room. In the morning when they were checking out they bumped into him in a hallway. "And we talked long," she said, "and we were ready to leave, and the conversation kept going. And we walked away and we were like, 'God what a really nice friendly guy! And he's so well spoken!' I mean, he just kept carrying the conversation, and he always had something to say about everything."

On the drive home from South Bend, Shelley, Chris, and Kelly teased Gail that Dennis would be a nice guy for her. And they found themselves reevaluating his Elvisness. Everyone agreed he had an excellent voice, but needed work on his movement. "I guess probably a word we were using often was he's got *potential*," Gail said.

They had exchanged phone numbers but neither called the other. By the next contest that January, Dennis had slipped Gail's mind. But once she got there she felt nervous. She found herself scanning the room for him. Months later, after they became close, he admitted to her that he kept searching the room that weekend, looking for her. Not me, she told him. I didn't do that. But almost in the same breath she admitted that she had been searching for him, too.

At first they hung out as a group, with Shelley, Kelly, and Chris. He invited them to a show at the Sabre Room in Hickory Hills. They invited him to Milwaukee. Eventually he started driving up just to see Gail. They learned they had a lot in common.

Gail grew up in Milwaukee, the youngest of three daughters in a German-Polish family. Her sisters were eight and eleven years older, and though she remembered hearing Elvis music or catching snatches of his movies around the house, she never considered herself a fan. Her biggest memory of Elvis revolved around her niece Shelley, eleven years younger and in love with Elvis since kindergarten. Gail remembered sitting at the organ in her grandmother's house, playing "I Want You, I Need You, I Love You" at the organ. They played and sang it over and over, Shelley tilting her head to look at Gail with her big brown eyes. Gail was sixteen, Shelley was five. It was the only Elvis song they both knew. "We thought we sounded good, I guess," Gail said.

Shelley always saw Gail as a rebel, and in some ways she lived up to that image. When she was a teenager, Gail told her mother that she could see herself being a mother, but could never imagine being married. Gail's mother told her she was crazy, but when she was twenty-six, she had Jennifer, whom everybody called Jenna, after an old roommate of Gail's—and a character on the then-popular TV show "Dallas." The fact that Priscilla Beaulieu Presley played the part was just a coincidence. While Gail was pregnant, she helped her boyfriend's sister clean houses for extra money. A year and a half later, she broke up with Jenna's father, quit her waitressing job, and totaled her car, all in the space of a month and a half. She decided to clean houses part time.

"All these changes," Gail said. "So I needed money—but how do you get money if you don't have a car? But I didn't have a car. So how do you get a car if you don't have money? And I had a lot of bills that were in my name. So I really needed money, and I said to my girlfriend, why don't we do this for extra money, we'll use your car and I'll handle all the business aspects of it." When her friend got married and quit, Gail took on all the work herself. After Jenna started school, she eased into cleaning full time. Eventually, she got more business than she could handle alone, so she hired some help. That was how she met Chris and Kelly. She cleaned mostly houses, though she also did a couple of small offices, a gymnastics academy, and a convent. For a while she cleaned a trucking company and some other rougher businesses, dragging Jenna with her because she couldn't afford a babysitter. "I was doing some pretty hard work, at a trucking company," she said. "Pretty grimy, and I didn't like it. But most of all I didn't like the hours. I had to go in the middle of the night. I found myself getting up, taking her sleeping at like five-thirty in the morning to an office, carrying her and laying her on the floor, then telling her, 'Get up—you gotta get ready for school.' You know, it was just way out of hand. I said, 'I can't do this any more.'"

Gail described her life as a chain of logical occurrences, no matter how hard things got: One thing happened, and another had to be done. It made her sound like an independent person. "Yeah," she said, "I guess I am." She paused, then burst out laughing, as if she'd never imagined herself that way. "Yeah, I guess I am! Wow! Well, because I always just felt like well, you gotta *do* it, you know? Even like when I had her, people were always saying, right when I was pregnant, 'Well, go on welfare.' And I was like, *No.* I guess I've always been that way. You gotta do what you have to do. And I did."

She and Dennis soon found they shared this attitude, along with a love of travel, the beach, and what she called "silly things," like miniature golfing. They also liked Elvis, of course, but only to a point. Once Dennis told Gail about an Elvis clock Dennis got as a gift.

"I never hung it up," he told her, "because I thought it was gaudy. I'm like, God, I'm not gonna have an Elvis clock in my house. That's gross! I'm funny about that stuff. Hey, I'll leave my dirty socks on the floor, but I won't hang up an Elvis clock!"

"When you allow that to enter your living area," Gail said, "then it becomes too much."

"There has never been anything," Dennis said, "I don't care. Even religion, and I have respect for God. I see people who get all goofy on God, and the first thing I think of is, those people have usually screwed up so bad in life they have nowhere else to turn. So anytime I see anybody who's a fanatic, right away I don't care what it is, I think, there's something wrong with them. Don't you?"

"Yes," Gail said. "It's awful hard to explain sometimes to people that you are not a fanatic, an Elvis fanatic."

They also encountered differences other than the distance between them. He liked to stay up late. She rose early to send Jenna to school. He loved to eat; she ate a couple of crackers with cheese and sausage and called it a meal. She was excitable, always worried something would go wrong. Dennis approached most things in life with the attitude that it all would shake out OK. He loved to work out at the gym; she always worried people were staring at her because she couldn't work the machines. Dennis teased her about how she could never decide what to wear when they went out, flinging glittering dresses around the room before choosing one using no logic he could detect. But he admired her independence, and that she would take turns driving to see him on weekends, and the way she supported him no matter what he did.

The main difference between them in those first months remained Dennis's hair, or more precisely his hair's future. Gail learned only to tolerate the wig. She appreciated the reasons he resisted changing his own hair. She understood that he didn't want to look like Elvis every day, especially at work. But every time she laid eyes on him in that wig, she liked it less. The harder he tried to succeed, the more the wig mocked his progress.

Though they could talk on the phone for two hours straight, they never agreed on the subject. It wasn't that Dennis refused to discuss it. It was that he lacked the words to articulate his fears and insecurities.

He realized he had turned into two people the night he performed at Greene's West.

That warm June night, when he sang and swiveled and the top of his head rose like fresh bread, Dennis assumed his illusion worked. He knew he had pulled at the wig, but reasoned he had moved so smoothly no one ever saw. After his second set, after the six Elvises shut things down with "Can't Help Falling in Love" from the movie *Blue Hawaii*, he rushed to the lobby to hug friends and relatives, still wearing his black Spanish Flower jumpsuit. He was shiny with sweat and breathing hard from the hot lights and excitement. "So . . . what did you think?" he asked them. Reports were cheerful yet sketchy.

He headed home, flushed and a little triumphant. Gail brought the video she had recorded, and with Shelley, Chris, and Kelly, they gathered in his living room to screen it.

He had never witnessed anything so miserable. He had never seen himself in profile wearing the wig. He could barely stand to look at himself, yet he couldn't tear his eyes away. When he wrenched the wig halfway through the second verse of "Patch It Up," everyone laughed. Actually, for most of that thirteen-minute set, they laughed. The minutes slithered on, and Dennis's perception of himself began to change. For thirteen minutes—really, for the first time—Dennis saw himself as others did. Not as a smooth interpreter of the king of rock and roll, but as a fool in a floor-sample jumpsuit, entertaining in ways he never intended: The sliding sunglasses. The piston-driven pelvis. The evil slipping wig.

Thirteen minutes is a long time to watch a dream die.

It sickened Dennis to see how far he had strayed from his dream of doing Elvis justice. And, for the first time, he wondered if he should leave Elvis alone. The entire time he watched with Gail and his friends, he did the only thing that felt right, the only reaction that made any sense: He laughed. Sunk into black leather in his living room, surrounded by friends, he laughed and tried to hide the depth of his shame and humiliation.

Finally, everyone left. Dennis sat alone and watched himself again. And again. It made him sick to see it, but he replayed the tape after work, on weekends—fifteen times, twenty, he lost count—those thirteen minutes spinning into hours of hard study and self-doubt. "Oh, my God," Dennis said to the man on the screen, "what a dork. You are what everybody makes fun of. You are that bad Elvis joke."

It was like that day in grade school when he talked about *oranja juice* and felt foolish and angry when his classmates laughed. But this time, he felt as if he deserved ridicule. Until he watched the video, he had managed to keep his perspective because he recognized that his appearance, and often his very life, bordered on the absurd. Unlike a lot of other impersonators, he recognized the inherent silliness of his situation. "I have to tell you," he said, "although I like to believe that I'm the sanest guy in the world, I must admit: If I wasn't me—let's say I was another guy. And I had a sister. I might hesitate before bringing me over to meet my sister. Because I'm thinking: 'OK, let's see. He does Elvis. He's an insurance man. He drives a Corvette. He's going on thirty-seven and never been married.' I think: Goofy son of a gun."

After all, he felt that way about some of the other Elvises. Sometimes at shows he would stand in the dark in the back of the room, nursing a gin and tonic and staring at the other impersonators with their strobe-jeweled suits and their big sideburns and most of all their monumental heads, as they trailed admirers behind them like the tail of a Las Vegas comet. The sight would make him laugh and shake his head.

"You have to admit," he said, "if you're a steadfast type of person, there is something very humorous about seeing a bunch of guys running around with these pork chops. And these guys who walk around on a daily basis wearing an Elvis hairdo, which is really kind of outdated—what are you thinking? I mean, *what's going on in your mind?*"

At the start of his first serious year as an Elvis impersonator, he had to ask himself the same question. He did consider quitting, but not seriously. "More than twenty times in the last year," he said then, "I've second-guessed myself. And I've said, Am I a goofy son of a gun? Am I doing the right thing here? Should I maybe be spending more hours at my insurance office, trying to earn a more quote-unquote legitimate living and quit dreaming in the stars?

"But I don't want to be one of these guys who's seventy years old and in a rocking chair who always wondered, Could I have done it? At least this way, if I tried it, and people just said, 'Oh, just go back to selling insurance,' I know I did the best I could, and maybe it just wasn't in the cards for me. But at least that way I could say I tried."

Once again the salesman in Dennis surfaced. He spent hours studying the situation and drew a conclusion: Since he fully understood and accepted failing this badly, he could proceed with the business of getting better. So he set out to unlearn the punch line to the joke he kept telling on himself. First he visited a hair stylist; he showed him the wig, explained his troubles with tension and gravity. The stylist took the hairpiece in his hands and examined it. "No wonder," he said. "It's a woman's wig."

Now here was a revelation. The stylist explained the wig was designed to fit someone with a smaller head—that explained the slipping and bunching—and its hairline was designed to sit lower on the forehead than a man's, which accounted for the persistent cowlick. That meant he wore the crown of the wig on his cranium's downward slope. Though not as painful as wearing a pair of women's boots two and a half sizes too small, the situation threatened more far-reaching effects. The hairdresser offered to cut and style the wig to streamline it and install wig clips Dennis could pinch into his own hair to make it stay. He quickly agreed.

This decision baffled his friends. Gail decided that he was stubborn. She had hoped that seeing her Greene's West video might finally convince Dennis to dye his hair and grow sideburns. But to Dennis, no other choice made as much sense. Greene's West began what promised to be a major summer of Elvis. A few weeks after that show he would perform twice in Las Vegas at the annual convention of the EPIIA. Barely a month later he planned to leave the office late on a Tuesday afternoon and drive the Corvette through the night, stealing naps at rest stops, until he reached Memphis and the Images of Elvis contest. So he had an illusion to maintain.

What if he ditched the wig? Two options. He could spend up to $1,000 on a wig shaped and sewn to fit the contours of his head. This he resisted, because he had already sunk thousands into Elvis. The karaoke machine had cost $800. The speakers for his machine totaled $500—he bought two of them at a church and they gave him a break on the price; the microphone was $250; the amplifiers set him back another $500; a reverb device was about $150; he spent another $200 for a tape deck; the eliminator cost another $300.

The total cost of karaoke tapes, plus the CDs to study Elvis Presley's sound, he estimated at around $3,000. He saved money on his two jumpsuits by purchasing floor samples from Butch Polston, who made his jumpsuits based on Elvis's original patterns—around $2,000 for both, less than half the normal cost of one. All that passion added up. In March he had traded in his 1986 Fiero for the red Corvette and gone from having no car payment to owing $612 a month. Plus he planned a remodeling job on his den and two major road trips, so spending another thousand on hair felt reckless. He wanted to be Elvis, but he had to be practical.

The cheapest course would have been to grow his own hair and dye it black. But to Dennis, the psychic costs of a pompadour amounted to more than he felt able to handle. He admitted that he cared what people thought, and that an Elvis Head might hurt his credibility at work. Most impersonators with pompadours did Elvis as a full-time job, where their appearance counted as an asset, or they held jobs in factories and other places where they either could avoid the public or wear hats. Dennis had trouble imagining himself selling people insurance—the intangibles of future and risk—with a hairstyle that telegraphed a message of excess and questionable taste.

"Most of what I do is based on residuals—people I've signed five, six, seven years ago," he said. "I doubt if these people would get up and leave because I had darker hair and thicker sideburns. However, they'd probably mutter as they're leaving my office, 'That goofy son of a gun.' I'm not necessarily saying that they wouldn't buy the insurance from me, but maybe think it's a little humorous and maybe not take me seriously. They'll be waiting for me to jump on top of the desk and sing 'Big Hunk o' Love' or something."

He wondered how people he met for the first time would judge him if he wore a pompadour. "As it is right now," he said, "when I tell people that I do an Elvis impersonation, one eyebrow goes up and goes, mmmm. Already a warning bell is going off: Goofy Son of a Gun."

And most of all, he saw nothing wrong with the way he was. It wasn't that he didn't appreciate the power of transformation. After all, it had taken years of weightlifting and miles of forklift rides to shape him into the man he was. But the same milestones that had led him to impersonate Elvis had also taught him to resist turning into him. To blacken his hair and upholster himself with sideburns, to imitate someone else's appearance every moment of his life when he had grown to value his own, struck him as stupid, a strange kind of vain. He couldn't change now.

It wasn't that he was stubborn. He was scared.

The deeper Dennis got into Elvis, the more he felt Elvis's grip on his identity. His own life continued: He worked all day, quit around 6:00 P.M., visited his father, stopped for something to eat, hit the gym for a dozen sets on the weights and ten minutes on a stair-climbing machine—enough to look good without appearing compulsive. Sometimes he would meet friends for a beer. But Elvis had insinuated himself into the contours of Dennis's days. He sang in the car. He spent less time in the office, and the days he worked, melodies coursed through his head. When he glanced up, he could see hanging on his office door a certificate he had received for performing in South Bend the year before. Shows disrupted his workouts at the gym. His circle of friends stretched to include fellow impersonators. He dated Gail, a woman he met at a show. When he started impersonating, it bothered him that people would think he was living in a fantasy world. And now it scared him to think that he could.

When Dennis Stella was nine, he sat in a movie theater and wished he could be just like Elvis. Twenty-eight years later, he struggled against the deeper meanings of that innocent wish. How do you pursue a dream without it consuming you? How do you embody something so full of bald-faced absurdity and still move people to respect you? Could he accept attention and minor fame—which, to his delight, felt like those high school plays all over again—in exchange for his very identity? He impersonated Elvis to show feelings and affections he lacked the words to express. But more and more, people saw him only for how he looked and not for what he meant.

Careening into his big Elvis summer, Dennis found himself defending an identity even he wasn't so sure of anymore. Still, he held on. He paid $75 to have the wig styled and bought several products formulated to give it lifelike shine. He took it home, tried it on. The wig looked the same, but smaller. Better? Maybe. He spent a lot of time studying his image in the mirror. "What do you think?" he kept asking everyone that summer. Including himself.

"See, I think Elvis was a great man, but he was exactly that—he was a man," he said. "No better than me or you, he was a human being. And I happen to think Dennis is a pretty good guy, too. So I don't ever want to forget who I am. OK, maybe I didn't have a ton of hit singles, and I wasn't adored by fans all over the world, but I think I'm a pretty good guy. And I like to be myself."

Las Vegas

6

"Vegas is Elvis is Vegas"

        Late one afternoon in 1970, Mike McGregor got a call from one of the boys at Graceland. The caller relayed a message that Elvis wanted to see him and his wife, Barbara, right away. This struck McGregor as strange. Elvis often called him up to the house if he needed something. But why would he ask to see Barbara?

They left their trailer behind Graceland and walked through the back of the house and out the front door. Elvis was standing on the porch waiting for them. Before him was parked a brand-new, copper-colored Coupe de Ville with a beige roof. McGregor saw the car and thought nothing of it. There were always nice cars parked in front of the house, Cadillacs and Lincolns and who knows what else. They never impressed him much.

"Hey, boss, you want me?" he asked.

"I want you to take a look at that car," Elvis said. "What do you think?"

"It's a pretty car," he said.

"What do you think about the color?" he asked.

"It's a real pretty color," McGregor replied.

Elvis asked him: "You ever owned a Cadillac?"

McGregor said: "No, I ain't the Cadillac type."

Elvis said, "Here's the papers, the key's in it. It's got some gas in it, I'm not sure how much. Better check that before you and Barbara go very far.

"That's yours. I want you to have it."

McGregor's first reaction was that he didn't want it. He already owned a car. He didn't need a fancy Cadillac. And he hated to feel obligated to anyone. In fact, he had given Elvis's father Vernon $125 for the RCA New Vista Victrola that had been in the den at Graceland—the same one he and Elvis had listened to the country album on—rather than just take it outright. Vernon was auctioning off some things the family didn't need, and when McGregor saw the hi-fi he asked Vernon to name a price. It was a nice piece of furniture, with a fine walnut cabinet. No way could he buy anything new for close to that amount. Vernon probably would have let him have it for free, but McGregor didn't like getting anything he didn't work for.

But this car was different. He knew it would be hard to say no. Elvis had gone to a lot of trouble to pick out a color he thought the two of them would like. He looked so happy, standing there on the porch. And McGregor had to admit it made him feel good that Elvis wanted to give the two of them something so nice.

So he shook Elvis's hand and thanked him; Barbara gave him a hug. Elvis was visibly pleased. "Get in it!" he told them. "Go somewhere!" They did exactly as he said—climbed in and eased through the tall trees, down the driveway toward Highway 51.

They drove the car a few years, then traded it in for a new one. "It's probably in a crusher somewhere," McGregor said with a shrug, standing near the front door of his store in Oxford, the one with the ceiling made of Graceland's pine fence posts. He built everything in the store himself out of rough pine. It was an interesting contrast—the delicate gold and silver jewelry, the mirror-bright belt buckles and pearl gun handles inside the rough-hewn cases, all made by the same man. McGregor was much the same way. He looked like a cowboy, but he was an artist and a philosophical man. He could see why people would be amazed that he hadn't saved his copper Coupe de Ville to sell for a big profit down the road. But even after knowing someone like Elvis—or maybe because he had known him—he never believed people would stay so crazy about him for so long.

"I try to look at everything as real," he said. He smiled, which deepened the amused expression he usually wore. "Maybe that makes me weirder than most people."

McGregor was a handsome, tan, and wiry man in jeans, brown boots, a denim shirt, and an ever-present ivory straw cowboy hat atop his silver hair. His shop, next door to the house he built himself, was eight miles from downtown Oxford, but it felt farther away. Just down the road stood a country store made of corrugated metal. A big metal box out front had a sign on it that promised "Ice Cold Watermelons." McGregor's store was quiet but for the rush of passing pickups and cars and the gurgle of a small stream a step off the front porch. During the day neighbors came with their tackle, sat out front and fished while inside he made jewelry beneath a sign that read, "Silence Please—You're in the Presence of a Genius at Work." In the front of the store there was an Indian blanket on one wall, a steer's head with feathers lashed to its horns over the door, and a box of shotgun shells on a log beam above the counter. When he showed off his work, a fat-pawed cat with fur of black and tan and brown sat atop one of the glass cases grooming itself. Its name was Ten, after Bo Derek in the movie. In McGregor's Mississippi accent, it came out "Tee-un."

It was a typical summer day. He rounded up some fence-jumping cattle he and his son, Bill, owned out of a neighbor's field, then sat down to polish some .38 shell casings, hang them on some nice leather cord, and sell them as necklaces at thirty bucks a pop. He had picked up the casings off the ground at Graceland in 1973 and 1974, after Elvis and the boys had fired them during one of their target practices. McGregor, whose knotty-pine walls were covered with guns he had collected, hated to see perfectly good casings go to waste. Twenty years later, he gave a woman he met at an Elvis show three or four of them as a souvenir. "And she called me back," he said, "and you thought I'd given her the back side of Graceland, you know? I mean, those were Elvis's. And I said, Wait a minute. I got a moneymaker here." He laughed. "And you got 'em, why not sell 'em?"

McGregor knew the reasons why people wanted to buy the casings. What he could not grasp is why anyone would want them. Just because Elvis might have touched them or shot them out of a gun? That was nothing he could consider real. The TCB necklace or the engraved watch Elvis gave him—those were real, a part of his life. But while Elvis fans confounded him, they also paid his bills. He happily admitted it: When Elvis hired him in 1967, he gave him the means to support himself for the rest of his life. "The whole thing comes from the association with Elvis—and I'm smart enough to understand that," he said. "Now that does not make a better artist, having been with Elvis. That is in me—that is there, and it's how hard do I want to work to get it out. But it gives me an outlet that most artists would not have. Had I never been with Elvis, you would not be standing here in this shop because it would not exist. I would still be doing it, but I would not be making a living from it, because this community will not support an artist enough to make a living. But with the Elvis connection, I'm supported from all over the country and over part of the world. So I got a lot to appreciate from Elvis."

He met Elvis in 1966, soon after he went to work at a saddle shop near Graceland. Though he didn't recognize Elvis the first time he visited the store, they soon became friendly. After a while Elvis, who had taken up riding horses, hired McGregor to make him a pair of chaps. Whenever he stopped by the store they always got to talking. Then one day Elvis walked in, slapped him on the back, and asked if he'd like to come work for him. "I said, 'Man, yeah,'" McGregor recalled. "And I didn't ask him how much he paid or nothing. I went, 'Yeah. Let's do it.'"

He cared for the horses Elvis kept at his ranch in Mississippi, and he lived there with Barbara and their son, Bill. When Elvis sold the ranch they moved their trailer behind Graceland, where McGregor cared for horses and did odd jobs—which, when working for Elvis, might have meant driving a car to Los Angeles, then flying home. "You had a pocketful of money," he said, "and all the time in the world."

It was an incredible story, considering where the journey began. McGregor grew up on a small cotton farm in Sledge, Mississippi, the river about 150 yards from his house. His father died when he was just a boy, so he farmed from the time he was twelve or thirteen. When he was twenty-one and out in the fields he lifted his eyes to the sky and prayed, "God, if you'll let me out of this field, I won't be bothering you about rain and stuff like that." To this day when he plants a shrub for Barbara he jokes, "You understand this is just an ornamental bush. I'm not farming."

His love was saddle making, but even charging $2,400 a shot he could not build enough of them in a year to earn a living. So he designed and made jewelry, a craft he took up so he wouldn't have to shoe horses all his life, and big leather belts just like the ones that Elvis wore with his stage clothes. He created some of Elvis's early belts before Bill Belew was hired to design the jumpsuits. A couple of them are on display at Graceland. That is the replicas' prime advertisement. Making the belts for impersonators, he said, was "like having a license to steal." He charged anywhere from $135 to $310 for one of the three styles. The more eagles, studs, and chains, the higher the price.

Though he moved to Oxford in 1976, McGregor never really left

Graceland. When he attended Elvis shows and conventions, people clamored to hear stories about Elvis, and he was pleased and flattered to supply them. His encounters with fans ranged from merely strange to heartbreaking. Once a man tried to get McGregor to admit there was a room upstairs at Graceland where Elvis parked his mother's 1955 pink Cadillac, which is actually on display at the car museum across the street from the house. McGregor told him he'd been all over the house and he thought he'd remember seeing a thing like that. Another time a woman related a tale of how her father had abused her as a child. Her solace was the only record her father hadn't busted, an Elvis record, that she played again and again. And after she told McGregor her story she asked him, "Do you think Elvis would have loved a kid like me?"

"Yeah, I think he would have," he said.

"You know, I always thought he would have," she told him. "And I think that's why I survived. Because I always thought that if nobody loves me, Elvis loves me."

"I hear stories like that all the time," he said. "And you know, you get tears in your eyes. It's those kind of things that Elvis did that nobody knows."

He came to love these people because they were so sincere. And he liked to pull little surprises, just to watch them react. At shows he would wear the TCB necklace—short for Elvis's motto, Taking Care of Business—that he placed around McGregor's neck in 1970. When a fan asked to look at it, he would slip it off and hand it over, just to see the expression of shock and awe. He liked to think it would please Elvis to know that a gift he gave has made so many people happy. On his travels he also carried a ring he made from silver and a stone off one of Elvis's jumpsuits. Sometimes, when he handed the ring to a woman, she would start to cry. It never ceased to surprise him, that anyone would still shed tears over Elvis after all these years. He pondered this as he polished a .38 casing, musing over the machine's whine. "It's amazing, the impact or whatever you want to call it, that the man had on people," he shouted. He examined the brass for shine, then set it aside and chose another. "And so I honestly still don't know how to read the fans."

He had come to count some of these people, fans and impersonators, among his best friends, yet he couldn't imagine why anyone would mourn for so long a person who, in McGregor's opinion, was just sound and images to them. But at the same time he could not guess why anyone would consider that behavior strange. If somebody wanted to dress up like Elvis, what should it matter to anyone else? If a person loved Elvis impersonators, did this make them strange? The way McGregor saw it, it was one thing not to understand someone's motivations. It was another thing entirely to call them crazy just because you didn't. Or to assume you were even the right person to judge.

"Which ones of us are not crazy?" he asked. "I mean, I guess nuts is all the way you want to view it. I have never worked as a living, breathing cowboy in my life. And I'm not sure that I actually would want to, because I know enough about the work to know that I do not want to be out there babying a bunch of cows in snow this deep trying to keep them suckers from freezing to death and hauling them hay on a wagon or a sled or something like that, and I'm out there freezing, and I'm trying to keep them from freezing. And I like horses, but it's kinda like roughing it to me. Really roughing it is a motel room without quite enough hot water or the television ain't working. And I don't even want one if it don't have a telephone. But you know, I have always leaned toward a cowboy image type thing. Now I guess you could say that's nuts. A kid off a cotton farm off the Mississippi Delta, where our whole livelihood was cotton, didn't have nothing to do with cowboys. I guess I pushed it about as far as you could push it by becoming a saddle maker and everything. But still, you could look at it and read that on the real nutsy end of the whole thing. So I don't feel the same way, I don't see Elvis the same way, and everything that the fans do. But you gotta remember, I was there."

The idea for the Elvis Presley Impersonators International Association originated not with the Elvis impersonators themselves, but with a husband and wife living in Aurora, Illinois. Ron and Sandy Bessette never thought of themselves as pioneers or promoters of popular culture. At first glance they looked more like any comfortably married couple than they did visionaries. Ron had slick dark hair and wore subdued suits, and Sandy had blond hair grown long on top, a graceful neck, and an easy laugh. But Elvis had always been a constant in their lives. One of the first things Ron told people he met is that his father served as Elvis's company commander in Fort Hood, Texas, and that as a boy he saw the enlisted idol around the barracks, doing chores and cutting up just like any other soldier. As a boy, Ron was impressed that Elvis elected to stay with his unit rather than sing for the USO.

Sandy would let it slip that she and Ron first met at a drive-in showing an Elvis movie. Neither remembered the name of the movie, partly because of the passage of time and perhaps because it is sometimes hard to tell one Elvis movie from the next. But that was not the point. What matters was that it was Elvis, and he brought them together.

Another interest they came to share over the course of their married life was square dancing. Ron became a square-dance caller, and they joined a callers' association. As an account manager for the Union Pacific Railroad, he was transferred around the country. He and Sandy loved the idea that they could move to a town not knowing a soul, and through the association's network of sources meet nice people like them who enjoyed square dancing. Their two interests merged when the Bessettes attended the World's Fair in Vancouver and they encountered more than forty Elvis impersonators. The scenes the performers inspired astounded them—the electricity, the affection, the sheer unexpected Elvisness of it all. They had to know more.

This desire arose at a crossroads in their lives. Ron was considering ending his career with the railroad and buying some kind of franchise. Sandy also wanted a change. Before Vancouver they never really thought about impersonators. But back home in Chicago it seemed they bumped into one everywhere they went. They began attending shows and introducing themselves to some of the guys. Ron and Sandy were shocked to learn that although there were hundreds of impersonators, there was no way for them to meet, just to talk and swap tips the way square dancers did. The Bessettes suggested to two of the area's veteran Elvises, Dave Carlson and Dave Ehlert, that they start an association for impersonators to meet people with similar lifestyles, raise money for charity—just like Elvis did—share trade secrets, and gain strength from each other. Ron thought Elvis impersonators were a lot like square dancers. He saw this new organization as a version of the callers' association, where thousands of people could be united under a single common goal—in this case, continuing Elvis's legacy of entertaining and doing charitable works. Carlson had doubts you could organize a group of people with few professional standards, but agreed to do what he could.

The Bessettes registered the Elvis Presley Impersonators International Association in Illinois as a nonprofit agency and drew up a charter. They also wrote a creed for its members to follow:

1. I have an obligation to all associations, groups, and businesses who purchase my entertainment services, and to provide those services in a professional and ethical manner.
2. I have an obligation to the activity as an Elvis performer and thru [*sic*] all my personal, business, and social contacts, be conscious of my image and what I represent and conduct myself accordingly.
3. I will provide leadership and direction in continuing the music and style of Elvis while lending strength and direction to the growth of the activity as a great world-class entertainment media in "continuing the legacy of the king."

The logo they chose depicted a man with black hair wearing a jumpsuit and playing a guitar in front of a globe while stars swirled around his kneecaps. Except for tiny ink spot eyes, his face was blank.

This was slick and ambitious stuff. The Bessettes intended to not only encourage impersonators to support each other, but also to encourage society to surrender its acceptance and respect. They saw no lack of potential ambassadors. Ron told reporters that there probably were about 2,500 Elvis impersonators in the world, an estimate that was 1,000 higher than the one from Legends in Concert's John Stuart. An average of about 200 impersonators, mostly from the United States, belonged to the association. "We feel that in five years we should have a pretty good handle on what is out there in the world," he said that first year. If their plans worked, the Bessettes imagined impersonating someday becoming a valued profession, like medicine or law. To reach this goal they chose veteran impersonators to help their cause, like Dave Carlson and Dave Ehlert.

They also drafted Rick Marino, the Jacksonville band singer who, in the years after envisioning Elvis meet Jesus in heaven, had become an impersonator himself. Ron Bessette called him and briefed him on the aims of the EPIIA. Then he invited him to serve as the group's first president. Rick, owner of one of the premier Elvis Heads in the business, was impressed but asked for time to sleep on it; he didn't want the other guys to think he felt superior to them. A couple of days after their chat, Rick got a letter from Ron thanking him for accepting the post. Just thought you needed a little push, Ron told him. Rick accepted on the condition the guys could vote on it later.

Rick compared his new job to that of an ambassador or union steward. He could listen to the impersonators' concerns and then explain them to Ron, who as a non-Elvis didn't always understand. He prided himself on being approachable. This was true; not only was it easy to talk to Rick, it was nearly impossible to stop. Ron joked to Rick once when he phoned that he'd like to talk, but he couldn't clear three hours on his schedule. He exaggerated only a little. Call to inquire about his career and, after a half hour of small talk, Rick would respond with a story about how being stranded overnight on the Matterhorn wearing shorts and, thank God, gloves made him reconsider his fast-living ways, or how putting on his jumpsuit makes him feel exactly like Captain Marvel, though he doesn't like to tell people that because they will think he is a nut. He peppered his stories with the word "son," stretching out the word like Elvis did so it came out "sawwwn." Once you got used to it, the talking was a big part of Rick's charm. He needed to illuminate all the reasons he loved Elvis and valued the association.

"When we did the first convention, the guys were pretty tacky, to be blunt," he said. "And they're all looking good now. They're all looking sharp. They all got nicer-looking outfits and they look a whole lot more like what Elvis wore. And the quality in the last five years has really gone up leaps and bounds from the visual presentation."

The greatest thing the association had done, as he saw it, could be summed up in one word: networking. Hang around enough impersonators, he thought, and any beginner was bound to learn how to look better and earn more money. "You're basically in a marketing situation," he said. The way he figured it, you could charge 25 percent of the price of your jumpsuit. If he owned a $100 suit, someone would pay him $25 to show up as Elvis. If he owned a $2,000 suit, he could demand $500. "It doesn't matter how good I am, or that I can sing or not," he said. "I'm gonna show up in a costume that costs me two thousand dollars, it's gonna cost you five hundred dollars for your people to see it. And that justifies your price."

A practical streak ran through all of Rick's views on life, not counting heavenly visions or Matterhorn epiphanies. "I believe in Elvis," he declared. "The thing about Elvis is that he was a good man. Everybody wonders: Why is everybody so crazy about him? Because: Who *wouldn't* have wanted to be like Elvis? Who wouldn't want to grow up in the projects and be able to buy your mama a new car and a big house? Who wouldn't want to be a movie star? Every movie you make, you're the hero. You look great. Who wouldn't want to have been that good looking? Who wouldn't have wanted to be able to sing that way? Who wouldn't want to walk into a store and give somebody a Cadillac?"

Rick could even offer a practical explanation for bodyguards, an accessory almost always frowned upon in the impersonator world as too self-reverential. Everywhere Rick went in Las Vegas, he would be flanked by Bruce and Joe, two friends who doubled as a security detail, decked out in those red satin Elvis on Tour jackets sold in the Graceland gift shops. Why would someone pretending to be Elvis require bodyguards?

"Because I don't like people messin' with me," he said. "It's just that I like being unapproachable. I like being able to walk around and if I don't want to be talked to, or something like that, I just walk on. People just think that they can just come up and: 'Hey! Can we have a picture with you?' Or: 'Hey! Let us tell you about our life's story and our relationship with Elvis!' I don't have the time for all that."

Attention was best, he had decided, when you could control its thrill and severity. "Unless you're one of these idiots that walks around that really doesn't care—you know, these guys are so full of it they *don't* really care," he said. "It bothers me. Bothers most anybody that's normal, when somebody goes, 'Hey, Elvis!' across the room at you."

In 1990, 250 people applied to perform at the first EPIIA convention. Sandy chose thirty-two of them. They gathered one weekend in June at a Sheraton in Rosemont, a heartbeat from O'Hare International. Right away everyone involved sensed they had hit on something big. For the first time, these people could walk into a room where everyone looked like them and, better still, feel that everyone understood and accepted them. After a long, often lonesome journey, this weekend felt like a welcome home. It also meant something new: attention that, for once, they welcomed. The media sign-up list included more than fifty names from outlets such as ABC, the *Boston Globe,* the Associated Press, the *Seattle Times,* the *Detroit News,* and, inevitably, the Memphis *Commercial Appeal.* Impersonators went from being ridiculed to being interviewed. As TV lights shone down on them they explained their lives and their ideas about how Elvis had changed the world. People may have laughed, but they were listening. The Elvises's promotional packets would now include news spots and clippings from well-known sources.

The mood at the hotel reflected their new status as cultural commentators. No one slept. Strangers serenaded each other in the hallways, in the lobby, lying on the floor. Men who performed for years in anonymity or some tabloid-fueled alternative received awards celebrating their dedication. Men who hadn't been chosen to perform lined up on standby to get a turn with the band. At the awards ceremony three impersonators sang songs they had written in honor of Elvis. And senior impersonators and people who had worked with Elvis, like his drummer D. J. Fontana, conducted continuing education seminars. Dave Carlson conducted a session in which he taught impersonators the importance of marketing and learning to think on their feet. Elvis impersonation, he told his students, meant more than climbing on stage and blurting out "Blue Suede Shoes." He also explained that Elvis windmilled his right arm in his Vegas numbers and sneered mainly by curling the upper left corner of his lip. Most people who study photographs and films don't think to reverse what they see. The true impersonator does.

At the end Sandy stood on stage and told the gathering that it all was like a dream come true. "Many lasting friendships were made and new bonds were established," read an entry from the group's newsletter after the convention. "Standing ovations were given by EP performers to each other. What tremendous feedback on how warm and friendly all the EP performers were and the great brotherhood displayed. Everyone was rooting for each other to be outstandingly dynamic . . . and they were."

The second Chicago convention was not as successful as the first, which led Ron and Sandy to make a bigger but to their minds more logical move—to Las Vegas. After all, it made sense to play where Elvis did, plus it made a nice line on the guys' résumés.

The third convention took place at the Hacienda Hotel during what the mayor proclaimed as "Viva Las Vegas Week." The shows went well, but they were held too far from the Strip to profit much from the move. The fourth year they moved to the Imperial Palace Hotel, a vaguely Oriental-looking structure with a tiki bar in the lobby, across from Caesar's Palace. The fifth convention was set for there, too; the Bessettes decided they'd found a good home for it, with a big enough show room and an ideal location for tourist traffic.

Early association members recall the first convention with fondness. Jerome Marion had been impersonating Elvis for just two months when he was named one of the thirty-two performers. He had already performed for Legends and toured Russia, but now he would perform in his hometown with people he had admired since he was young.

"This was a whole new thing for us," he explained, "to walk up and pick up moves and pointers. I remember giving my shoes up the first year to a guy—on the plane, he lost his shoes. I gave him my shoes, and he was like a size ten, I was like a size eight and a half. He squeezed into these things, and he was a big, fat guy—real nice guy, though—but it was just kind of hilarious that I'm standing there giving up my shoes to this guy. But everybody was so outgoing and so friendly. And there was so much energy in the room, and the interviews, and the excitement—everybody felt like celebrities. And everybody felt like they were the star—they were the King, you know? And when you walked into the room, everybody's dressed like Elvis, when they show up at the hotel, they got limousines pulling up with Elvis guys getting out. It was really done up like, you know, bigwig. It was just awesome. And that was one of the first things I remember: It was fun."

In the short life of the EPIIA Jerome Marion had grown from starstruck novice to major player. He loved the convention; it lent his profession respectability, especially with its continuing attempts to raise money for charity. "I don't want to sound like we're some kind of weird cult," he said, " but you know, we all believe in the same thing. We follow the music because we enjoy it. They're all down-to-earth guys and we have a great time. It's kind of like any other convention—a doctors' convention or a lawyers' convention. We're all members of the same thing, and we all follow that one main cause, which is bringing back the music and the style of one of the greatest entertainers who ever lived."

Jerome discovered Elvis when he was thirteen. He would put on his mother's Elvis records and sing to them. When he was sixteen he taped himself on a tiny recorder and played it for friends, telling them it was Elvis to see if they noticed a difference. He worked for seven and a half years driving a forklift on a shipping dock in Chicago. He got passed over for a promotion on a Wednesday, and that Friday he quit to pursue Elvis as a career. He progressed from doing $35 deliveries to charging a minimum of $250—and often up to $400—for corporate appearances. He earned on average $50,000 a year. He owned two celebrity look-alike businesses, first with his former father-in-law and then on his own, in which he provided one of a nationwide stable of celebrity impersonators—Marilyn Monroes, James Deans, the occasional president—for photo shoots and private parties. "I don't like being a follower," he said. "I like being on top. That's why I like being my own boss."

Yet Jerome acknowledged that he had become a leader by co-opting someone else's persona. "Right now he's my life," Jerome said of Elvis, "and it's kind of weird to say that you live off a dead man, but hey—whatever it takes. Beats that nine-to-five job."

His success sprung from an ability to mix business savvy with the sense that what he did was something he could joke about. "I'd like to be Elvis," he said. "Who the hell wouldn't? There's two advantages—if we were Elvis we'd be rich, and if we were Elvis we'd be dead."

Jerome joked a lot because he had survived bad times. His mother died when he was a teenager. His first marriage broke up, partly because it became hard to remember who he was when so many pretty girls thought he was Elvis. But the defining moment of his life came when he was fourteen. A pleasure trip he took in a four-seater plane ended in a crash behind a factory in Richland Park, Illinois. The pilot and his young son, both friends, died in the crash; another friend wore a body cast for a year. And Jerome lay pinned in the wreckage for forty-five minutes before he was rescued.

"The plane stalled and we went down, nosed in and the pilot was killed instantly. His son lived for about forty-five minutes, he was a good friend of mine, and I was—shit: broken pelvic bones, ankles, I severed my toe. Not only did I almost die, but I cut my tongue off in the accident. My tongue was severed completely, all but about a sixteenth of an inch of tongue, from when we came down, the impact of teeth. And what's really bizarre is that I came within a sixteenth of an inch of not only choking to death, probably, on my own tongue, and dying, but this is the thing that makes my living now—and I may have never been able to talk again. So I look at it like, God had a reason for keeping me alive, keeping my tongue on, or whatever you want to call it. It's so bizarre when I think that I could have never been able to talk again, and now I sing for a living."

He never concluded that God let him live so he could be Elvis—that would sound too strange and self-important. But in all the bad times he would listen alone to Elvis sing "Bridge Over Troubled Water" and "Mary in the Morning," and he decided that if he could make other people feel the way Elvis made him feel, he could live with anything else. He had gained perspective, and it gave him nerve.

"It's something that made me not afraid to die," he said of the accident, "because I realize that life is short and you can go at any minute. But it's also something that made me realize that you live life to the fullest, and you don't wait your whole life to do something that you may someday never be able to do. So you kind of take that goal and you go with it."

It also simplified matters when people asked the hated question, "Are you one of the Flying Elvises?"

"No," he would reply. "I crash in planes, I don't jump out of 'em."

Preparing for the fifth annual EPIIA convention, he sensed that everything would work out. He had just gotten married again, to a woman named Michele, who helped with his business. After the 1993 convention, the Imperial Palace felt like home. And his own band, the Exspence Account, had been hired to back the performers. He never minded trading the rush he got from being on stage for sleeping six hours in four days. Like so many others, Jerome had borrowed from those who came before him to achieve his piece of the American Dream. That he had succeeded by being Elvis surprised him as much as it might anyone else.

"I would have never dreamed it possible," he said. "I would have never dreamed I'd be doing Elvis, I never dreamed that I would perform in Vegas and travel all over the world doing it. And hopefully, ten years from now I'll be standing back and making fifty million dollars a year, going, 'Boy, I'd never dreamed it possible, man.'" He paused for effect. "Hopefully I won't be sitting in a little home with four little walls, going, 'I thought this might happen.'"

In four years the conventions had evolved from elaborate jam sessions to taut small concerts—showcases, they began calling them. The seminars were shed for lack of interest, with the emphasis placed on the reason everyone came: the singing. Sandy Bessette rated uniting the impersonators the association's greatest achievement.

"They have learned a lot from coming, just coming and watching, even if they're not in the show," she said. "And they see all these guys in real nice costumes, and they listen to them, and watch them on stage, and they say, 'Boy, this guy really put a lot of time into this. I'm gonna go home and I'm gonna study.' We had a guy, when we first started the association, who was only doing this in car shows. And he wore a jumpsuit and he used to zip it up all the way to the neck, and he had a scarf stuck right here at the neck. He invited us to come out and see him for the first time. We went out there and he said, 'How did I do?' 'Fine as far as the voice, but zip that zipper down and take that scarf out of the neck and get closer to those women.' You ought to see him today. He is one of the top entertainers. He's doing a cruise ship now. They love him."

Things looked more polished, but not everything was perfect. Media coverage died down some once the novelty wore off. Many veterans dropped out, including Carlson and Ehlert, for a number of reasons. Some impersonators who used convention exposure to build solid careers felt they no longer needed the networking. Others elected to stay home and do gigs to make money rather than spend money to go to Vegas and sing for free. Members who paid their $36 annual dues and didn't make the cut felt excluded. Ron offended a few of them by saying that the association didn't want "K-mart Elvises." And a few top impersonators resented the fact that anyone could join the association, regardless of ability. These disputes, along with the constant problem of finding money to finance the shows, weighed on the organizers.

"Used to be all the guys got together, we had a great time—we had the sing-alongs, we hung out," Rick Marino said. "It was a lot of fun, a good time. But we didn't raise any money. We were in the *hooole*. We weren't organized, we were just having a big party. And from that standpoint, you know, I kinda miss that. I enjoyed it a lot when it used to go like that.

"But we've lost a few of the guys because they really—uh, how can I say it—they were a little more interested in themselves than they were in the big picture. Which is basically trying to establish ourselves as an organization, get some credibility, and have people respect us a little bit."

And even among the members who remained, dissent simmered. To raise money, the Bessettes printed up $1 raffle tickets for members to sell. Many resisted selling them, in part because they wondered what really happened to raffle proceeds and showcase ticket sales, which were supposed to go to charity and convention expenses. They wondered among themselves if the Bessettes weren't skimming money from the association for themselves. It seemed unlikely that they could take in money for admission and raffle tickets and still come up short.

Such talk vexed Ron and Sandy because they thought they made it clear that the opposite was true. They had poured more than $22,000 of their savings into the association, booking venues and paying operating costs, trying to make things fly, and they saw little chance of recouping. "It's like a hobby," was how Sandy explained it. "Sometimes hobbies are expensive and sometimes they're not. This happened to be a very expensive hobby for the last four years, and Ron and I just had to say,

'Look. We've invested all we can invest. We don't have any more money to invest.'"

Some impersonators also wondered if the association really raised money for charity. To be sure, the group's attempts to interest other nonprofits in its ventures proved to be disappointing. They did collect about $3,800 for one group, the Association for Retarded Citizens of Lincoln, Nebraska, in 1993 by selling raffle tickets. Other organizations were reluctant to associate themselves with the association. Ron didn't think this was because they disliked impersonators, but because all they wanted was money. He envisioned a group like the Elks or the Veterans of Foreign War putting on an impersonator show and keeping all of the proceeds but paying the band and the Elvises. No one shared his vision. "They've all got their hands out," he said before the 1994 convention. "They don't want to take any risk, they just want everything to go to them, and of course what we want out of a charity is somebody to help us promote the show and not that we do all the promoting and hand them all the money. So we haven't found too many groups that want to do that."

The EPIIA's future had eroded enough that the Bessettes talked to Jerome and Rick about not holding a convention in 1994 because they could no longer assume the cost. They had begun two new ventures, a karaoke business and a business called Celebrity Superstar Doubles, sort of an offshoot of what they had learned from their impersonator work, with Elvises and a Charlie Chaplin and a Joan Rivers whom Ron called a "knockout." Jerome and Rick agreed to help Ron and Sandy keep the EPIIA afloat. So Jerome held the miniconvention at Greene's West, and Rick mailed letters suggesting a $50 donation from each of the forty-eight performers to help cover costs.

Having financed their own shows, Jerome and Rick sympathized with the Bessettes. They didn't understand why the other Elvises suspected dark motives. "You don't rent a hotel for four days and put together promotion and media and all this coverage for nothing," Jerome said. "And I've seen the receipts, being executive chairman. I get the breakdown of where the money goes. And I don't think that Ron and Sandy are skimming anything. I think, if anything, the association is screwing them. But these performers have their own opinions of it. And the people who have their opinions are people who have never, ever had to deal with an event. Meaning that they go in and they perform. They've never attempted to set one up or promote it. Because they don't realize that every time you put a dollar out, you've gotta sell four more tickets to make that up. That everything costs money, nothing's for free.

"And also, I think, there's a lot of attitude, because of the fact that not everybody who is involved in the association can perform. Unfortunately, we have our limitations—there are only so many people that can perform, and again, we want the quality performers on stage."

It was ironic that an organization begun as a means of uniting a maligned group of people carried within it the seeds of discontent. But the major players hoped that with a secure home in Vegas and an extra day of shows, things would be the way they were the first time, and that the guys would come around. As Jerome put it, "Vegas is Elvis is Vegas."

Reunited

*T*he day before he sang at the 1994 EPIIA convention, Dennis Stella found salvation in an unlikely source—the person who probably hated his wig most.

Randy Hottinger pulled up in the Corvette at Dennis's house around 10:00 P.M. Thursday night, thirteen hours before Dennis performed in Las Vegas. Randy's mother, Chris, sat in the passenger's seat, happy to be alive. It wasn't that she didn't trust her son's driving. She just preferred to be the pilot.

Chris had convictions, and one thing she felt certain about from the first time she saw Dennis's wig was that Dennis needed to forget it and go natural. Chris, whose own ash blond hair was cut in a stylish long shag, had loved Elvis since she was a kid. "He's my generation," she would explain. Ugly Elvis Heads offended her deeply, even more so when they belonged to someone she cared about, someone with the potential to succeed.

When they got inside the house, Randy suggested to Chris that they open the bag to make sure the wig was really inside. Chris knew Dennis's mental state these last few weeks well enough to consider this an excellent idea. They found the bag right where Dennis had said it would be, in the spare room on top of the pinball machine splashed with pictures of Charlie Chaplin and other old-time movie stars. But when it came to that wig Randy wanted to leave nothing to chance. It was in there all right, nestled on a white plastic foam head, just a hank of black synthetic hair held together by flesh-toned netting and lace.

But for everyone who knew Dennis, the wig had taken on an evil identity all its own.

Randy and Chris left Milwaukee in the Corvette around 8:30 P.M. Chris volunteered to go with him after none of Randy's friends expressed interest in driving to Chicago to put a wig on a plane. The drive to Dennis's house in Calumet City took about two hours. The trip to O'Hare took another forty-five minutes, so it was around 11:30 P.M. by the time they arrived. Randy, lugging the bag, ran through the airport while Chris tried to keep up. Both were tired after working all day and driving half the night. Chris wore no makeup and the beat-up shirt she'd had on when the wig debacle began, and Randy wore shorts. Both looked stale and rumpled. The bag weighed at least fifteen pounds, and carrying it got more awkward the longer Randy carried it through the airport. As he jogged along he decided Dennis must have stashed bottles of cologne under the wig because he could hear glass clinking. He could imagine the scene if somebody tried to rob him: "Before you rob me, just look inside," he pictured himself saying. "Take everything but the wig." Chris joked that the way they looked, people probably thought they were a couple of terrorists trying to smuggle a bomb.

For whatever reason, no one seemed to want to ship the bag overnight. They went to one airline, which had a flight that arrived about ninety minutes before Dennis went onstage. Too close. The agent referred them to another airline with a 9:00 A.M. Las Vegas arrival. They left the terminal and walked down what looked to Chris like a back alley to another building. The woman at the counter directed them to a counter in another building, but it was closed so they'd have to wait. They returned to the terminal they had just left and went back to the first airline. The woman at that counter said it would be no problem to ship the bag. All she needed to know was what was in it. "Some hair and a blow dryer," they said. They paid her $60 and got out of there as fast as they could. They rode the airport train back to the lot where they'd parked the Corvette. They shared the train car with a man in drag—evening gown, wig, earrings, mustache, the works. Chris couldn't believe anyone would do something like that to themselves.

On the way home they missed the exit for 294 north back to Milwaukee and found themselves headed for Chicago, so they had to backtrack. It started to rain. Randy, blaring a Nirvana CD—one of only two non-Elvis selections he found in the car—passed a semi going 120 in a construction zone. As he flew he said, "You know, Ma, I know if I had done something like that, I would want someone to help me out."

They finally arrived in Milwaukee around 3:00 A.M. Both of them had to get up for work at 6:00. At the door, they realized that in their rush to leave neither had brought a house key. Chris leaned on the doorbell until Kelly woke and let them in.

Dennis would later give them an extra $75 for going to all that trouble. Chris felt funny taking so much money for something she would have done for free. "Even though I hate that wig on him," she said, "he wanted it so bad."

It was a weird night, Randy had to say when it was all done. The only thing weirder was he didn't regret any of it.

Dennis was grateful for the support. Being new to the convention scene, he was nervous. Ron and Sandy seemed nice—they had seen something special in him, after all. He agonized less over potential improprieties in their event and more about scoring a repeat of the wig incident at Greene's West. He also worried that the songs he had been assigned to perform wouldn't display his vocal prowess. When he received a tentative song list for the shows, he noted with some amusement that a guy from Ringwood, New Jersey, named Tony Grova had been slated to sing a few of the songs he wanted.

If Dennis's inner voice about his Elvis appearance could have assumed human form, it would have looked just like Tony Grova. Dennis felt a kinship with Tony—both were Italian, both blunt talkers and proud to say so, at great length if necessary. But Tony maintained an ease about his Elvisness that Dennis could only imagine. And the one time the two had spoken he'd felt just as comfortable informing Dennis about the shortcomings in his hair and sideburns. Dennis wasn't sure he wanted from advice from Tony. Once he saw him walking around Memphis in ninety-degree heat, wearing a seventies-style Elvis suit and a belt buckle the size of a slice of bread. He stood several inches shorter than Elvis did, so seeing him was like seeing Elvis in a more concentrated form.

Tony Grova had a reputation among other impersonators as a guy who held a lot of opinions about Elvis and didn't hold any of them back. "Hey, look," he said, "Elvis was Elvis, but he was a normal person. You know what I mean? We're all normal people. You know, people are people, you know? We all bleed the same and everything. That's why Elvis's downfall was—because people, us, the fans—we put him on this pedestal. You know what I mean? We made him a god. We did this to him, really. It's pretty heavy when you think about it."

Tony Grova thought about it a lot. He believed that Elvis was put on this planet for a reason. He tried to imagine what the world would be like if Elvis never existed and concluded his own life would be much different. He joked that he probably would have ended up with purple and yellow hair, following the Grateful Dead. Instead he got to meet Priscilla Presley when she was promoting one of her fragrances. He wore a black jacket with a pattern of shining black triangles. When he bent to kiss her on the cheek, she smiled and closed her eyes.

He discovered Elvis while growing up in the Bronx. "When my mother had forty-fives around, I used to play all her records," he recalled. "And the Elvis records happened to be the ones I seem to have worn out. So then time went by, and then I saw the Comeback Special in sixty-eight, when my mother woke us up. We were in bed, we were kids and she said, 'Come down and see somebody from your mother's era. So I saw this guy and the next morning, I don't know what happened, I was puttin' my father's VO5 in my hair and greasin' my hair back. At like ten years old. I don't know, I just became an Elvis fan."

In high school he performed at assemblies and dances. In 1978, he saw Rick Saucedo on Broadway. Inspired, he decided he wanted to impersonate Elvis professionally. He took his work seriously. "I've studied Elvis. I don't want you to think I'm a nut or anything like that, but I studied," he said. "Like, you look at him. Why is every picture, every picture he takes—same guy, but every picture's different? If you look at Elvis— don't think I'm crazy, but he has one sideburn that was always longer than the other. Yeah. Look at the pictures. A lot of his pictures—especially if you got the *Aloha from Hawaii* video, OK? Watch that video. His right sideburn, compared to his left sideburn, watch how small the difference in the sideburn is. I mean, it's a major difference. I don't know how he could shave himself like that, or somebody did it as a joke to him, whoever shaved him. But I mean, it's a major difference. That's why he has so many different looks, this guy."

Tony's own look had remained unchanged for much of his adult life—the curving perfect pompadour, the sneering smile, the mannerisms he picked up from years of watching video footage. He took seriously his commitment to looking as much like the early-seventies Elvis as possible while remaining his own man—a philosophy he summed up as "Do what you gotta do and that's it." Impersonators who had never met him would just stare when he walked by wearing his replica of the sky-blue suit Elvis wore at a press conference before a concert at Madison Square Garden in 1972, complete with the black-and-white shirt with a test-pattern print and slab of gold-buckled belt. Like Dennis, they had to admire the guy. They enjoyed imitating him, speaking in an always disappointing copy of his heavy New York accent.

At the same time Tony prided himself on maintaining his own regular-guy style on stage. People came to hear Elvis, they ended up liking Tony. A lot of people liked Tony. For his major shows, he drew about 300 people at $15 to $20 a ticket.

"And I get a lot of compliments," he said, "because before I leave the stage, and do my last song, I'll say that, 'Before I go, no matter what you see me do up here, or whatever you think of anybody else, always remember that there are many kings and queens and presidents, but there will never, ever be such a man or an entertainer as the great, one and only, Elvis Aaron Presley.' And usually it takes the house down."

Tony saw no contradiction in copying Elvis's appearance while claiming to be his own man. To him this approach was both noble and justified: The more an impersonator man looked like Elvis, the more dedicated he was. That made him a good guy. He respected Elvis so much he could not understand why anyone who impersonated him would not try every means possible to pull off the most flawless illusion. In April of that year, Tony had come across Dennis at Steve Chuke's first Kentucky showcase and told him he needed to work on his look—particularly his hair. He never considered that his advice, delivered with his usual bluntness, would hurt Dennis's feelings. But it did. When you insult a man's Elvis, you insult him. It's not the kind of thing you can separate.

"Tony's kind of rough in his ways," Dennis said. He slipped into Tony talk: "He's 'Hey, yo, you're either gonna do this all the way, or don't do it at all—what's with the hair, and those sideburns?'" Dennis mulled over Tony's remarks, along with all the other doubts and criticisms doing battle in his brain, and decided he couldn't look like Elvis every day. That was what led him to buy the wig.

Tony considered his bluntness an asset. He preferred to see someone bruised over his advice than going around looking like a walking punch line. "Sometimes I guess people take it the wrong way," he said. "Because they're not used to people being straightforward. What inspires them, a guy like—I mean, I don't want to choose any names, OK? I guess in your own mind you can think of somebody that has gone into this field of business and is doing Elvis and shouldn't. You know what I mean? What inspired them to just get into this business? I mean, loving the guy's one thing—don't you look in the mirror?"

Of course, Dennis had more pressing concerns as he flew to Las Vegas. But he wanted Tony to see him wearing his new wig. And he wanted Tony to think he looked good.

That Thursday night, as Dennis and his wig flew in separate planes to Vegas, the convention opened with a jam session. Sandy Bessette sat at a table toward the back, listening to the Elvises, applauding wildly at the end of every song. Next to her sat Rick Marino, wearing cream-colored tennis shorts and white sneakers. She was talking about the fans.

"Has it ever crossed your mind why they scream?" she asked. "Why these girls scream and go crazy? Now you're not really seeing Elvis. You're seeing an Elvis impersonator. What it is to me, when these girls are screaming, is these Elvis impersonators up there are creating such an illusion that people are forgetting who they're watching, and they're screaming just as if they were at Elvis's show. So that's what it feels like to me. Now I myself never saw Elvis, OK? When I go into the Legends, and I see a really good performer go up there—and they're all good, but I do have my favorites—and you know, I hate to say that, but I do. I'll go up to the stage and get a scarf, just like everybody else, to get my little gift, too." She laughed. "It's something that I enjoy doing. And I know these girls do, too. All the women do."

It was obvious that Sandy was enjoying herself. She loved to walk into a room full of impersonators and hear them call her name and embrace her like a sister. In a way she thought of them as her kids. She enjoyed giving advice and helping others improve themselves. "I have guys in here tonight, came at noon, they wanted to do know if they could wear their jumpsuits through the hotel. And I said, 'Well, I really don't think that's a good idea. If you're going to be doing a benefit or something like that, sure. Put it on, and wait for your limo, or however you're getting to do your benefit.' But to mill around in a costume in a crowd—you know, this is a massive crowd—it kind of leaves a bad image or a taste in a lot of people's mouths. And I'd like to just keep that image clean, and just keep it as a show. Because there's a lot of Elvis fans out there."

For all the worries and doubts that preceded this event, she had a good feeling now. She sensed a vibe in the air that reminded her of the first show in 1990. She closed her eyes, just thinking about it. "Yeah, the first one in Chicago, they had a lounge in the hotel and everybody gathered in this lounge area and we were all singing and the guys, they were singing with guitars. Then they went out into the hall, they were singing in the hall, and they all got into a great big circle and a couple of them were laying on the floor, looking up, singing—they had a ball. They were up late at night and didn't want to go to bed. Nigel was there." She nodded at Nigel Kingsley, an Elvis from Switzerland sitting next to her with a shopping bag of Swiss chocolate. Nigel began and ended many conversations with the word "aloha." His life took its course in 1973, when an aunt took him to see Elvis's famed *Aloha From Hawaii* concert. He had a broad face and a sunny expression, and everywhere he went, including on stage, two girls with long blond hair accompanied him. "Remember all the singing that we had in the hallways?" Sandy asked him.

He turned in his seat and smiled at Sandy. "Those were real nice days."

"Those were the good days," Sandy said.

"No bad days," Nigel agreed. "We would stay up until five-thirty, six o'clock, play the guitar. It was so warm. Everybody said hello to each other." He looked around. "Now you get a funny feeling. But those days were nice. Really, really nice."

"Well," Sandy told him, "we just need to open up these guys a little more. There's a lot of them that are real new. And they're not really sure what to expect. So you older ones, the Hall of Famers . . ."

"We gotta pull 'em in a little bit," Nigel said.

"Ahem, ahem," Sandy said.

"Oh, yeah, no problem," Nigel said in his dusky voice. "We can handle that reeeal good."

Friday, July 22, 10:20 A.M. Dennis walked into the Legends Theater and blinked until his eyes adjusted to the show room dark. He surveyed his first Las Vegas venue and declared it impressive. Soon he would be standing on that stage, singing the opening lines of "Patch It Up." What happened before he strutted out in front of the band in his white-and-red Pinwheel jumpsuit promised to be, in many ways, more important than the show itself.

He still considered abandoning his wig a boneheaded mistake, but felt grateful for one thing. It took his mind off how nervous he was about performing. By now he figured he would be shaking, and as he stood there calmly he surprised himself. "Don't get me wrong," he said, "I'm a little jittery. But you know, it's kinda funny. After you perform for a while, you become almost numb, you know what I mean? It's like, what's the difference? All right, it's Las Vegas—it's a little bit of a bigger room, but when you're onstage, it's dark out there. And all you really see is the first row or two anyway. So it makes not a lot of difference, I don't think. I don't *think* so. The main thing is that you come prepared and I think I'm a little more prepared than I was last time—except for the fact that I left my wig at home."

The wild card in this situation would be how well he responded to the pressure of completing three important tasks: fetching the wig, fitting it on his head, then wearing it while he sang and danced before a lunchtime crowd. He remembered how frazzled he'd been when he hosted the party where he unveiled the wig. And he'd felt so scattered leaving his house the day before to come here that he forgot the one item, next to his jumpsuit, that he needed most. Now here he stood, packing about four hours sleep and a hundred bucks more than he had when he'd arrived. Unable to sleep because of, as he put it, "the wig, the money, how big a dummy I am," he'd won the money soon after he, Gail, and Shelley had arrived by playing blackjack in the casino downstairs. Dennis watched Jerome fiddling with some equipment on stage and hoped his luck would hold.

His winnings would help offset the cost of what he had to do ten minutes from now: catch a cab—a hotel shuttle would take too long—head to Hartsfield International, run to baggage and be reunited with the black bag and the wig, due in at 10:49 A.M. Then he had to jump back in the cab, return to the Imperial Palace, reach his room, put on the wig using the spanking-new clips, glue on the sideburns (his main source of worry, because he had to get them straight) change into his jumpsuit—or should he do that first?—and take the extremely slow elevator to the lobby, past the banks of slot machines, past the tiki bar, up the escalator, past the showroom, through to the backstage door. The way he explained his itinerary, it was obvious that blackjack had not monopolized his attention overnight. Tight but possible—that was how his plan sounded, considering what time he went on stage.

"You perform at twelve-twenty?" I asked him.

"Please, I hope not," he said. He thought he went on later in the afternoon.

I thumbed through the hot pink program I'd found on a table by the door. Oh boy. "Twelve-ten."

"Twelve-ten?" Dennis said, practically screaming. That was an hour and fifty minutes away. "Oh, God. I might ask if I can be bumped."

He approached Ron Bessette, who despite the early hour, already wore a blue blazer and a tie. He stood talking to a circle of pompadoured men, who parted to let Dennis in. On stage someone was belting "Amazing Grace."

"Excuse me, Ron? I'm Dennis Stella."

Ron turned, lifted his eyebrows, extended his hand. He was several inches shorter than Dennis, and looked smaller because his hair was slicked back tight. "Hey, welcome! Finally get to meet you! Good to see you!"

"Good to see you, too. I had a little bit of a hectic thing happen to me, Ron." He unspooled the whole sad scene, the resulting mad acts, the slapstick strategy.

"Oh," Ron said. He began to laugh.

"It's costing me a bundle," Dennis said.

Ron told him that Jerome would most likely find a way to swap his time, if he needed to. Dennis thanked him with genuine emotion and let loose a roomy sigh.

"Boy, they got a lot of equipment up there—my God!" He slowly turned, taking in a three-sixty of the theater. "You know what, though? The room is not that big! I thought it was gonna be BIG."

Jerome got close, and Dennis collared him. They talked, Dennis with a pleading, puppy-dog look, Jerome brisk and efficient in his tank top and baggy shorts. Jerome assured him they would wait for his wig. Feeling safer, Dennis decided to try to perform at 12:10. He left right after that, but not before he'did a quick sound check. He wailed "Fever" over a tape of Bonnie Raitt singing "Nick of Time." Even if things went according to plan, when he returned he'd have no time to warm up.

In a half-moon booth closer to the stage, fifteen minutes to showtime, Steve Chuke sat, fighting sleep. His eyes looked sleepier than usual—he'd flown a redeye and hadn't gotten to bed until 6:00 A.M. Fort Thomas, Kentucky, time. He hoped performing would rouse him. It always gave him the sensation of someone jabbing him with pins, only the pain felt so good. "Sometimes," he said, "you feel like crying. You know, sometimes you get an eerie feeling, you get chills. It's not butterflies, it's just an eerie feeling. And you think, God! What a feeling! And you're just getting a little fraction of what he did."

It had been a strange couple of months. Just before his first impersonator revue in Erlanger a woman visited him at his store. She had heard of his fondness for Elvis memorabilia, and she was prepared to sell him a wild specimen—the RCA New Vista Victrola stereo that Elvis had kept in his den at Graceland. What's more, she told him, a man named Mike McGregor who had worked for Elvis had bought it, then sold it to another man for $1,000, who then sold it to her. Now she wanted to sell it to Steve.

He thought she was crazy. A country boy from Kentucky could never afford anything so otherworldly and cool. He took the documentation she offered him and told her he'd think about it. And he did, to the point of obsession. He showed the pictures to some of the other Elvises. He brought it up in casual conversations. And he kept asking himself, what if she were telling the truth?

As he sat in the booth trying to wake up, a friend of his from Kentucky walked over. She'd flown to Vegas to hear Steve sing. She was flying high that morning, too, because she had witnessed a Wayne Newton show the night before. She sighed just remembering, her round cheerful face glowing.

"Out of this world," she said. "I didn't think he could play what he played. The guitar, violin, trumpet—I mean, he put on a show. Fantastic."

Backstage, Charlene Ziemann, whose plane had touched down just forty minutes earlier, was shuffling set lists. She was a Chicago EPIIA associate whose job it was to make sure the Elvises performed in order. "Okey dokey," she told the first few guys lined up and ready to go. "There's a light system on the stage. Green light means you got eight minutes. Yellow means you got two. Red means he wants you off."

On stage, keyboards were building. "Ladies and gentlemen," Jerome shouted, "it gives me a great honor to present from the Imperial Palace in Las Vegas the nineteen ninety-four Elvis Presley International Impersonators Association. Our first performer today, from Mount Lake Terrace, Washington, ladies and gentleman, Mr. Tracy Moore!" The band vaulted into the opening for "C.C. Rider." The spotlights swirled and swooped. The crowd burst into cheers.

It was an exciting moment. Dennis missed it. At that moment he was hurtling down the Strip in a cab toward Hartsfield International Airport.

Friday morning, 11:39 A.M. "Now, don't let this scare you," Dennis said. "It's gonna take some work."

He stood in front of the bathroom mirror in a pair of green plaid boxer shorts, studying his reflection in the mirror. The wig, freshly lowered on his head, looked as if it had survived some kind of violent coup. Hanks of it jutting up looked more like feathers than fake hair. He picked up a brush. "Through a period of combing and spraying, it does start to take on a nice look—a much better look than it did last time you've seen it, anyway," he said. "You may already notice that it fits my head a little bit better." It looked shorter, the hairline slightly higher, though not much. He asked the time. For all his attention to it, Dennis hadn't packed a watch. It was 11:40—thirty minutes to showtime. "Oh boy," he said. He picked up his nasal spray and took a couple of hits. The bathroom, roughly the size of an elevator, filled with the smell of flowers.

Just minutes earlier he had burst through the hotel doors, past the front desk on the left and the slots on the right, past the escalator that would carry him to the Legends Theater. At the airport he had abandoned his usual easygoing ways after he was told he would have to wait for his duffle bag until someone unloaded the plane. "You don't understand," Dennis said. "I go on at twelve-ten. I'll go out and get the damn thing myself!" He got the impression they weren't used to that sort of thing. They finally dispatched a supervisor, who went into the cargo hold and retrieved the black bag. Dennis dashed back to the cab, which was waiting with the meter running. The ride cost $32, not counting tip. The whole adventure cost him $125. As he ran through the hotel another Chicago Elvis, an aspiring actor named Mark Hussman, was finishing his set in the theater with the ballad "Kentucky Rain." Four more Elvises, a dozen songs, and Dennis was on. He had to contend with singing in Las Vegas with a band he hadn't rehearsed a single song with. And he had to change into someone else when he wasn't feeling too sure of himself.

His breath fogged up spots on the mirror. Toilet-paper snowflakes dotted his chin and neck. His shaving supplies were in the wig bag, too. 11:42 A.M. "Gonna be doing a lot of heavy breathing in the next couple of minutes—don't let that scare you," he said. "I'm not hyperventilating. I'll be OK. I'm kind of a nervous person by nature and I tend to put myself into these very stressful situations. But you never know—see, I haven't had an awful lot of time to deliberate over what's gonna happen in about the next half hour, so maybe it's better."

The wig adjusted and brushed, he proceeded to the sideburns. He patted them lightly onto his face, stared at his reflection and turned his head rapidly, as if he were taking punches. He worked in bursts of silence and long sighs. 11:45. He did not take his eyes off the mirror. "How does that look? Does that look all right? Now they haven't been glued in, of course, so they're not gonna look exactly right this second. I have to go back and once I got them in place, line them up and then I'll go back and glue them." More silence. Sixty seconds. "Do these look fairly lined up? They look OK. Now I gotta comb it and clip it—oh, God! I just got those clips—I'm telling you, I never worked with them before, so you can imagine this is gonna be a very . . . This is the glue. I gotta be real careful about this because if I don't put this glue on right . . . You notice the netting kind of blends into the face." He sighed again. "I'm sorry if I can't be more sociable. I'm holding up better actually than I thought I would, but I have to tell you, I'm a nervous wreck right now. My hands are kind of shaking."

11:50. "How do I do this?" he said under his breath. He held his hands away from his head, so as not to touch the wig with the sideburn glue. "I can tell I didn't do this exactly right, but—I guess I can't complain. OK— all done." He rinsed his hands in the sink, then grabbed his Pinwheel and closed the door to change. A minute passed. The door opened. Almost there. "Gonna style the hair," he said, "and then I'm gonna get out of here."

He grabbed a couple of bottles from a remarkable lineup of hair-care products out of the black bag, pump sprays decorated with pictures of beautiful people with hair more exquisite than his. He aimed the first, a mist to make the synthetic shine: Grunt. Fftt. Sigh. Ffffft. Pause. Fft. Brush. Fft. Fffffft. Wait—he remembered he hadn't snapped the wig clips into place. "I don't want to have another incident," he said, smiling. He took his time; he had tried them just once before.

"And then the finishing spray." He sprayed his hair with it eleven times. The wig gleamed like a freshly waxed car. He sighed. "Well, what do you think?" He rotated his head slowly before the mirror, side to side. "Adequate. The illusion has been created. I mean, considering I'm not Elvis —" He looked over, wanting me to complete the sentence.

"I think people will know who you're trying to be."

Dennis smiled and fluffed the hair with his palms. "I think so." Five minutes to noon. Fifteen to showtime.

He talked to himself: "I've got everything, right? OK. I'm set. Maybe I should take a glass of water with me." He filled one, then picked up a fistful of the scarves Gail had sewed for him and encouraged him to autograph with a gold-ink pen she borrowed from her daughter. "Well," he said, "no one will ever accuse me of getting there too early." He slid on his sunglasses. He opened the door across from the bathroom and strode, with great purpose, into the closet.

He stepped out and sighed. "Now the most embarrassing part of all: I have to walk through the entire casino. Oh, Jesus. You *know* I'm gonna be looked at in there. Sideshow."

"Does that bother you?" I asked.

He started to consider this but laughed instead. "Well, what the heck?" he said. "I'll never see these people again."

He located the proper door, and we walked the 100 yards or so to the elevators. His boots struck a steady beat on the carpet; his pants swished. A woman approached us, tanned and smiling. She smiled at Dennis as if she knew him. All the doubt Dennis exhibited in his room lifted like mist from all those wig sprays. He seemed to grow six inches. He stuck out his chest. "How you doin', honey?" he asked.

"I won."

"I'm sorry?"

"I won!"

"You won? Did you? Well, that's fantastic."

"Thanks," the woman said. Flush with cash and blessed by Elvis, she floated down the hall.

We stood in front of the elevators. Dennis fidgeted. "I have come to the conclusion that I am blind with these glasses on," he said. "Do the sideburns look like they're fairly on?"

"Yeah."

"Oh, God," he said, out of the blue. The heels of his boots clicked together. "I just looked in the mirror. I scared myself."

The elevator doors parted. Inside a woman stood alone. She stared. Her mouth fell open. One heartbeat. Two.

"No," Dennis said, "this is not a nightmare."

The woman, a curly-headed brunette, laughed at that. They stood a moment in silence, descending. "These outfits are fun to wear in one hundred-degree weather, too," he said.

The woman looked him up and down. "Yeah," she said.

The elevator doors opened. About thirty people who stood waiting for it burst into a cheer: "ALL RIGHT! Hey, Elvis!" Dennis nodded solemnly. The crowd parted to let him pass. He turned right, past the first lineup of slots. All you could hear was the sounds of voices and machines. Deafening. Lights like Christmas.

"Hey, Elvis!" a man said.

"Hey, how you doin', baby?" Dennis had suddenly developed a drawl.

"Whassup?" another man asked.

Dennis reached the second bank of slots. Arms poised to pull down, eyes focused on rows of fruit and diamonds, hands black from nickels, the people stared, but not at him. Dennis studied them with amazement in his eyes. No one looked up. His reflection caught on every shiny surface. The gamblers were surrounded by Elvis, but they couldn't care less. Dennis frowned. "You know," he said, "it is kind of odd, but you can actually walk through a place like this and people don't think that much of it. I notice a lot of people haven't even looked at me, and I'm thinking, well, you know, you're in an odd type of town."

"You're disappointed, aren't you?"

He laughed. He had just realized it. "Yeah! I thought I'd have people running up, asking for my autograph." The only thing worse than dressing up like Elvis and having everyone stare at you is dressing up like Elvis and having everyone ignore you. The machines blooped their music; quarters slapped into trays. "Oh," he said, "this is like a Death Row inmate walking to that last cell." The escalator lifted us up. Dennis studied himself in the mirrors alongside. "See," he said, "we are complex creatures: We don't want the attention, but we do."

Past the theater entrance, through the backstage door. Down the hall. One more door. Randy Black, yet another Chicago Elvis, barreled through the last song of his set, "Promised Land." Randy was a heavyset man wearing a lipstick-red jumpsuit his mother sewed for him, its most intriguing feature a cape emblazoned with a web and a furry black spider in one corner laying wait. Four minutes.

"What do you say, guys?" Dennis said. Lisa Parks, the band member who handed the Elvises their scarves and water onstage, stood smiling in the wings.

"Am I the next person?" he asked her.

"I think so," she said, looking amused.

They ironed out scarf strategy. Jerome said, "Ladies and gentleman, let's give a big round of applause for Mr. Randy Black." Then he added, "Let's give Elvis Presley a big round of applause. There's over thirty-five hundred Elvis performers in the United States, and there's one thousand that do this on a full-time basis. That's all they do . . ."

"I should be more nervous," Dennis said. "Why aren't I nervous?"

He looked up and noticed Jerome staring at him from the bandstand. "Are you ready?" Jerome asked, all business. Dark circles stood out on his boyish face. "OK. This next performer also comes from Illinois. He comes from Calumet." He paused. The first show of the weekend and already he was tired. "Comes all the way from Calumet—Calumet City, Illinois. Ladies and gentlemen: Mister!—Dennis!—Stella!"

The band sprung into "Patch It Up"—*Dah-dah-DAH-dah-DAH*—and Dennis strode out to cheering. Gail and Shelley, sitting in the center of the room, applauded, then Gail squinted at him through the eye of her camera. His hair looked believable, and his suit spangled in the lights. Behind him on the bandstand a sun made out of flashling lights rose and set. He started right in. His voice rang out clear and strong, better than it did at Greene's West. His movements looked much the same, maybe a little less jerky. There is always a moment in an impersonator's set where the audience decides whether to keep applauding or to turn polite. They kept applauding. The muscles in his face visibly relaxed.

"Thank you. Thank you," he said when he finished. "Thank you very much, ladies and gentlemen. Hey, we got any water over here for us cool guys?" He was panting like a dog.

"What would you like to do, Dennis?" Jerome asked, his voice smooth.

"Oh, I don't know, Jerry."

"You ready to do that second SLOW song?" Jerome asked. People in the audience got the joke and began to laugh.

Dennis smiled. "I think that would be appropriate. Slow it down a little bit, ladies and gentlemen . . ."

The band clacked into "Fever." Dennis's voice sounded looser but still a little higher than usual because he hadn't quite caught his breath. With this song, that didn't hurt too much. He shouted the refrain—*"Fev-ah!"*—and popped his hips when the drum rolled. The women whooped and laughed.

"All right. Thank you. Oh. So far, so good. OK. I'd like to sing a beautiful song, ladies and gentlemen." He was still breathing fast, a little hard to understand. He sunk into his last number, the ballad "Just Pretend." His voice still sounded higher, but you could tell he felt at ease with the ballad, nailing every note, hushing with the church-organ keyboards. The audience sent him off on a rolling wave of applause. Except for a little mussing, his hair never moved.

"Good job, brother, good job," said an Elvis standing at the curtain. He reached out and slapped Dennis on the back.

Still panting, Dennis balanced on a tangle of wires held down by tape and collected himself. Despite the mess with the wig, the taxi ride and the rest, he barely felt nervous, and he hadn't scared himself by counting heads in the audience. He had entered a bad stretch and come out of it stronger and not at all humiliated. Every time he went onstage, he learned something about himself. "I don't think I cracked. Good sign," he said, and then he laughed. "Well, I could say now, if lightning strikes me down, I sang in Vegas!" He was dripping sweat and exuding, for the first time all day, confidence. He walked into the hall in search of a towel. Seeing a waitress from the snack bar next door, he asked for directions for the men's room. She turned around, grunted in surprise, then pointed the way. By now he had caught his breath. "Lady," he said, "you should be used to this."

He walked through the front door of the theater and peered into the blackness until he spied Gail and Shelley sitting in the center of the room. They squeezed his arms and complimented him, taking a moment to examine the wig. "You know, it's like almost a fantasy, a dream come true," he told them. "Even if I never make it, to say that I was able to come to Las Vegas and perform, that's nice to say, you know?" They turned their attention back to the next Elvis onstage, but Dennis kept up a constant happy patter. So much had just happened: "Hey, Gail? Gail? I impressed myself. I got ready in a very speedy fashion. And I didn't touch my wig once, if you noticed. No wig touching! By the way, did I cut down on my herky jerky?"

Steve Chuke stormed onstage in his black leather, singing "Lawdy Miss Clawdy." His voice sounded raw and mean.

"Well, that was one of the biggest mistakes I've ever made," Dennis said to them. "It was so important to me and then to do something so stupid, I just can't get over how much of an idiot I was. You should've heard me to talking to myself in the car. I kept going, 'You big dummy! You big dummy!' "

Steve Chuke lit into "Trouble." Gail nodded in Dennis's direction, trying to listen to him and watch Steve's act at the same time.

"I will tell you," Dennis kept on, "this wig is very hot. I feel sorry for women who wear wigs all the time. I don't know how they do it."

He was pumped so full of adrenaline and relief they finally had to walk out into the hall, where Dennis could raise his voice. "Now I really do have three things on my agenda," he said. "Food is number one. Sun is number two. And this incredible urge to go back to a blackjack table."

As they stood in front of the theater doors, Tony Grova strolled over. He wore a sport shirt and shorts. His hair was perfect.

"Hey, how you doin', man?" Dennis asked him. "I didn't recognize you!"

"I haven't slept yet, that's why," Tony replied. "I'm a wreck! A wreck! My plane was delayed five hours, I got in five this morning, I haven't slept. The day before, four hours. I'm a wreck—look at me."

"Hey, now, Tony," Dennis said, "I gotta tell you something. You notice a little different look on me, right, hair and all that? Who do you think is responsible for that in big part? Do you remember giving me a hard time about the hair?" He turned to Gail. "He looked at me and said, 'He needs not to do it or do it right.'"

Tony shrugged. "Hey, I tell it like it is—if you don't like it, the hell with ya, you know what I mean? I'm honest!"

"Pulled me off to the side, said . . ."

"Do it, or don't do it. I'm just tellin' ya to help yourself, that's all."

"Well, you know what? A lot of people fought me on it! They were like, 'Oh, be yourself!'"

Tony cocked his head and looked at Dennis's wig. He wouldn't be caught dead in a thing like that. "It looks good, though," he said.

"Oh, thank you. I'm tryin' to get that Elvis look."

Tony smiled. "I like that look."

That night, the EPIIA held its annual awards banquet. Ron and Sandy thought it would prolong the life of the organization and boost the morale of its members if everyone received some kind of recognition for their work, be it doing charitable endeavors, or sticking with Elvis for so long, or just appearing in the showcase. As Sandy told them when it came her turn to speak, "I love you all."

Rick Marino had told Ron before the dinner started that he should explain to the impersonators as plainly as possible why it cost so much to put on the show. Ron hesitated; he feared being too blunt might sound crass. "The hell with crass!" Rick told him. "I call it being direct!"

Anyone who ever doubted the wide-ranging appeal of Elvis Presley could well be converted by attending an event like the banquet. Men— and one woman this year, four-time conventioneer Janis Waite from England— of every age, size, race, nationality and profession sat around tables swapping small talk. They dressed mostly in casual clothes, the most notable exception being Tony Grova, who wore his sky-blue Madison Square Garden press conference suit with a black shirt. Only one man brought a woman dressed to look like Priscilla Presley in the sixties, with a double-dip beehive. With that exception, things were business as usual. All but a few of the men, and Waite, too, wore pompadours, which made a declaration stronger than any of those in the association's charter. Hair quality varied. Some resembled weatherbeaten convertible tops, while a few called to mind the original. It appeared that it was possible, though not very pretty, to have both a pompadour and a receding hairline.

The banquet room was located on the left of the Legends showroom on the second level, across from a few rows of slots with padded chairs. The head table, where the officers sat, rose directly in front of the Exspence Account's instruments, set up for a jam session later on. Behind the heads of the association leaders cymbals tipped like flying saucers.

Steve Chuke sat at one of the round tables with still another of the Chicago Elvises, Joe Tirrito, as always sporting a breathtaking tan and a brace of gold chains around his neck. For this night Steve had selected his best rebel wear—black trousers, black short-sleeved shirt unbuttoned halfway down his chest and sleeves rolled above the biceps, hair freshly dyed to match. He'd had a few beers—a habit he seldom indulged in at home. Drinking somehow put him to sleep and woke up the country in his voice.

As the waitresses darted between the tables, refilling the men's coffee cups, Ron Bessette held forth on the dais. It was an act made less impressive by the fact that he spoke softly and rapidly. The Elvises kept shouting that they couldn't hear. But Ron didn't seem hear them, and he strolled along the elevated head table in his black tuxedo, introducing the people who had worked and sacrificed to make the weekend a reality. His wife, Sandy, sat next to him. She glowed, twisting her long neck back and forth, wearing a sequined top that winked back flashbulb light every time someone snapped her picture. After praising Sandy, Ron introduced Rick Marino, who also wore a tux, though he accessorized his with gold-rimmed Elvis glasses and a shirt with ruffled cuffs. Asked for a few remarks, he removed his glasses and kept it short: "About the only thing I'd like to say is I would like to see all the guys, really, three hundred sixty-five days a year, make a little bit more of an effort to make Ron and Sandy's job just a little bit easier. Like he said, write back to them, let 'em know how many shows—what it is you're doing. If you see something in your area, anything to do with Elvis, or anything you can do to help Sandy with the newsletter, you know, it would really be a big help. . . ."

He wagged his left hand for emphasis. "We all have our own careers, and it's tough—you know, it's very tough to find the time to be able to give a little bit. But I think if everybody just spent about an hour a month—which is not a lot to ask—and just sit down and wrote Sandy a nice letter, tell her what's goin' on, maybe tell her some of the stories about somebody you know, something that's happening, it would be very helpful. Thank you very much."

Ron thanked Rick and moved on, introducing others at the head table. He moved to the second table directly below and stopped at a man with silver hair and a broad smile wearing a Western shirt, his elbows resting on the table. "We have down here Mike McGregor," Ron said. "And for those of you who don't know Mike . . ."

Steve Chuke had performed the tiring '68 Comeback Elvis a few hours earlier, he felt tipsy, and his jet lag haunted him like an uneasy dream. But at this he perked up. Mike McGregor?

"Want to say something, Mike?" Ron asked. He handed him the mike.

Resting a hand easily on his hip, Mike talked a moment about Elvis and how much he loved working for him. "It makes me feel really good to have been a part of the whole thing," he said, "and then to come to somethin' like this, like we've been doing year after year, and seeing all ya'll folks, just keep supportin' it, and keep helpin' out Ron and Sandy. Thank you."

"Mike McGregor," Steve Chuke said. "Where the heck did I hear that name at?" He sat amid the clinking of silverware on china, the impromptu snatches of songs and Rick Marino's booming laugh, trying to remember.

The rest of the banquet dealt with two themes: happiness that they all had come this far and fear that the association risked losing everything they had achieved these last five years. After recognizing Nigel Kingsley and Tony Grova for their many years of impersonating Elvis, Ron introduced Jerome Marion and praised the work he had done over the years for the association. By turns halting and heartfelt, Ron's speech updated the members on what had happened since they last met. As he spoke about the mission of the EPIIA, his mike cut out and when it came back his voice was a dull mumble. In the audience, impersonators groaned. Ron continued. In January of that year, he said, he and Sandy had bought a business. "Our lives change," he said, "just like your lives change." The result of this change, he explained, was that the two of them could no longer afford to foot the bill for the convention. They contacted Rick and Jerome and told them how it was: "We're not gonna be able to pay the bill this year. We cannot commit ourselves to that debt. If we're gonna do the showcase, somebody's gonna have to pay the bill."

They were happy to hear Jerome and Rick wanted the convention to continue. "We said, well, we want this to continue, too," Ron said. "It's just that we're not able to make the financial commitment. And the financial commitment, with appreciation, is . . ." He hesitated. "We're twenty-two thousand dollars in the hole. And the association is six years old, it costs us four hundred a month to operate, and that comes from telephone bills and postage and all that stuff that we do." It had become even harder to hear him. Rick, who had excused himself, returned and whispered something to Ron, who reached back toward the band setup and found another mike. This one worked better, and the audience burst into applause. "Thought you were going to sleep out there, huh?" he asked. He then offered the floor to Jerome, who stood and propped one foot on his chair.

"Ron has talked a little bit about the association and what we stood for, and what we stand for, and I think that we've done in the last five years what the association really stands for," he began. His white shirt, open at the collar, blazed under the bright lights. "And what the association stands for is basically keeping the legacy of a great entertainer alive, but also at the same time raising funds for worthy causes. We're here for you, but you're here for us. We would not exist without you, and vice versa.

"Five years ago, when this association started, I'm sure Ron and Sandy hoped that it would be much, much larger, as we all did. But we kept a lot of the members, we kept a lot of the fans going, we're still around. And that is that name of the game, and I hope to be around for a long time, and I think we will be, as long as we still have people like you who come out to help us every year celebrate the legacy of a great entertainer." The audience applauded warmly. Jerome swept his arm across the room. "I think *you* deserve a round of applause," he replied.

"As Ron had mentioned, back in January he had contacted me regarding the financial difficulties. And I kind of anticipated this was gonna happen eventually, because I knew a lot of the behind-the-scenes and what was involved in the financial end of it. Working with the performers and with Ron and Sandy very closely over the last five years I learned—and with my own business—it takes money to make money. It costs, I don't even know, thirteen thousand or some dollars just to put this event on. And the total breakdown would just astonish you, what things cost—and it's all part of what it costs to do this. I mean, before we can ever do this, it costs that much just to get the door open, before we can walk in.

"We need to offset the cost of this convention," he concluded. "You guys, we want you to come out every year. And I don't know about you, but I want to keep coming out here every year. You guys want to come out here next year?" They applauded in response. Jerome then handed out certificates to those who had performed at the miniconvention. Dennis Stella was the only one not present to accept.

Ron and Sandy stepped down to a table topped with a white tablecloth and began handing out plaques with large gold stars in the centers and certificates to the performers. Ron presented a plaque to Jeff Scott, who had donated a jumpsuit with an estimated value of $2,500. It was displayed a few seats down from Mike McGregor; it was covered with sequins, with a gold eagle screeching across the chest with wings that looked something like lungs. It was the object of a silent auction, with bids starting at $500. They would repeat the process with an Elvis belt to match the suit.

Ron said: "What we're going to do with that money—what we want to do with that money, the jumpsuit and the belt, is we wanna start a fund. We want to put a fund in for our sound, lights, and the band. That totally costs us, to give you a number, just the sound and the lights and nothing else, and the band, seven thousand dollars. Just to think about walking into that theater. I'm not talking about promotions—promotion's two or three thousand dollars. Fliers, phone calls—four hundred dollars on phone bills. So we're talking about fourteen thousand dollars to put this on. To walk in that theater door, just for the hotel, costs seven thousand dollars. And if you want to keep that theater, we need the seven thousand dollars a year."

Up at the head table, Rick Marino broke in: "And I would like to say one thing, Ron. I would like to say I think it looks pretty good on everybody's resume to say they performed in the show room here in Las Vegas, the Legends, such as we have. It's an opportunity a lot of us wouldn't get to do and I think it's very important you all remember that. And Ron has worked very hard to take us from a convention room in Chicago to the main stage at the Legends show room in Las Vegas." More applause.

"That's what we want," Ron said. "We want to continue the professionalism. And that's the only way you can keep professionalism, is having and performing in a professional location. And I don't want to go back to a hotel ballroom. That's not what I want for us, for you guys. I want you to be represented professionally, to be in a first-class place, in a first-class organization. Then you can go back and say, 'Hey, I'm first class, and I'm always gonna be first class and work first class and deal first class.'"

Everyone applauded again. They accepted more awards and certificates, including the coveted twenty-year trophies, and then they moved to the front of the room to pose for group pictures to remember the occasion by. The cameraman had to stand on a ladder to fit them all in. After that, a jam session began. Jerome kicked it off around 11:00 P.M. with a rousing cover of "Viva Las Vegas."

Dennis never showed at the ceremony to accept his award that night because, he, Gail, and Shelley attended the early show of Legends in Concert. Each show, no matter who else appeared, featured an Elvis impersonator last on the bill, and Dennis thought it would be fun, not to mention instructive, to watch someone who had hit the big time. They arrived early and took a back booth to the left of the same stage that Dennis had stood upon just a few hours before. They sipped their drinks and chuckled at two men who portrayed the Blues Brothers. Gail and Shelley, showing off their tans in sleeveless, form-fitting evening dresses, rolled their eyes at the Madonna. Dennis regarded the Liberace, who floated above the stage supported by wires, with mild alarm. Finally, the end: A man appeared in black leather. Dennis nudged Gail, his eyes round and white in the dark: Trent Carlini! From Chicago, Trent

Carlini! He had seen him perform at home before he made it big. Dennis watched Carlini's entire Comeback recreation with his mouth half open. At the next table, another conventioneer, a seventies Elvis in a red satin jacket, grunted and left the room.

Carlini had everything Dennis coveted—sharp moves, classy costume, strong voice—and as critical as Dennis tended to be, he could find little fault. If he could follow Carlini's example, he decided, he might do Elvis proud. It wasn't that he expected to accomplish such feats overnight, but after his wig slipped he'd wondered if he could do it at all. He'd surprised himself once today. Maybe he wasn't crazy after all.

Powerful thoughts shot Dennis out of that theater into the neon-lit night. First he went up to the room, where Steve Chuke joined him for about ten songs on the karaoke machine. Then he, Gail, and Shelley wandered out on the Strip, basking in all the lights. It was 5:00 A.M. before he finally closed his eyes.

8

Viva Elvis

*S*aturday morning. When Dennis and just about everyone else involved with the convention opened their eyes, they found themselves in much the same state: conscious, yet not quite awake. Jerome retained, though weakly, some pleasant memory of eating a salad on Friday between shows; other than that, comforts such as food and more than an hour's sleep a night became something he associated with home, which seemed very far away. He had reached a point sometime the day before where it felt more professional to laugh at the mistakes he made introducing the performers on stage rather than apologize for them.

Steve Chuke had reunited with his good buddy Ronny Craig, the strapping dinner-theater balladeer from LaCrosse, Wisconsin. Ronny had taken advantage of their current location and hit the casinos. To him, gambling is business and meant to be taken seriously. At one point—with all those damn lights, God knows how late it was—Steve found himself at Caesar's Palace with Ronny, who was losing money and feeling lucky at the same time, a combination that made Steve's brain bubble, seeing that he was the one holding all their money.

Rick Marino contended with the usual fatigue and the fact his throat kept squeezing shut—not a happy fact, considering he had to sing at 3:40 that afternoon. From Thursday on, he smelled like eucalyptus cough drops. Flying from muggy Florida into Nevada always sucked the life out of him. Plus he got sick to his stomach, as he did every year—too many buffet meals, too unpleasant to explain, though, being Rick, he tried.

Dennis, meanwhile, was moving through his day in a happy haze. He woke, got dressed, and went backstage to see Charlene Ziemann. He was marked down to sing an encore of "Patch It Up," plus the ballad "I'll Remember You," which was pretty, he could handle that, then "Steamroller," a sexy number he didn't much want. He walked in, hoping to change two out of three. He reminded Charlene this was the last time he would sing this weekend. She perused her list. Song choice is always a hotly contested issue at these events; few impersonators ever walk away completely satisfied. "I've got 'Suspicious Minds,'" she said. Dennis started getting excited. She had to be kidding—a good, fast song that most people, fans or not, recognized?

He burst into the lobby and found Gail and Shelley standing in line for the next show. "I got 'Suspicious Minds,' 'In the Ghetto,' and 'I Can't Stop Loving You,'" he said. He was bouncing like a cheerleader, and they laughed at how happy he was, after everything that had come before. He showed them a couple of moves the guys backstage taught him when they heard he was singing "Suspicious Minds": "All right. I turn to the band, the last time I'm going to do it . . ." He flailed his arms over his head, jumping two feet off the carpet. ". . . and then it'll go, '*Dum, dum, dum, dum duuuuuuuuuum!*'"

"Dennis, you're going to punch somebody!" Gail said, laughing. She had been watching him closely all weekend, worried that the hair caper would wreck his nerves.

"I'm fired up! I'm all fired up!" he said, and he did a little dance. "Can you imagine?"

Saturday afternoon, 2:30 P.M. Dennis was due on stage in half an hour. Sigh. Riiip. Ffft. "Shoot," he said. He stood before the mirror in his black Spanish Flower jumpsuit, the one with the glass emeralds, regarding a sideburn pinched between his fingers. It looked like a caterpillar he'd just peeled off the sole of his shoe. He soothed it on. He smoothed the wig. "Maybe I should've just stuck with insurance, huh?" he said. But he nailed everything down and ran out the door with ten minutes to spare before his set.

The elevator doors slid apart. Another woman stood inside. This one gasped.

"Hello, how are you?" Dennis asked.

"Oh, no," the woman replied.

"No, I'm not Elvis," he said. "I'm just a guy who pretends to be him." This could have been the very thing she feared, but she let him on anyway.

In the lobby, a woman called, "Hey, Elvis!"

"Hey, baby," Dennis said, slurring the words. Slot machines giggled and squealed. "You know," he said, "I keep looking at myself in the mirror and still cannot believe that is me."

Near the tiki bar, a little girl said: "Hey, Elvis!"

"They must like this outfit better," Dennis said. "I'm getting that attention that I so desperately seek."

Up the escalator, through the backstage door. "Looks good, Dennis," Sandy said, eyeing the black suit, the imitation emeralds, dozens of gold studs. She spent most of the show standing outside the theater door, taking tickets. She hardly got to see anyone perform.

"Wish me luck," he said. "I need it."

Actually, he did all right. During "Suspicious Minds" he got so fired up he swung his arm like he was throwing a shot put and nearly keeled over. At one point during his second song, "In the Ghetto," he got to the line "And his mama cries" and folded it into the one about when the young man in the song dies so it came out as, "And his mama dies"—an entirely different tragedy. Once again Gail and Shelley felt terrible and at the same time couldn't wait to tease him. When he came off stage, Charlene wrapped her arm around him and whispered in his ear that he truly had improved.

He walked out into the hall to catch his breath. A man with thinning hair and a satin baseball jacket opened the door. "I love your voice," he said.

Dennis's eyes opened wide. "Really?"

"Yeah," he said, "you wiped the rest of 'em out."

Dennis's voice arced two octaves higher. "Really?"

"Yeah. I grew up with Elvis—I'm fifty years old—so I know. As far as the sounds, the rest of 'em aren't too clear, aren't gettin' close. You're the only one to me that sounds clear."

Dennis's face shone like the moon. "Really?"

"I think you've got a good voice there," he said, and he disappeared into the lobby.

Dennis called after him, "Thank you! I appreciate that very much!" He stood there a moment, blinking, then tried to steady himself by telling a woman about the benefits of satin linings in jumpsuits. On-stage Angel Peña from Fremont, California, was singing "Hurt." At the 1993 convention Angel, a beefy man with a large pompador and side-burns like skinny peninsulas, was married in the We've Only Just Begun Chapel at the Imperial Palace. The ceremony was open to the public or anyone else who wished to be married. When the justice of the peace pronounced Angel and his bride man and wife, a man in the front of the chapel shouted, "Hunka hunka burnin' love!"

The woman walked away and Dennis could stand it no longer. "By the way," he said, "that guy gave me a very nice compliment." For the first time in his Elvis career, this was one thing he didn't attempt to analyze.

He went up to his room and changed to lie by the pool. Down in the theater Nazar Sayegh, an emergency-room physician from Yonkers, New York, emerged in a skintight red Pinwheel and did such a power-house "Polk Salad Annie," all lariat arms and piston hips, that when he finished all he could say was, "It's hot up here, baby."

Jerome looked down and said, "Are you hot now? Because I'm hot just watching you." Nazar, a personable and well-spoken man offstage, just smiled. His mind appeared to be someplace else. As he meditated on the opening of "American Trilogy," someone in the audience let loose a long *WHOOOOO!*

Nazar snapped up his immaculate Elvis Head and pointed into the darkness. "Thank you, baby," he said. The crowd went wild.

That afternoon by the pool, Dennis bumped into Tony Grova again. The more he got to know him, the more Dennis respected his opinion. The more impersonators he met, the more firmly he believed that there was no one way to present an illusion of Elvis. No performer captured it ex-actly, but some of them did it with more style. Dennis still saw himself as a work in progress, but he suspected—and hoped—that Tony saw something good in him. When they met again, Dennis asked Tony one more time what he thought of his look.

"Well, Dennis, do you want me to be honest with you, or do you want me to tell you what you want to hear?" Tony asked. "Because I'll be hon-est."

"No," Dennis said, "I want your honest opinion."

Tony told him the hair was passable, but the sideburns had to go. "I don't mean no disrespect," he said, "but you're asking me my opinion. It looks OK from a distance on stage, but when you're up close it looks terrible. I mean, you asked me a question. I'm gonna answer you. You want me to say, 'Oh, it looks great!' What do you want me to tell you? Don't ask me—I'm not gonna lie to you."

This time Dennis didn't feel intimidated by Tony. He had worked hard and gotten a compliment from a stranger in a satin jacket. For the first time, he felt bold about his Elvisness. "Tony, you're a handsome man," he said. "You'd be a handsome man even if you didn't do Elvis. But to be honest with you, I think you'd be better looking if you shaved off those stupid muttonchops and cut your hair. You've kind of, in my opinion, lost perspective of what reality is. You're a damn good-looking guy all by yourself, just as Tony. You don't have to be Elvis."

"Neither one of us is right," Dennis said, "and neither one of us is wrong. You have chosen to look like him on a daily basis and I have to respect that, whether I like it or not. And I'd appreciate it if you felt the same way with me. Just because I don't look like Elvis on a daily basis, don't put me down for it. Because I have a right to be me, too, and I happen to think that being Dennis is OK."

Later, after they changed and met each other downstairs, Dennis and Tony posed for pictures together for a photographer named Patty Carroll. One of the shots wound up on the cover of an impersonator-a-month calendar. In it both of them were lunging deeply, and both wore knowing sneers.

"You are what you look like, basically, in this industry," said Butch Polston, a lanky man with a blond mustache. Polston was a rare breed of man—neither Elvis imitator nor intimate, he still managed to make a living in the impersonator world. He traveled to events like the convention, setting up a display table and dressing a couple of mannequins in his products. His job was outfitting Elvis impersonators with their work clothes—or, as his catalog put it, "Replica Jumpsuits with That Edge of Reality." Polston quit a job in a factory making wood veneer for walls to make jumpsuits full time. One of the reasons he succeeded is that he understood the reasons somebody would want to have a suit like Elvis. He'd had those urges himself.

"What had happened," said Polston, "was shortly after Elvis died, I wanted to collect something unusual. Because I'm an unusual person myself." In the impersonator world, however, Polston fit right in. He fell in love with Elvis when he was a child, growing up with two brothers in

Clarksville, Indiana. His family was poor; one of the few times his parents would splurge on a family outing was when a new Elvis movie came to the local drive-in. Love of Elvis was passed down to him like an heirloom, and he accepted it without question. "Besides him being the ultimate performer as far as I'm concerned—I mean, he had charisma, he just had an air about him," he said. "Just had something about him. I just absolutely fell in love with the way he sang."

When Presley died, Polston told his wife, Kim, that he wanted to own something special to remind him of Elvis. The story goes that Elvis loved jumpsuits because they reminded him of Captain America, a childhood hero. Polston understood. The suits whispered to him of a world of glamour and flash. If Polston owned a jumpsuit, he would possess something most other fans didn't. But the prices of originals Elvis had worn were out of reach for a man who worked burying phone cables and gas lines for a living. So he hired a seamstress from Louisville to sew him four jumpsuits. She had made a few for her little boy, so she understood exactly what Polston was searching for.

He studied pictures of Elvis wearing jumpsuits and memorized the intricate patterns of studs and glass jewels. Then he studded his four suits, using bric-a-brac he'd bought at a crafts store. He was so proud of what he had done he convinced Kim they should drive to Memphis and show the suits off to fans during Elvis Week. They scraped together some money and rented a room at the Days Inn on Brooks Road, a base of operations for some of the more serious fans even before Graceland opened to the public. Butch spread the suits on the bed in their room and propped open the door so people walking by could see. Fans passing by marveled at his handiwork.

"And I had these Elvis impersonators," Polston said, "which was a totally new type of animal to me. I had never met any of them. They started coming into our room and oohing and ahhing and saying, 'Wow, I paid x amount of dollars for my costumes and they're nowhere as authentic as yours. Yours is the most authentic.' And they just ranted and raved. And so what happened was, they were actually made to fit me. I'm six-foot-two. And this one gentleman my same size, height and everything, he came in. He was a big Elvis impersonator back at that period of time. He looked at the costumes. He said, 'These are great!' He said, 'I've been paying nine hundred apiece out of New York to have mine made, and they don't look nowhere near as good as yours.'

"And my mouth dropped open. I said, 'You have got to be kidding me.'

And he tried them on and he says, 'You wanna sell these?' And I said I had no intention of selling them.

"He says, 'Well, I'll tell you what: I'll have all four of 'em and give you five hundred dollars apiece for 'em. Right now.'

"Well, after I picked my jaw up off the ground, I sold them to him. Because that was two thousand dollars, and back then, to my wife and myself, two thousand dollars was like all the money in the whole world. You couldn't see nothing but enamel from our teeth smiling all the way home."

He and Kim decided to make Elvis suits as a sideline. Butch set out to learn how the real jumpsuits were made. His path took him from Graceland, where many of the original suits were displayed; to Ciro Romano, a former tailor to Elvis; to the designer Bill Belew; who supervised Elvis's wardrobe for much of his career; and finally to a man named Gene Doucette, who worked for a design house and who had designed many of the jumpsuits Elvis wore under contract to Belew. Doucette explained secrets about embroidery and patterns, and let Polston study some of his original sketches. They became close friends. Doucette gave Polston an Aztec-style appliqué for a Sundial suit he'd hand-beaded himself.

With Doucette's help, B&K Enterprises became a force in the impersonator world. The company could produce 140 suits a year, between Butch, Kim, and a seamstress they employed. The suits took anywhere from thirty-five to 250 hours to build, depending upon the intricacy of their design. Some impersonators groused that the suits cost too much. Indeed, they were not for pretenders: A copy of what is probably the best known jumpsuit, the one Elvis wore in his *Aloha from Hawaii* concert, costs $2,100, $600 more with the cape. The cheapest jumpsuit, the Cape Fringe, is $1,300. The Gypsy and Sundial suits, decorated with embroidery done on a chain-stitch machine, cost $5,000. Polston also offered satin shirts with puffy sleeves for more informal outings at $100 each and custom-made chrome sunglasses for $250.

The complaints that he overcharged frustrated Polston. It was harder for him to recreate the jumpsuits as original materials used twenty years earlier became more scarce. He sewed his suits out of a hand-washable polyester gabardine, rather than the more durable yet fragile wool gabardine Elvis wore. "Last time I bought it was like sixty-two dollars a yard," Polston said. "And it takes about almost five yards to do a costume. If they want the suit and the cape, it takes about seven yards."

Studs and cabochons, foil-backed jewels of polished glass, were still easily imported. The stones cost from 75 cents to $5 each; often Polston punched them in by hand because they were so fragile and expensive. The sapphire stones on the Aloha suit, as it has come to be known, cost $2 each. The suit contains 400 of those stones.

Although some impersonators disliked his prices, they could not deny what he had done to increase respect for their profession. Polston would never boast about his skill, but he would declare that serious impersonators told him they considered one of his jumpsuits an investment in credibility: "That's just if like you go to a custom-car show, and you put a Volkswagen that's a plain painted Volkswagen in with a bunch of real elaborate painted Corvettes, which one are you gonna tend to look at the most? And which one would you prefer to drive around in? Certainly not the Volkswagen. That's unfortunate, but that's the only way that I can make the point." His regulars also confided to him that they got less attention from tabloids and other media outlets that ridicule impersonators.

"One of the things that happens is people who wear our suits, and I mean no disrespect to anybody, so please don't take it that I'm making fun, because in no way am I. I really feel for a lot of these guys," he said. "People who wear our suits, generally people like the *Enquirer* and those tabloid ga-ga papers, they tend to stay away from them. They home in on the guys that have taken a painter's suit, or had their sister's second cousin by marriage or whatever make them a costume, and they throw all kinds of little spangles and doodads on it, and it looks nothing like something Elvis actually had. Or they'll get sequins. Well, none of Elvis Presley's costumes had sequins on them—not one of them had a sequin on them. And what they'll do is the media tend to focus on those guys. And what they do is, these poor guys think, 'Oh, wow! I'm gettin' all this attention.' But they're simply doing nothing more than making fun of them. And I really feel terrible for those guys."

Polston never intended to become a jumpsuit designer. After all those years he still couldn't sew. And he could hardly believe his luck. "The way I look at it," he said, "it's where the good Lord pointed his finger for me to go, and I just followed his finger."

In the process his own edge of reality had expanded beyond anything he'd ever dreamed. He was famous in impersonator circles—if you said Butch Polston made a jumpsuit, an Elvis would nod knowingly. He had granted interviews to newspapers all over the world and toured Australia, where he showcased his jumpsuits in a shopping mall. But he insisted, "I'm not into it for fame or anything like that. I mean, God's sakes, I'm recreating something somebody else did for people who are doing something that somebody else has done. You see where I'm coming from?"

Polston stood at his table and talked to his friend at the table next to his. Impersonators never bought much at these events, so having Mike McGregor to talk to had become a highlight of his weekend.

It was Sunday, the last day of the convention, and the longest: Twelve hours, ten of them nothing but Elvis. People smiled weakly at each other in the lobby. Everybody was running low on money and sleep. They were having a wonderful time.

The sets seemed to run together now, a mix of sex and death and showmanship. Gary Sanders, a miner from Cullman, Alabama, introduced his last number, "You Gave Me a Mountain," which features a line saying the singer's mother died giving him life. "This next song has a meaning for everyone," he said, eagles on his jumpsuit writhing in the light. "It has some meaning for me. Matter of fact, this story, and this song—Elvis, I believe he wrote this song for me. [Actually, Marty Robbins wrote it.] Because my mother, she died the day I was born. And so I want you to enjoy this song as much as I do." Robert Washington, the shipbuilder from Auburn, Maine, came out in the Concho jumpsuit, silver discs running down the chest and legs, did the medley of "I Got a Woman" and "Amen," then did an extended "Polk Salad Annie" that ended with him running up the steps on stage, flying off, landing on his knees, then collapsing backward, the audience applauding the whole time. It was the most electric moment of the weekend.

Steve Chuke was tired after countless hours in Caesar's Palace with Ronny Craig. He had roamed around until Ronny would approach him again and ask him to spot him some money, shouting, "Come on! I feel lucky!" It had been fun, but Steve couldn't rest until he straightened out something in his mind. He realized where he had heard of Mike McGregor before that night at the banquet, but he wanted to be sure. As the show wound down, Steve strolled the banquet room, checking out the vendors until he saw the man he had come to see. McGregor had the table to the right of Butch Polston's along the back wall, and it was laid out with fat leather belts. He wore his straw cowboy hat, Western shirt, and jeans. Another Elvis stood there talking to him, but Steve was so excited he walked right up.

"Mike?"

"Yeah?"

The other Elvis gave Steve a look like he was butting in, but Steve had to ask it now, before everyone packed up and headed home. He introduced himself, explained how he put on shows down in Kentucky.

"Somebody approached me with Elvis's stereo that he gave you," he began. "And they wanted to sell it to me."

"Hold it," Mike McGregor said. He turned to the other Elvis: "It's been nice talking to you," he said. The man left and McGregor turned his attention back to Steve. "Hold it right now. I want to tell you something: Elvis Presley never gave me anything that I didn't work for."

Great—he'd just met the guy and he offended him. "OK," Steve said, "I'm sorry. I didn't know, you know?"

McGregor sized up Steve. He considered himself a good judge of character, and this guy seemed all right. "If you got time," he said, "I'll tell you exactly how the story is."

Next door the entertainment continued, suffused with fatigue and factors more mysterious. During the second Sunday show, as I watched Charlene Ziemann direct the flow of Elvises past her tiny table, I felt someone staring at me. I looked up to see a man with a pompadour and eyes that looked as if they were peering through thick smoke. He handed me his business card and began to sing "Loving You." To me.

He stood so close I could see how the dye coated his hair. He handed me his card. "When was the last time you had a guy sing to you?" he asked.

"About half an hour ago," I said. This was true. Someone was always singing backstage. Often several impersonators clustered and echoed whoever was on stage, creating a stereo effect.

"Half an hour ago since a guy sang you a love song like that?" Smoky Elvis asked. "Wow. So I'm two or three down in the line, huh?"

"You're a lot more than that," Charlene said, twirling her pen between fingers that, for all her hurry this weekend, featured immaculately manicured nails. "We've had it all day."

He shared with us secrets he invoked to enhance the suppleness of his throat and then sang again, this time "For the Good Times." He fixed me with his smoke-stung eyes as if it all meant something, and I suppose it did, though what I was ill-equipped to say. Ace Crye, an Elvis from Texas, and Rick Ardisano from Chicago exchanged glances, then strolled over from behind the table to sing harmony.

"We're immune to it all," Charlene shouted over the sound. Smoothly, Smoky Elvis handed me his card.

"You gave me your card already," I said.

"I gave you my card and you're gonna call me and we're gonna have a party someday, honey. That's right. You're gonna remember me. What other guy do you know would stand here for this long—sing all these love songs? I mean, only real love does that. Isn't that right?"

"Want to run down the list, hon?" Charlene asked.

"If you say so," I told him, "it must be true."

He looked hurt, then slunk into "You've Lost That Lovin' Feeling." From near the curtain someone yelled, "Bring out the hook for this guy." That worked. As he walked out the door I almost said, "Who does that guy think he is?" Then I realized I already knew the answer, and that it didn't begin to explain anything.

Fifteen minutes later Steve zoomed past the slot machines on the Legends floor, licking his lips and blinking. "I wanted to tell you, I was down here talking to McGregor," he said. "Did I tell you already I'm gonna buy the stereo? Oh! I am so pumped up, man, I could scream. Man, I didn't know it was original. Now I do. I'm gonna go back, I'm gonna try everything in the world—I'm gonna put the sucker on display in my store." He took off running to change. He was singing "I Got a Woman" in the convention's big finale, about an hour after Jerome closed the 6:00 show with a rousing version of "How Great Thou Art."

Dennis did not perform in that final show, "Viva Elvis," a separate production from the convention, but he put on his black Spanish Flower anyway and sat in the audience with Gail and Shelley. Backstage, impersonators dashed on and off stage, peeling off their sweaty suits behind a small black curtain in the corner. Someone yelled for a full-length mirror so he could make sure his hair hadn't gotten mussed when he changed. Some of the other Elvises rolled their eyes; just as many walked over to use the mirror once it arrived. As the show ended Ron Bessette stood backstage, hands clasped behind his back, watching the performers take their bows. "Too soon, too soon," he said, softly. The impersonators closed "Viva Elvis" with "I'll Be Back," the last number in *Spinout,* only they changed the refrain to "We'll Be Back."

When the convention ended, tradition held that all the impersonators were supposed to unite on stage to sing one last song—this time, the ballad "Memories." Ron, wearing a brown suit, walked out to join them. Among all the jewels and lamé, he looked out of place. "Where's my wife?" he cried, and Sandy came out, wearing a black sequined sweater and white pants. They put their arms around each other's shoulders and swayed to the melody, and the Elvises took turns singing a line. Dennis wanted to jump on stage to join them, but he was unsure whether this was part of "Viva Elvis." A lot of the Elvises assumed the same thing and stayed off the stage. No one had told them the plan.

The show ended, and everyone milled around the Legends lobby in front of the glass case that contained color pictures of the show's cast for sale. Dennis roamed the crowd, debating whether he should throw a sing-along party in his room or just go there and sleep until just before his plane left the next day. He did look tired. He had applied some makeup for a photo shoot, and his eyeliner had smeared. But he was smiling and in a philosophical mood. He hid out from the crowds in the backstage hallway and leaned against the wall to let the last three days sink in.

It had cost him $150 to get his wig from the pinball machine in his spare bedroom to the stage in Vegas. The bad news was that the whole mess was his fault—he couldn't blame anyone but himself. His inability to portray someone else had eroded his own self-esteem. The good news was that his success—taming his hair and doing the best shows of his young career—had nothing to do with Elvis. It was a victory of his own design. He knew he needed work on attitude and technique, wisdom and glide. But considering that he was an amateur with luckless hair and a bad case of nerves, he transcended expectations. The pride he felt reminded him of when he graduated from college at twenty-eight. Maybe that attitude, he mused, had carried over into his Elvis.

"You know, I pulled something off that people told me I couldn't do," he said. "People told me, 'You're starting way too late. You can't do it.' And I said, 'Maybe they're right—maybe I can't. But I'll find out.'"

He returned to the lobby. There was barely room to maneuver, and in the middle of the crowd some joker was warbling "O Sole Mio." The guys hugged and shook hands and swore they couldn't wait for next year, then shouted goodbyes as they rode the escalator downstairs. Sandy's laughter rose above all the voices. She was tired—her eyes were bloodshot—but still angling to squeeze in another stretch at the slots. A couple of hours later, at the annual post-show strategy meeting with Ron,

Rick Marino, and Jerome Marion, she would look down at an empty plate that had contained steak and eggs and not remember eating them.

By the Legends case a woman with frizzy hair and a bashful expression on her round face held out paper and pen to Dennis. "Could you?" she asked. Dennis took the paper, asked her name then signed "Much love, Dennis," in his careful looping script. As he finished, another woman waited to take her place.

After the officers caught up on their sleep, they agreed the show, from a professional standpoint, had improved upon previous years, even that ideal first one. In fact, most of the talk centered on what they could do to make the sixth year even better, rather than repeat mistakes of the past.

Rick suggested a new gimmick with national stature. "I'd like to come up with some kind of award where you became a knight, you became Sir Somebody, you know—Sir Richard, Sir Galahad—and you were really a special person. The king depended on you. And I told Ron it would be great if we could come up with some award that most exemplifies not so much the Elvis person who looks the best or sings the best or is the best but the one that throughout the year did the most in the name of Elvis professionally with his own personal career, helping charity—just all around did it all. Let's make a nice ring or something—you know, like a gold ring? Come up with a name for that, call it the Something Award. Something cool. And really make it a big deal, make it something the guys would really want, because there can only be one of them a year, and it's something that, if we had enough media saturation on it we could get Oprah or one of these shows or something, or 'Hard Copy' or somebody to kinda cover it when we do it, and then follow this person around or something, this and that. Make it really special."

"I was a little concerned that this might be the last year," Jerome said. "But now I feel very kind of confident that it's going to go on next year and continue."

More than any of them, Sandy felt something good had happened during those three days. For at least a year she had worried that the association would fold. Now she allowed herself to think that maybe things could change. The band was hot, the guys were polished, the mood was optimistic. "This year is the first time that I've actually seen the guys get out and sell raffle tickets in the lobby when the crowd came out of the theater," she said a few days after the convention. "The very first time I've actually seen them work. Previous years, it's been 'Me, me, me, I'm gonna be on the stage, and I'm not doing anything but coming to Vegas.'

"You know, I get downhearted sometimes. Because Ron and I are doing this for them. And there are just a small handful of people who help. And if we could get more help out of the guys, to make their association grow, it would be much better. Much, much better. I'm not saying they don't really appreciate what we're doing—I'm sure they do. But they need to be a little more involved than just showing up in Vegas and getting on the stage."

If help didn't come, she suspected things would end. She thought that if the association folded the guys would probably just go back to the way they'd been before. The brotherhood would disappear. Yet she couldn't seem to convince them they needed to help. "They kind of more or less take it for granted that, yes, there's going to be a show," she said. "Somebody else is going to roll the ball for them. But when it ends, there's going to be some very, very sad men."

She and Ron always began planning next year's show as soon as the previous one ended. But this year, there was a difference: After they got some sleep, they started kicking around the idea of christening the show with a new name—something snazzy that would lure the curious and match the show's attendance with its organizers' ambition. If they could market this thing right, she reasoned, more people would see it. And maybe they would see it the way she did. Driving to her job at the hospital, she listened to cassettes impersonators had sent. And she brainstormed, and she gave herself permission to dream. She had a lot of ideas, but she liked her first choice best. It was "The Illusion of Elvis."

On August 4, about two weeks after the convention and seven days before he sang in Memphis to mark the seventeenth anniversary of Elvis's death, Steve Chuke bought the stereo that was once in the den at Graceland. When he returned from Las Vegas and his meeting with Mike McGregor, he tore through his store, looking for the papers the woman had left him as proof that the stereo had once belonged to Elvis. When he found her phone number, he called her right up. He wanted to ask her a couple of test questions.

McGregor had told him in Las Vegas there should be holes on the underside of the hi-fi. He had removed the original legs to make the stereo fit in his trailer on the Graceland grounds. And if the stereo was authentic Steve would see a deep nick on the right side because McGregor had bumped it when he carried it through his door. The woman checked and reported to Steve that there was one big nick and a lot of small holes. Steve told her to haul the thing up to Fort Thomas. If he didn't buy it, he would pay her $100 for her time.

She brought up the stereo in a pickup truck. It was in great shape. The speakers had shiny tan-and-bronze webbed covers. The walnut, except for a few faded spots, still looked warm. On the arm of the stereo curled a feather in gold. The turntable had four speeds, from fifteen to seventy-eight. Steve crawled beneath it and peered at the stereo's underbelly: Four holes in front, just like Mike McGregor said. The nick was there, too. Steve handed the woman $1,000—the price they'd agreed on—and he gave her a ring from his store worth about $500. McGregor had sold the stereo two years after Elvis died for $1,000—a fair return on his $125 investment.

Steve waited until the woman's truck pulled out of sight. Then he jumped straight into the air and hollered. He ran inside and spent some time with the stereo, just looking at it. Owning it made Steve feel the way he did the first time he slid behind the wheel of a Corvette and looked out at the road stretching ahead. The world held possibilities for him. He could go places. This link to Elvis and his music reminded him of who he was and who he wanted to be. It didn't fit in with the furniture in his sitting room, all those antiques. In a way that made sense.

He tuned the radio to his favorite oldies station, the one that sponsored his impersonator shows. He forgot the first song the speakers sent out. But after all these years, the stereo still sounded good.

Steve called McGregor some time later and asked him what he thought the stereo might be worth. "Thousands and thousands," he said. And it wouldn't have surprised McGregor if someone would fork over that much, just because Elvis had owned it. He never could see it himself. Now if someone ever offered to sell him a gun like the ones that John Wayne owned—good and old with worn ivory grips—that would blow his mind. And if someone had wanted to sell him a gun John Wayne had actually owned, you bet he would have been excited. After all, John Wayne was his hero.

Memphis

9

Images of Elvis

*E*very year, tens of thousands of men and women come to Memphis, as so many did for three days in August 1977, to remember Elvis Presley. About 30,000 of the 700,000 people who visit Graceland every year come during the seven-day stretch known as Elvis Week. About 10,000 gather at Graceland every year on August 15, the eve of Elvis's death, for the candlelight vigil. They cradle single white tapers stuck into plastic cups and two-liter soda bottles sawed in half and they file past the graves of Elvis and those of his closest relatives in his old refuge, the Meditation Garden. His final resting place lies separated by a fountain and a sidewalk from his kidney-shaped swimming pool. During that week in August, people meet to relive a time when Elvis lived along with their dream, and to lean on each other for solace.

Of course, no one wants to mourn forever, especially when they are on vacation. Imagine a town filled with 30,000 perpetually mournful tourists every August—and to a lesser extent, during the birthday celebration around January 8—and it becomes easy to see why Memphis tries to talk folks into having some fun. So the days before and after the anniversary of Elvis Presley's death have evolved into a celebration of sorts. Widely known as Elvis Week, the city and Elvis Presley Enterprises, the organization that runs Graceland, offer enough activities to distract visitors from the fact that the basis for the occasion is that somebody died. Graceland sponsors a number of happy attractions—reunion concerts starring Elvis's backup singers and band members, chats at Humes

Junior High School with people who knew Elvis, a bus trip to his tiny Tupelo birthplace, a breakfast for the presidents of Elvis fan clubs worldwide. Beyond that there is a moonlight cruise on the Mississippi, a laser concert tribute at the Pink Palace Museum and the Elvis Presley International 5K Run.

For people who love impersonators, there are no sanctioned activities. Elvis Presley Enterprises, the company that runs Graceland and oversees the Elvis empire, does not officially recognize impersonators. But the estate also respects the concept of people exercising their First Amendment right to imitate a rock and roll singer. This explains why so many people decked out in jumpsuits freely roam the highway in front of Elvis's house.

But even more than Graceland, the hottest spot in town for impersonators and their followers is Images of Elvis, Inc. It is probably the best-known Elvis impersonator contest in the world. Since 1987, impersonators have traveled there to honor Elvis while trying to make a name for themselves. To some Elvis fans, the contest has become an annual pilgrimage—a way to remember Elvis's life and reclaim a piece of their own.

Carol Rice met Elvis Presley when she was sixteen. It happened just as Elvis became famous beyond Memphis, that time in the mid-fifties when girls began pulling their hair and screaming over a young man who, like Carol, had spent much of his childhood in Memphis. Her parents had many friends and a reputation in town as music fans, which was why the man who managed the Ellis Auditorium called Carol's mother one day with a proposition. He knew the whole family loved music—Carol's brother Aubrey had even jammed with Elvis in a band—and, more to the point, included young daughters. So the manager suggested that if the girls wanted to meet Elvis, they could come to that auditorium that night. Elvis would be attending the gospel show—not to sing, just to sit backstage and listen. He had already reached the point in his life where sitting in an audience had ceased to be safe. "He will definitely be here tonight," the manager told her mother. "I've already seen the pink Cadillac."

They saw the Cadillac themselves when they entered the auditorium that night. And, when they were led through the stage curtain, backstage and into a little room in back that contained an old desk and a chair behind it, they saw a quiet young man sitting alone. "Elvis was sitting in a chair, with his feet on the table," Carol recalled. "Just kind of fooling with his nails—just kind of doing nothing, really, just biding his time, I guess. And I couldn't believe it! I thought, *My God, this is the man! I can't stand here and scream!* I just went into shock. I mean, just literally. My mouth was open, nothing would come out. And only years later did I realize, hey, I was in a position that just millions of girls would have liked to be in."

Luckily for Carol, her sisters Joan and Juanita, and her nine-year-old brother, Gary, their mother had no difficulty speaking. She introduced them and made small talk while her children gawked at the famous young man. He shook each of their hands—"And you're Carol," he said when her turn came—and her skin went cold, he thrilled her so. But even through her nerves she noticed that Elvis acted as shy as she felt. He stuttered some, and he hesitated before everything he said. He acted braver with little Gary. Said he was a fine-looking boy, rubbed the burr of his white-blond flattop. Afterward Gary's hair smelled so sweet that his sisters teased him that they wouldn't ever let him wash it again.

Carol had seen Elvis perform long before she met him. She watched him shaking on stage, wearing wide-legged black pants, a pink shirt and black-and-white shoes, hair flying everywhere, his complexion looking bad and her mother saying, "That's the boy that Aubrey was talking about." And Carol couldn't look away. "It was like an electrifying thing," she said. "It was like, hey, I don't have to decide do I like this guy, or not like him. He's different, so I'm gonna watch him."

But that is not what she remembers most about Elvis, or what makes her cry a little just thinking of him. Something else stayed on her mind all these years. It was the way he treated her family as if they mattered to him, as if they were doing him a favor by stopping by.

"His manners are the strongest thing I remember from that day," she said. "Because when we walked in, he had his feet up on that desk, not knowing a soul was around, I guess. When he saw us, he threw those feet down. He said, 'I beg your pardon, ma'am.' He's apologizing for being in that position! And we're total strangers! I thought, How many men would do that?"

About forty years later, Carol Rice, by then married and known as Carol Henry, met Cookie Mignogno in the ladies' room at a nightclub called Bad Bob's Vapors. Both women had dropped in on the second annual Images of Elvis impersonator contest. Carol looked behind her and noticed a petite woman with high cheekbones and elegant upswept hair, tugging on the bra that buttressed her strapless dress. Carol was struck by how attractive the woman was. Cookie had red hair, or sometimes blond, an aquiline nose and eyes that turn green or blue depending on what she wears. She called to mind an exotic tropical bird.

"Well, honey," Carol drawled, "I gave up on bras a long time ago with these cocktail dresses. I just try to just get the dress to fit."

Cookie took in Carol and her eyes locked on Carol's two most noticeable features: her platinum blond hair and her ample, generous, wondrous chest. "The Bible says that men are created equal," Cookie shot back. "Well, we know that's a lie. We sure as hell know women aren't created equal, from what I'm looking at. My God! There oughta be a law against those things!"

Something about the way she said it, this compact elegant creature, made Carol laugh so that her white teeth flashed against her tan. She teased her right back: "My God, though, what I wouldn't give to have your little bitty figure. It takes me fifteen minutes to get into my pantyhose."

"Oh, my God," Cookie said, "if you got boobs like that, who cares?"

And just like that, they walked out of the restroom friends. They rejoined the action and realized they were practically sitting next to each other. They chatted so much—Cookie in her husky alto, Carol in her sweet drawl—that Carol's husband Dwight finally said, "Why don't we just trade places so you two can talk?" In the early morning after the show, they went to breakfast. Later that day they went shopping. Cookie, being from Willow Grove, Pennsylvania, loved knowing someone who knew Memphis. Carol loved meeting someone who lived so far away. And they rejoiced to find they agreed on just about everything. They both loved flashy clothes. They both had suffered when Elvis died, and they still missed him deeply.

At home their lives followed the same routine, though on different schedules. Monday through Friday, Carol did the same thing: Worked from 8:00 A.M. to 5:00 P.M. as a secretary for a company called Buckeye Cellulose. Headed home, where her dogs nipped at her feet. Pulled together some dinner. Fell into bed. Rarely drank. Seldom socialized.

Cookie's real first name was Joyce, but her father gave her the nickname because she couldn't keep her hand out of the cookie jar. She kept it because, as she reasoned, nobody remembers a girl named Joyce. She started her working life at sixteen, as a salesgirl. She tried being a telephone operator, then a waitress, but she hated carrying the heavy trays. So she became a bartender. She preferred tending bar in hotels, but the older a woman got the harder it became to compete with the young girls managers consider a natural draw. No matter where she was, the work was tough.

"People think you just go in there and just make their drinks and pick up the money and run," she said. "They don't believe I have to carry cases of beer from one room around the corner over to the bar. And refill the beer cases every night. My nails are always messed up because of the glasses, the detergent and the sanitizer you have to put on to scrub the glasses and everything. It's a tough job. It's nothing like people think it is."

Most mornings she got home around 3:00 or 4:00. She often spent her days converting her bedroom into a small museum of the singer she'd loved since she was a girl. She had hung photos of Elvis, including one six-by-four-foot picture of Elvis in the Aloha concert framed in white wood, and dolls that play Elvis songs when you snap a cassette into their backs. She named her Sheltie puppy Elvis Charro Flaming Star, after two of his movies. Her husband tolerates these pursuits the best he can.

"I came home and I dropped the little puppy, it was only like *this big.* He was sleeping on the couch and I plopped him on his chest and I says, 'Hey, Daddy!'—that's what I call him all the time—'meet Elvis!' Woke him out of a sound sleep—like, what, is she going nuts? And then he spots the puppy. For the longest time, he wouldn't even call him by his first name. He must just have felt funny, I don't know what it was."

It wasn't that Cookie and Carol didn't love their husbands or their lives because they felt this need to flee to the contest. But they wanted something more. To find one thing in your life that stirs your passion and gives you something to look forward to is rare. To meet someone from a thousand miles away who understands how you feel is rarer still. And to remind yourself, while you answer three phone calls at once or mess up your manicure scrubbing lipstick off beer glasses, that you get to repeat the whole thing next year and the year after that—that is a small, priceless kind of heaven.

They sat together at the same front table off the right side of the stage every year, paying $100 each ahead of time for the privilege. In the winter they sent cards and talked on the phone, with Cookie making Carol laugh by moaning about how cold it was in Pennsylvania and how she was freezing off strategic pieces of her body. And they looked forward to August and planned what they were going to wear. Carol said, "We girls have a running joke. We call ourselves the members of the Sluts R Us Club. Our theory being, hey, if you can't be a slut, you can at least dress and act like one, you know? But at first, our husbands didn't buy into that thought too much. But then they've realized that hey, this is something the girls do enjoy and there's nothing wrong with it, other than the late hours."

They survived on about two hours sleep a night and what Carol calls a strange kind of high. All that Elvis acted as a kind of stimulant. She told her sister, Joan, another contest regular, "My goodness! These people must be on something!" Then it occurred to her that those people could be thinking the same thing about them.

Carol and Cookie had refined the art of impersonator watching. They sat at their round table with their chairs turned backward to face the stage; Carol positioned herself to Cookie's left. They crossed their legs and studied the acts, Carol with an amused look on her face, Cookie with her chin tilted up, both women singing along softly. When an especially handsome man would take the stage, they traded sly glances. When an impersonator sang a song that had deep personal meaning for Cookie, like "American Trilogy," "How Great Thou Art," "It's Midnight and I Miss You," or "My Way," her eyes misted and she dropped her chin just a little. She pretended to fiddle with her camera. "Oh, boy, I'm gonna smear my makeup," she would say, dabbing at her eyes with her fingertips.

"Certain songs just hit me," she explained, "and I start crying. I just— I miss him, I really do after all these years. I just wish I could go to a concert and see him again, you know? And it's never gonna happen."

"I think that's what makes it so wonderful, is even though you have some of the impersonators that are just god-awful up to those you think, hey, my goodness, why aren't they in Vegas or somewhere," Carol said. "I think the love that you feel from all the fans that are there—it's a uniting thing, I guess is the way I would describe it. It's like we're all there for the same purpose, because we just loved Elvis. And I know there are kooks around who think that he's still alive, but this really doesn't fit into the mode of the group that seems to be there. And it's kinda neat that most all the impersonators make it very clear in the beginning that, hey, I'm not Elvis. I'm just someone who enjoyed his music, and hopefully will keep his memory alive. I think it's just a wonderful thing. I don't know if I'll ever tire of it, and I hope that they don't stop having it."

In a city in which every kind of person claims all kinds of connections to Elvis, it is only right and possibly inevitable that the idea for the Images of Elvis impersonator contest sprung from the mind of his former veterinarian. Dr. E. O. Franklin, known to most folks as Ed or Doc, cared for Elvis's horses both at Graceland and at the Flying Circle G Ranch in northern Mississippi. He now runs the DeSoto County Animal Clinic in Southaven, Mississippi.

Franklin also operated nightclubs. One of them was called Bad Bob's Vapors on Brooks Road, the place he first divined a future in encouraging the imitators of his most famous veterinary client. "Of course, all of the Graceland people and all the entertainers who came to town were always looking for something to do at night, so they started coming in there," he said. "Elvis impersonators started coming in. I started messing with Elvis impersonators about nineteen-seventy."

On August 16, 1977, Jerry Lee Lewis sang at Bad Bob's Vapors. Willie Nelson, whose concert Mike McGregor had driven from Oxford to see earlier that night, showed up, too. And so did the fans, looking for comfort and, just maybe, something to remind them of Elvis. The impersonators did that. "Thirty days later, the fans are still coming," Franklin said of that time. "Ninety days—well, you know this isn't going to die."

He began hosting tributes during Elvis Week. In 1981, he started awarding prizes, though still nothing formal. But Franklin, who had long prided himself on his promotional skills, had for years been planning a full-scale impersonator contest for August 1987 that would commemorate the tenth anniversary of Elvis's death.

He suspected some would be skeptical, and he had a ready answer: "Of course, you've got some people who'll say, 'Oh, I won't enter a contest.' Well, my answer to that always is, 'Well, what's the first thing you ever heard of Elvis Presley as far as music goes?' And the answer is he won a contest at a fair in Tupelo, Mississippi. The next time he appeared he won a talent contest at Humes High School in Memphis." One of these early skeptics was his wife, Jackie. She is the kind of person who never dresses up for Halloween because it makes her feel creepy. Her first reaction to Franklin's idea was fast and heartfelt: She told him it was tacky.

Jackie, an energetic woman with reddish-brown hair and a wide smile, could boast her own connections to Elvis. Growing up just over the Mississippi border, she and her girlfriends would drive into Memphis, pull into Graceland's driveway, steal stones, and squeal away like they had pulled off something big. One of her cousins married one of Elvis's cousins. Their sons Arthur and Brandon had served as stable boys at Graceland. The notion of a contest struck her as foolish. She never heard of anyone wanting to be the best at being somebody else, and she wasn't sure she wanted to meet anyone who would. "I couldn't believe anyone would actually want to enter it," she said. "I couldn't believe people would come to see it."

They would and they did, until finally even Jackie began to consider the contest a community service and its participants her friends. She could laugh about her early reservations, eyes shining behind big round glasses. "I had this stereotyped image of an Elvis impersonator, I guess, at first," she said. "But now I've seen so many different people, in all walks of life and professions and economic levels that are into it. So there is no typical Elvis impersonator or Elvis fan."

The sincerity of the impersonators impressed her most, along with the devotion of their families and their fans. The fact they all loved Elvis so much fascinated her. "I don't think that there's been any celebrity or monarch or holy person or anything that has received this type of adulation after death," she said. "Not even the saints. I think there is a fan-like devotion, and these people are fans. But I think the thing that keeps drawing them is that there are so many other people, and it's part of a culture. You make so many friends. They draw each other, as well as the attraction to Graceland—I think the attraction is that there are all these other people there that share your interests."

Anyone who pays the $25 entry fee may enter the contest. "At first we were going to try to screen," Jackie explained, "but from the tapes we get, you really can't tell. And we found out that for so many people, just to perform is like a dream come true to them. There's no way I can say, 'No, you're not good enough.'"

The first several years the Franklins held the contest at the club regulars called either Bad Bob's or the Vapors. It squatted on Brooks Road across from a Ramada Inn in a part of town not known for its wholesome character. The old sign out front, its flashing panels yellow with age, quaintly proclaimed Bad Bob's a "supper club" and promised dancing, steaks, and seafood. The building itself was old and the plumbing vindictive, but the club held more than a thousand people—a crucial point, especially during the finals. It contained a room with pool tables and lots of nooks where people sat at tables with red-and-white table-cloths and watched the Elvises skitter across the hardwood dance floor, red globe lights on the ceiling tracing rainbows across their blue-black heads.

Even now contest veterans speak of Bad Bob's and those early years with fondness and nostalgia. "It was really great," recalled Robert Lopez, better known as El Vez, the Mexican Elvis. "Because from three in the afternoon to three at night, you could see a different Elvis every twenty minutes. And it would be Elvises from Tallahassee, Florida, to Bombay, Kansas, coming out of the woodwork. Lots of them had never performed before. And it was a really great rite of passage for lots of them because it was like human psychodramas on stage, these people who had never performed, had no sense of timing, and had no ability to perform, but would just do this out of their love for Elvis. And they'd be terrible as they could be, or stuttering on stage or leaving the stage crying. But you were watching their devotion in action.

"They didn't have the real jumpsuit and that was great—they'd just make a belt out of paper clips. Or they'd paint silver dots on their pants. And it was really nice, just because it was real heartfelt—you know, 'I don't know what I'm doing and I'm nervous as hell, and you can tell, but I'm gonna go up there and do this for Elvis.' It was really sweet. And then there were big egomaniac professionals, strutting in there in their jumpsuits, and big tall guys and stuff like that. It was like a real human parade of Elvis devotees, all the different types."

In 1990, a British documentary team visited the contest to tape segments for a program called "Viva Elvis." The show included an interview with Butch Polston—with more hair, he would later point out wryly—explaining the origins of the Burning Love jumpsuit; El Vez showing off the roll of toilet paper he stole from Graceland; and a boy named Bruno with a pompadour as tall as his head, at four the youngest Elvis impersonator in the world. Don Sims, a friendly, thick-waisted fellow from Mount Olive, Illinois, wore his Dragon jumpsuit and requested during his rendition of "American Trilogy" that the audience please observe a moment of silence in Elvis's memory.

In another scene Sims told an interviewer, "I don't think there's any competition, really." He sought out some off-camera colleagues for support. "Is there, guys? No competition. We're just here as entertainers and having a good time. That's what it's all about."

In some respects, that was true. But what it came down to was that the impersonator with the most points wins—and for one year, for what it was worth, could proclaim himself the world's top Elvis impersonator. And that was where things got complicated.

The rules, at least, were simple: The impersonators performed in semifinal rounds for nearly a week. On the last night of semifinals, twenty-four Elvises would be chosen to perform in the finals. Throughout the competition an unnamed panel of judges—said to be Memphis citizens or prominent visitors with no link to Elvis or to any particular impersonator—each received a packet of forms upon which to record their results. They were instructed to rate the impersonators on four separate qualities: 50 percent for vocal ability, 15 percent each for appearance and audience appeal, and 20 percent for stage presence. "There's been some up there that really don't look that much like him," said Karon Armstrong, a veteran judge, "but they move the eye or they move the lip, or they cock that head or they shake that knee."

The top three winners received a prize and something even more craved and coveted: attention. After all, winning usually means exposure, and exposure may mean fame, and fame just might mean acceptance. Some top finishers do return to obscurity. "A lot of people that don't even make it to the finals, though, get a lot of exposure," Jackie Franklin said. "Just to be in the contest—I mean, not that we're doing some great thing—but it's a good opportunity for somebody to be seen by a lot of people. Because most of these people are not from Memphis, they're from somewhere else. And they travel distances to see these Elvis impersonators. And a lot of them, I think, have become known to the fans from being in the contest here. Plus a newspaper will pick up the story on them, or somebody will do an article or a human interest story. That's exposure that they wouldn't have gotten. Everybody gets something out of it."

Doc Franklin liked to point to past winners who prospered after winning the contest. Kevin Mills, the pizza-shop owner from New Jersey who won in 1990, played cruise ships and other gigs for Legends in Concert. Doug Church, who took first prize in 1991, also graduated to Legends. Michael Hoover was visiting Los Angeles for a jumpsuit fitting soon after his 1988 victory and ducked into a deli across from the MGM Studios. Roseanne noticed him and broke into "Suspicious Minds."

Eventually they got to talking, and he wound up not only singing at her fortieth birthday party, but also appearing on her television show. "You get more recognition," Hoover said, "and you do get more bookings. And," he added, laughing, "you can ask for more money."

For Mike Albert, an auctioneer from Columbus, Ohio, a segment on a tabloid television show launched him into a second career as an Elvis, and he didn't even win first place. He performed in auditoriums with the Jordanaires, put on his jumpsuit and pompadour on camera for a television show called "Elvis U.S.A." and, for a while, retained a manager who drove a car with a giant chicken head mounted on the roof. " 'A Current Affair' picked up on him before the finals were even announced. They liked him," Jackie said. "So it didn't matter whether he won or not that year. He'd already had that. He'd won the biggest prize. Nobody else had anything that good."

One of the biggest success stories connected with the contest is that of El Vez. Robert Lopez, a Mexican-American who grew up in Chula Vista, California, never even learned Spanish until he was in high school. But he had an instinct for marketing. He had played in punk bands like the Boneheads. And he curated an art gallery where, while planning a promotion starring impersonators, he got the idea to translate Elvis Presley's appeal into Spanish. In 1989, the contest gave him his start.

"My original plan was I was gonna get a boom box and perform for people waiting in line at Graceland," he said. "But somebody had given me a number, so I conned my way in and said, 'Oh, I'm booking for Robert Lopez, booking for El Vez, the Mexican Elvis.' And they said, 'Oh, yeah, we've heard of him!' Which was a lie, because he had never existed before."

He handed out flyers before his performance with the help of some German rockabilly kids he met near Graceland, then went to Bad Bob's dressed in gold lamé pants and a matching sombrero and a jacket with "ELVIS" written across the back. He debuted his songs "Está Bien Mamacita," "You Ain't Nothin' but a Chihuahua," and "Huaraches Azul."

"It was really funny, because I just rewrote some of the words on the plane, and then practiced dancing in the hotel room," he said. "Just by fluke, it worked, and people liked it. And by the time I got home from that trip it was in the *Los Angeles Times,* and it just kind of snowballed and backfired and here I am, on my sixth album, on my umpteenth tour—I leave for Europe on Monday, and it's my life, and I'm a happy guy." He has toured the world with a six-piece band, including his backup singers the Elvettes, Lisa Maria and Priscillita. As of 1996, he had released six albums—the most recent called *G.I. Ay, Ay, Blues*—and was planning three tours of Europe. What started out as a joke ended up paying the bills.

This is the kind of story some fans of the contest like to mention, a success that sprang from a contest that grew out of tragic circumstance. If all stories of the contest ended this happily, perhaps the view of it would all be positive. But it doesn't work that way. The rules of the contest may be simple, but the people these rules are applied to are not. How could anyone who dresses up like Elvis Presley ever settle for being simple? This is where rivalries and heartache begin. Because for a contest that hinges on illusion, the hope it inspires, and the anger it triggers, are real.

Many impersonators refuse to compete because they say the whole concept of choosing the best impersonator is a dubious science. "Who is to judge, to say that you're better than so-and-so or vice versa?" asked Jerome Marion, who quit contests because he found them too political. "There is nothing. And then all it does is put the bad blood in your mouth. It makes you think bad about the next guy—and why? Because this guy can beat you and you had four judges up there that don't know their rear end from . . . you know? First of all, they're going, 'Who's Elvis?' And then, 'Oh, yeah, we're supposed to judge this guy?' And they're judging in categories like originality? How can you have originality when you're performing somebody else?"

Another problem with the contest is, of course, that for every winner, there are losers. And for every loser, there are plenty of people in the audience who wonder why their favorite Elvis didn't rate. Although everyone agrees on their passionate, lasting love for Elvis, the ideal human form this love should take provokes wild debate.

People develop theories about who wins and why. One popular story: Whoever places second one year finishes first the next. This has often not proved true. Mike Albert finished second and didn't return for years because his career zoomed. Ronny Craig tied for second in 1993 with Steve Chappell, but never placed again. Robert Washington, the only black Elvis impersonator ever to finish in the top three, placed second in 1992, behind Japanese impersonator Mori Yasumasa. The next year he didn't place at all—a verdict that so angered him that he would boycott 1994, Dennis's first year at the contest. "My performing was OK," Washington said later. "I'm never completely satisfied with one of my shows. If I get a copy of the video, I'll nitpick it, critique it to death—I could have done *that*, I could have done *that*. But ninety-three, it was politics, I'll put it that way."

Others agreed. In dark corners by the back bar, in front of the mirror in the women's room, at all-night diners serving steak and egg breakfasts, around hotel pools—people mumbled their suspicions.

"That whole thing over there at Doc's is a propaganda game anyway," said Fred Wolfe, who dyed his hair black after his first visit to the contest. "It's not really based on talent or looks or any of the above. You can't judge everything by what you see, and that man and his little contest, quote-unquote. Not much of a contest—you can't see any of the scores or anything. So it's kind of a crock. I accept it as being a crock. So I just go along with the flow and don't bitch about it too much."

When Denese Dody, a manager of around fifty Elvis impersonators, took impersonators to the contests, she told them to hold no hope of winning. "We're going there to have fun," she said. "Don't worry about trying to get into the finals. Don't worry about winning the contest. But just go have fun. It's a learning experience, a learning tool for them. And they can meet a whole bunch of neat guys down here, pick up a lot of hints, a lot of information, by watching, listening to guys, the experience that some of these guys have gone through. I mean, they can pick up on moves, they can pick up on how they get the sound. For some reason, it's easier for them to copy so-and-so's voice and what he does with his voice as opposed to Elvis. I don't why."

"I did it one year," said Tony Grova. "And to make a long story short, I think it was the second year that they held it. I was in the club, and they were forcing me to get up and sing, and so I went up and sang. I sang a few songs, then I sang 'Hurt' and then that was it. Next thing you know, my parents are sending me my jumpsuit overnight express, and I go through the whole contest, make the finals, everything. I was one of the top finals—and I didn't even place in the top four. I even have it on video. The people went nuts. So I just never really got involved in contests anymore—because they don't prove nothing!" He snorted. "Contest for what? There's only one Elvis!"

Even Shelley and Gail, who try to refrain from contest gossip, once sat next to a judges' table at Bad Bob's and watched them drink all night long. They wondered how accurately you could judge an Elvis if you were drunk. But ask people for proof—of someone approaching an impersonator with a deal, or overhearing some truly incriminating statement—and no one can point to a specific, definitive incident.

The contest organizers deny any wrongdoing. "Since I've been doing it, there hasn't been any politicking involved," said Karon Armstrong, a veteran judge and the one Jackie Franklin says she trusts most. "And I don't think there has ever been." Armstrong is a square-jawed blonde from West Memphis, Arkansas, who loves sprint car racing and Elvis. She explained her first name by rolling her eyes and saying, "My mother decided she wanted to spell it different." She was popular among the performers because she has tended bar for Doc and Jackie Franklin.

"I'm a people person and I love meeting the people," she said. "If the outside world could see these people and just realize how nice they are—all of them are so nice."

That was why arguments over cheating puzzled her. "I think they just get so bent on themselves that—I don't know." She screwed up her face; her forehead creased. "And it's not really what they mean it to be. It's just the fear or the scaredness or the competitiveness."

"I guess any kind of contest, really, has that kind of thing—that kind of cloud of suspicion—hanging over it," Jackie Franklin said. "We don't have any local boys. We don't have any personal or financial interest in any of the contestants." She shook her head, and her mouth pulled tight. "I don't know why anybody would think that we would throw it anyone's way. To us, it doesn't matter who the winner is, you know? We're going to give the prize to whoever wins." It already pains her, she said, to announce the winners as things exist now. It would only offend more people if she and Doc skewed the results.

"I feel bad, I really do," she said. "That's one reason why I didn't want to have a contest. I hate saying you're not good enough to be in the contest, you didn't make it, you're not quite good enough." Her voice went soft. "I don't like being like that. That's why I don't even like announcing the winners. I hate that! There's going to be twenty people mad then. Or hurt."

Cookie Mignogno judged the contest a couple of times at Bad Bob's and saw nothing that led her to believe the contest was rigged. A few friends of impersonators came up to the table and tried to sway her vote, but she said that didn't affect the scoring. "We marked each guy according to what we think, what his ability was or whatever," she said. "And then they're turned in. So we have no control of them once they're out of our hands. But I don't see where they would be rigged or anything in the back, whoever counts or tabulates everything and comes up with who's the winner."

One reason suspicions continued to flourish could be traced back to Doc Franklin himself. He annoyed some contest fans by being, in their view, too eager to make a buck. Impersonators complained about having to pay for glasses of ice water at Bad Bob's. Franklin also forbade video-taping of performers during shows so that a crew he hired could tape the entire show and sell the result. A video of one night's final performances, distinguished by odd camera moves and poor lighting, has sold for $45. Buying a videotape of just one performer's set cost $25. Franklin also allowed gaps of twenty minutes or more between sets. Before breaks he urged patrons to visit the bars or try some food from the kitchen.

In some cases, Franklin's way of doing business drove people away. "The guy kinda got kind of greedy," was how El Vez put it, "and was charging the guys to be in the contest, and not even letting people film their own performances. So he was making money off all these people. And then I started to play other clubs, and he goes, 'Oh, you can't—if you're playing other clubs, you can't play my club.' I was just like, I don't need this."

El Vez took his career on the road and away from Bad Bob's, though occasionally Robert Lopez returned just to watch and remember his beginnings. And every year other impersonators, even the ones who complain, still paid their $25 entry fee and took the stage. And the fans followed close behind. Hope always triumphs over suspicion, and a week of Elvis always wins out over staying home. Besides, they all reasoned, this could be the year that things go their way.

Carol Henry tried to ignore people criticizing Doc and Jackie. She preferred happier memories, like the times at Bad Bob's when Doc arranged to have someone walk her and Cookie to their car, or how nice he and Jackie were the nights they had dinner together. She, her sister Joan, and Cookie were regulars, and the Franklins respected that.

"I've told them that I'm not gonna question it," she said of suspicions that the contest was fixed. "Because I know even if it were—you know, there's always a possibility of anything, we've got to be broad minded enough to know that. But the point is, I know that they're not going to be able to say, 'OK, it's fixed.' So I'm not going put them in the position that they feel that they've got to say that to me. Because they're putting it on, I'm not. Maybe I'm wrong in my feeling, but I feel like, hey, if I don't want to go, I don't have to pay them. They didn't call and beg me to come. Of course, it is upsetting, when you think about the chance of it being fixed. But I try to go, and I know that the little group that I'm with, we've said, 'Hey, we're just gonna have a good time.' We're there to see the guys perform. That's it. Because if we're gonna spend our whole time saying, 'OK, I saw that, I saw Doc talking to that guy' and decide that it's fixed, we're just not going to enjoy it. It's gonna ruin the whole thing. So we've developed this thing that hey, I guess I really don't care."

Besides, now that she was older, she found herself asking bigger, more cosmic questions. As she sat and watched the impersonators, she wondered about life and death. She asked, "Elvis, up there, what do you think about this one?" And she could feel his love, as if he were looking down on her, on all of them. She really felt as if he were watching.

In 1994, she could have used a little divine inspiration. Jackie Franklin had asked Carol and her sister Joan to be judges, and they told her yes.

"He caught me as a unique individual, I guess," Ray Guillemette Jr. said of Doc Franklin. "In his own world. Initially, everybody's a good guy in my mind. And I really can't say anything too derogatory, obviously. I won his contest, so he can't be that bad. But he's got his own ways about him. Some that I don't necessarily agree with. But overall, all I can say is he gets his job done. People I've talked to, some are very pleased and there's some that are very dissatisfied, but all in all I think he accomplishes what he wants to accomplish. I mean, granted it's a very big and intense week, so there's a lot going on in his mind. But I'd do a few things differently, especially in respect to the performers. He's just—well, he's OK."

One success story people pointed to when they talked about the contest was Ray Guillemette Jr., a chef from Chicopee, Massachusetts, who won first place in the 1993 Images of Elvis contest. With no planning or formal preparation, the twenty-four-year-old entered the contest after hitching a ride to Memphis with a disc jockey he'd met just a week before and zoomed past the pack of veterans to take first place. To long-time contest watchers, Guillemette appeared out of nowhere. But in fact, his arrival had been years in coming.

From the time he was seven years old, Guillemette played with the idea of singing like Elvis. He remembers going to bed at 8:00 every night. But some nights, his mother would wake him at 11:00 or midnight and bring him downstairs in his pajamas to show him this dark-haired singer on TV in movies and documentaries. "So for a little kid to see this and to maybe put two and two together and figure, well, something must be up with this guy," he said. "Something must be special about him."

In time, something special happened to Ray. Elvis died when he was eight, and he began collecting magazines and records to remind him of his hero. When they no longer satisfied, he went to see impersonators. They made him feel deep emotions. Like hate. None reminded him of the Elvis he had been allowed to lose sleep over.

"What you started to see was a lot of people getting into the business of doing it because of the money," he said. "Some of them might initially had it from their heart, because they enjoyed it, but if they knew the material and they liked to do Elvis, they figured, I can make money at it as well. What happens now is too many of them have made a mockery of it. And too many of them made a mockery of it in the seventies. Because it was easy to take to get the punches in. You can continually see it, whether it's in the tabloids or whether it's on TV, or a commercial or it's a joke, you get Elvis and the jelly doughnuts, Elvis and some kind of thing tied in with food, the overweight, when in fact Elvis was overweight for maybe two years of his life."

Not that he ever imagined he could do Elvis better. In high school, people knew him as "the kid in the chess club." He attended the Culinary Institute of America in Hyde Park, New York, where he kept an Elvis poster in his dorm room, punked his hair into a pompadour circa 1956, and cheerfully answered to the nickname "Elvis." The hair made him look most like Elvis; he was shorter and stockier than Elvis, though he could mimic his facial expressions eerily well. Sometimes he would sing at karaoke bars, and people would approach and ask if he were a professional. His voice got their attention. It had that rasp that Elvis's did in the beginning, dangerous yet totally in control. And after spending his childhood watching Elvis on TV, he knew how to bounce one leg while sliding the other across the stage, taking in the crowd through the hair swooping loose across his forehead, wagging his head every time the women screamed. Which was often.

He graduated from the institute, after internships at the Opryland Hotel in Nashville and in a restaurant in New Orleans, and got work closer to home, in Springfield, cooking in mostly traditional Italian restaurants. This was not his first choice. "I kind of prefer the continental French style of cuisine," he said. He also fit in a little singing on the side. In early August, 1993, at a fiftieth birthday party where he appeared with Marilyn Monroe and Buddy Holly impersonators, he met a disc jockey who liked his style and clued him in on Images of Elvis. Knowing nothing about the contest, he drove down with the DJ and walked into Bad Bob's.

What he found was a lot of other guys with a dream that looked just like his and, in some cases, better. "I was rubbing shoulders with all the other boys in the business, and I had seen some of the outfits and the gear that they had," he said. "I just felt so out of place—like walking into a war with a water pistol. But I think what I had going for me was more so what was inside and what I felt and how I felt about it.

"It wasn't necessarily the outfit and things like that that won it for me—it was more so what I had inside, the drive, things like that. It makes it a lot easier to actually deal with, just going out buying a suit coat and throwing on some pants and making sure people know where you're coming from inside, more so than what you've got outside."

But when he performed, this kid with the dark swinging hair no one had ever heard of, something happened that people still talk about.

"That contest Ray won, he won it fair and square," said Tony Grova, who has since performed on double bills with him. "I mean, he should have won that contest. He's got him down, he has a certain look about him."

Gail said she and Shelley stepped out of the contest to take in another show and when they returned, someone told them, "You probably just missed the winner."

"It was Ray," Gail said. "And we were like, 'Ray Guillemette? Never heard of him.' So you just never know."

When Ray stepped off the stage during the finals, other impersonators came up and told him he had the thing won, until even he allowed himself to imagine he had a chance to be first. "I think it was a situation where they would have definitely had problems on their hands if it didn't happen that way," he said. "Only because I have never in my life felt such a rush from the audience. From the people. I think I would have been a very big job for them to suppress that idea and that feeling that was created those four days. I think there would have been a lot to answer for. But again, if it was the verdict that I was second, third, or didn't place, I was prepared for that. Because I went to just watch and learn."

Instead, he taught people that anyone could win the contest, as long as they fit the judges' idea of an exemplary Elvis. And he proved that anyone, with the proper talent and feeling, could totally reorder his own life by impersonating someone else.

He returned to Chicopee prepared to cook, but found instead that people were starved for his Elvis. His appointment book filled with months of gigs. When the restaurant he worked for changed owners, he took that as a sign to change careers. He left behind all his formal training, a respectable career, to become something he had despised as a child—a development that struck him as funny.

"I didn't think in any way that I'd be even doing it part time," he said. "I just enjoyed his music, listening to it. And I might have played around on the stage, doing the karaoke in clubs and stuff. But to ever think that I'd even be doing it for any kind of income was not in the works. Some guys have said, 'Oh, yeah, I wanted to do Elvis, and perform Elvis for so many years.' That wasn't any plan of mine. And of course, the big booster was Memphis, yeah."

At first, he felt many of the Elvises treated him with suspicion. The idea of this unknown streaking out of nowhere and changing the rules— oddly enough, the same thing the man they imitated had done—made them question who he really was. "I did get a lot of cold shoulders," he said. "In speaking with people years after, a lot of them had thought that I was paid to be there, that it was kind of a scam, kind of a setup. And I kind of took offense to that. But people have gotten a chance to know me, and realized that obviously that was a bunch of B.S."

Indeed, fans and performers liked and respected Ray Guillemette. Not only was he talented, he never bragged about the unlikely feat he had pulled off in Memphis. He volunteered his time to charity, especially at Christmas, giving out teddy bears and pink-and-black pencils emblazoned with the name of his show, A-Ray of Elvis. "Which fits in my name, as well as being a nice, very bright and inspirational type of title, you know?" he said.

He tried to keep things positive. Which is why, heading to Memphis for the 1994 contest, Ray felt he had a good business relationship with Doc Franklin, no matter what anyone else said. "Overall, I had a great time at his contest," he said before flying down to Memphis that year. "I won the contest he put on, so that makes me happy. And it changed my life, so he can't I guess all be that bad. He is out to make money, I'll tell you that. And he does it very successfully, and sometimes without concern for how he's getting it. Those are my general feelings about it. The money he gets and what he puts out really don't balance out too well."

Franklin spoke highly of Ray, both on stage and to whoever would listen. He had hired Ray to perform several shows during the contest as a returning champion. Ray had some other plans for his time in Memphis, but he doubted they would interfere with his commitment to Doc Franklin.

Dennis Stella, in the heat of his first Elvis summer, had taken up dancing alone. Less than three weeks separated the end of Las Vegas with the start of Memphis, and he had to get moving. So he cued "Patch It Up" and some other fast numbers and whirled, kicked, dipped, shook, and did whatever else the joints of a man who lifted weights five days a week would permit. His Las Vegas adventure had left him feeling more confident about his burgeoning Elvisness. But in a strange way, this confidence made Dennis feel less sure of himself. The more certain he became about his abilities, the more he realized how much he needed to learn. It was as if he were running a race and every time his chest edged up to touch the tape at the finish line, someone pulled it another length ahead.

Memphis, he hoped, would provide a second wind. He had called Doc Franklin a few weeks before Images of Elvis began to see if he could still enter—late, as always—and Franklin told Dennis he was more than welcome to come down and try his luck. Dennis took this welcome as a good sign. He had heard the same complaints about Doc and the contest everyone else had, but chose to wait and see for himself. Something about dressing up like Elvis had enhanced, among other things, his tolerance and sensitivity toward his fellow man.

Besides, he wanted to see how he fared against the big guys. Could he win? Probably not—Dennis knew enough about the competition to understand that. Could he place among the twenty-four finalists? He considered this possibility often in the time before Elvis Week. He could not match the skill or experience of many of the veterans; in no way could he equal movement or timing or even voice. But he had one thing that matched or even surpassed his ability: The feeling that he had as much right as anyone else to propel himself on stage, walk front and center, and feel in his heart that, at that moment, he was as good as he could get.

"I will be disappointed if I'm not picked," he said after he talked to

Franklin. "But I have to be realistic and understand it's not so much a matter that I stink, but maybe just there are guys that are better than me."

In the days between Vegas and Memphis, he watched the video Gail shot of his convention sets and—he couldn't help himself—the notorious set at Greene's West. With some distance from that wig-slipping night he could see and hear that he had potential. But he still couldn't believe how he came across. Stiff. Tense. And, funny as he looked, dead serious. He had to admit that if he took himself that seriously, he deserved it if everyone laughed. He had been asking himself what made him different from more successful impersonators. When he watched the videos it hit him: The other guys seemed to be having more fun. Somewhere along the way Dennis had confused looking serious with being taken seriously. He had been so set on preserving his own dignity and sense of self—not to mention his hair—that his Elvis never stood a chance. He needed desperately to perfect technical points—things like stage patter and controlling the band with a cut of his arm. But he had grown so obsessed with surfaces he had forgotten to enjoy himself. What was the point of walking around in a jumpsuit if you didn't plan to have a few laughs? Somewhere between the man he was and the impersonator he aspired to be waited a person he could live with. He had no choice. He had to loosen up.

So began Dennis's quest to flush out the fun guy inside —insurance salesman by day, dervish by night. Anyone who passed his house after sundown could have looked in and caught flashes of some goofy son of a gun funking out at full speed, stiff but still trying, unleashing lasso arms and crazy legs, wheeling past the windows, through the den, across the kitchen, all the way to Memphis, Tennessee.

10

Contest

𝒥n 1994, Images of Elvis took place at a low-slung club down the road from Bad Bob's Vapors called the Head-liner Club.

Doc and Jackie Franklin, wanting to get out of the nightclub busi-ness, sold Bad Bob's and shopped for a venue to rent that would hold up to a thousand people. Up the road, signs stating that Elvis had definitely left the building abounded. Now called the King's Club, the former Vapors was painted flamingo pink. Cutouts of scantily clad women vamped across its roof. The old regulars drove by and sighed.

If the Headliner Club was any indication, Doc and Jackie's search for a new venue had proved difficult. Headliner was known as Club Obsession when the contest first relocated there in 1993. In a former life it was a roller-skating rink. The building had a buzz-cut roof and a narrow parking lot. Inside was worse. Wheels and feet had flailed the wax off the hardwood floors. The walls were painted gray on the left and a bruised blue on the right, colors that only increased the feel-ing of closeness to one's fellow Elvis fan. Long fluorescent tubes sput-tered on the ceiling, which was covered with acoustical tiles—some bloated, some stained a strange aqua. In the center of the ceiling, a mirrored disco ball spattered chips of light. On the bruised walls hung fluorescent pink signs proclaiming this the site of the contest. The club had one saving grace: By contrast, dreams burned even more brightly in such a seedy place, like a flawless blue-white diamond in a setting of tin. The site embarrassed the Franklins, but they knew the man who owned it, and they could find nothing nicer that fit the contest's needs.

The contest opened on a Monday, exactly one week before the annual Elvis Week candlelight vigil. There were five nights of semifinals and two nights of finals, with bonus sets of past winners thrown in each night. A half hour before the show began, fans and the curious paid their admission and filed in to take seats at tables dressed with tablecloths of frothy pink. Closer to showtime, regulars made their entrance. The first two nights at Image of Elvis provided plenty of evidence that dreams take many shapes—and that any man or woman with $25 and a little nerve can pursue them.

Walking into the club for the first time gave the non-Elvis a clue about how impersonators must feel because at first, Elvises outnumbered spectators. Some of them needed help, and maybe salvation. Men and women wandered the room festooned with shredded-wheat sideburns. Their jumpsuits had puckered seams and yards of braided sequins. Their belts drooped with what looked like chunks of dog chain. The belts squeezed their midsections so tightly some of the men resembled water balloons. One impersonator wore a wig that called to mind a cheap cut of meat. Another conducted informal lectures about his art with a fat gob of blue toothpaste stuck to the front of his fifties-style shirt. Some came to laugh at these people, but veteran contest-goers ignored them out of courtesy, or at least kept their comments quiet. Gail admired these people for at least having the courage to get on stage after they had seen that this contest was serious business. "I often wonder," she said, "If you don't have anybody telling you, if you just kind of hear about it somehow, how would you know just how in-depth they are?"

Almost all of the impersonators made cracks about the less polished Elvises, but no one would begrudge their right to compete. "I can't say all of them, but I would think that most of the guys that do it are probably big Elvis fans," said Irv Cass from Niles, Michigan, a past winner at the South Bend Ramada. "And they do it whether they're the guy who plays on stage in Las Vegas or they're the guy who does the American Legion club and draws twenty people. Whether they look like him, or whether they look like Bozo the Clown, I'm sure that each and every one of them puts their heart into it. They really want to make somebody happy, they want to be up onstage, they want to try to bring back the memories—I'm sure of that."

Monday, August 8, was the first night of the contest. It had been slow, featuring mostly unknown performers. On Tuesday, the usual rhythm took hold. The souvenir stand was set up in back, near the admissions table. Commemorative buttons sold for $2. Fans—hot pink heavy paper on a thick wooden stick—were $1. T-shirts of the same color cost $8 and matching program books were $5. Business was brisk. Carol, her shiny dress reflecting light, and Cookie, her black leather dress accented with silver studs, arrived together and beat a fast sashay to their table—as always, front row to the right of the stage. Gail and Jenna, Chris, Kelly, and Shelley took a table on the right side of the room near the center. The singing began around 7:00. Waitresses squeezed between the tables, trays cocked over their shoulders, through tangles of cigarette smoke and heavy cologne. The night began with some of the more unseasoned performers. One guy with a black beehive sported a large blotch of sequins on his left leg that looked like a rash and, helpfully, the word "ELVIS" spelled out on the back of his jacket. When he tried to lunge during the slow bridge of "Suspicious Minds," he nearly fell over. Everybody clapped anyway.

One of the people applauding at a long banquet table in the middle was Terri Jayne, a police dispatcher, mother of one and part-time impersonator of Jayne Mansfield. A buxom woman, she wore a platinum wig, scarlet lipstick, and a black beauty mark penciled on the left side of her face. She sat at a table with her friend Edie Hartman, a woman from Ohio with a pixie cut and a gap between her front teeth. If the need arose, and it has, Terri could also do Marilyn Monroe or Mae West. She preferred Mansfield, however, because her research led her to believe that Mansfield was a genius, with hidden talents the world never cared to see. "She could act, she could sing, she could dance," she explained. "She could make Ann-Margret look sad dancing. She could do everything. One minute she could be—what they call it, they called in something in the fifties . . . trying to think of the word. I don't know, it's a word they use for risqué. She could be that, and she could be loving like a preacher's wife the next. It's just many sides to her and I like that. 'Cause I've done a lot of things. You know, I've done security, I've been a waitress—I've been everything in the world, just about, except the stuff I want to be, which is a movie star." She laughed. "And you know, I just felt like this is a way to express myself. It's sorta like a lot of these guys here. They don't really have an identity. They're just nobody. Until they get up there and everybody claps for them."

Which was the reason she did impersonations. "Attention," she said brightly. "I love being the center of attention. I always loved it." Yet in her act, she would go only so far. She strove for authenticity with dignity. "I don't make the noise. You know, she made a little noise, it was like *'uhh!'*" She let out a two-tone squeal. "Like that. And I hate that! I mean, I know I'm not stupid. I got an IQ too."

At thirty-two, Terri Jayne had been married three times—once to a high-school sweetheart, once to a guy who needed a green card and then to her current husband—a history that led her to conclude that she has lived roughly five lifetimes. She met her husband, Paul, a Memphis police officer, while he was doing security during ticket sales for a ZZ Top concert. She knew she liked him because she waited in line for two days for tickets, and she didn't even like ZZ Top.

Most of her Jayne jobs she did for free at hospitals and old-age homes, wearing gowns that set her back a month's pay. And every year she returned to Images of Elvis, because what the impersonators did reminded her of herself. "I don't make fun of Marilyn in my act," she said. "And I don't make fun of Jayne, either. So behind them is a kind of remembrance, instead of the way people were, instead of what their downfalls were." She nodded at the stage. "Get up there, they could be heavy, they could be thin, or they can wear a jumpsuit or not, people still support them."

As the performers sang, Terri Jayne shimmied her shoulders, but she never shook her chest.

Three tables over sat Shelley, Chris, and Kelly. They had just arrived, but already their table groaned with purses, cameras, cardboard baskets of french fries, and bottles of locally brewed Zima, official beverage sponsor of the Images of Elvis contest. They planned their year around coming to Memphis together. They would visit Graceland once or twice during the week, or maybe venture out for dinner, but spent most of their time lounging around the pool at their motel, drinking beer and Diet Sprite, munching chips and crackers with cheese, comparing their acrylic-nail manicures and making plans for the evening while the Memphis summer sun fried the sky white at the horizon. As they talked, Jenna bobbed in the pool and played with other kids whose parents had come down on vacation. They all looked forward to Elvis Week, and they loved the contest.

"Your first impression, a lot of the guys walk around like they're unapproachable," Chris said. "But once you start talking to them, they're just, you know, normal. They're fun people. You come to something like this, and everybody's here for the same reason. It's a great way to meet new people—you know, just get outta town."

"I don't think we've seen one plate from Tennessee," Kelly added. "One guy's from England here." Her eyes widened. "All the way from England to do this. You know, if you're lucky, if you're in your own city, maybe in three months you'll meet somebody that's from more than one state away."

"And every time you come to something like this, it's like a reunion all the time," Chris said. "You come to this, you'll always know somebody."

The annual ritual started with Shelley. She and Gail had always talked about taking trips together when they grew up. In 1990, she convinced Gail it would be fun to visit Memphis for Elvis Week. They drove down to find nearly all the hotels booked—they had no idea the week was so big—and the people they met raving about a contest at a nightclub called Bad Bob's. "We walked into Vapors," Shelley said, "and we're like, oh, my Lord—red lights, worn-down carpeting, and it was just awful. The ceiling was caving in places. It was like, what in the world is this?

"I look at us now, how we act when we get into a place—it's just like we sit back—you know, 'Hi, how are you doing' to all the guys. That first year we had our camera with every guy: 'Can I have my picture with you?'" She laughed. "We have pictures with every Elvis guy, I'm telling ya. Now we're just a little more cool about it."

A couple of years later, Gail and Shelley convinced their friends Chris and Kelly Hottinger to drive down. The four women became friends when all of them, between other jobs, worked for Gail's cleaning service. "It's weird that we should actually get together and be friends and work together," Shelley said. "We work together, we go out together. And we're so different, but we kinda watch out for each other."

Chris and Kelly behaved more like friends than mother and daughter, though the resemblance was easy to spot. They shared the same fair coloring, the same high cheekbones, the same dry sense of humor. Kelly worked as a secretary for a marketing firm. Both women have done housecleaning for a living, but during Elvis Week their hotel room always looked as if they unpacked their suitcases by opening them and tossing in a grenade. The only time they opened the door to hotel maids was to accept clean towels.

Shelley considered herself the shy one of the group. Being a kindergarten teacher, she handled herself well in loud, large groups, which made her the perfect contest regular. She sat up straight in her chair and took in everything, her face showing infinite patience.

"Gail's more outgoing. She'll talk to anybody," Shelley said. Gail believed she was shy, though she knew most people would laugh at that, mainly because she was the most visibly emotional member of the group. She was high-strung to start with, and having Dennis competing only made things worse.

"Kelly's kind of like the—I don't want to say it . . . the bitch," Shelley said, giggling. "She's got that look on her face, like a 'What do you want?' kind of deal." The women still joked about the time a guy flipped up Kelly's miniskirt while she was playing pinball in a bar. She grabbed him by the ear, slammed his head down on the machine and told him that, if he had any brains left, he wouldn't be doing that anymore. But she surprised her friends constantly with her softer side. On cleaning jobs Shelley has watched her work wearing headphones, softly dueting with Elvis. And sometimes on a job she talked to Jenna with such kindness and respect it would make Gail sigh with pleasure.

"Chris," Shelley said, "is just looking for fun." Chris, who was divorced and had two sons besides Kelly, was always ready for a party, and she served as the group's most vocal critic. After her role in the wig debacle, she got bolder with her suggestions. She had begun to forcefully advise Dennis about dancing, song selection, and especially hair. She prodded him to dump the fake stuff and dye his own.

The other women joined in, each in their own way. As veterans of the contest, they knew competition could turn rugged, and that Dennis's homely wig would only detract from his performance. Gail worried more than anyone. But by early August, buoyed by his time in Vegas, Dennis felt he had reached a point where he could stop apologizing for his act. He had received his first fan letters—only two, but still. And he decided that if he gave himself time, he would mature into a fine performer.

After Chris, Kelly, and Shelley settled in at their usual table that Tuesday night—about halfway back on the right side of the stage—Fred Wolfe sauntered over. Fred, the former rock singer and a recent college graduate, was thirty-one years old and lived with his parents and younger sister, Sonja, in Royal Oak, Michigan, outside Detroit. He wore tight, light-blue Levi's shorts, leather deck shoes, a lot of gold jewelry, and a pompadour the color of ink. Fred dropped into a chair and commenced one of his favorite contest pastimes—critiquing the other Elvises. "Let's face it," he liked to tell people, "most of these guys suck."

Gail and Dennis walked in a minute before 9:00 P.M. They stood in the doorway, searching the room to see who else had arrived. Gail wore a blue-and-white sundress, a white jacket, and white pumps. Dennis eyed his surroundings, hunched the shoulders of his cream-colored blazer and made a sour face. He had expected something classier. As he came to the table, his friends were watching the performers and making notations in a notebook, each using a different color marker. A star next to an impersonator's name meant he would make the finals. A check meant no way. A circle meant maybe. Dennis swung his Lambda Chi Alpha key ring onto the table. He seemed relaxed. On his way to the table he had met Doc Franklin, who'd told him he could sit in tonight to get the feel of the band. Dennis thought he had detected what he called "a half-phony smile" as Franklin took him in and told him it cost $25 to register. Still, he got good news. "Tomorrow night I can perform for real," he said. He took in the action, and he started to laugh. "You know what's hilarious? Two weeks ago, we just spent a weekend with a ton of Elvis performers, almost none of which are here. It's another ton of guys. Which just tells you how many Elvis guys there are throughout the country. There must be, what do you think? Three hundred? A lot of guys are in the closet, if you know what I mean."

Gail, sliding into the old routine, leaned over the tip sheet. "He has a good Elvis Head," she told Kelly, pointing at a guy on stage. Jenna got her mother's permission to run and play with some of the other kids. One of the Memphis impersonators, Joe Kent, had a son about Jenna's age named Sal she hung out with. Sal was an impersonator, too, with a mean hip shake.

"Do you guys like this place better than the old one?" Dennis asked his friends. "What was it called—Big Bad Bob's Vapors?" They shook their heads no.

"I'm not saying this is a great place, but I expected worse," he said.

"Wait till you go to the bathroom," Kelly said.

As always, talk turned to his wig. He told the women he had triple-checked everything before he left his house around 8:00 P.M. the night before. He acted out rifling his trunk for the black bag with the wig. "I kept going back like: It's in there. I didn't take it out. It's still there."

He pantomimed hugging the bag to his chest as he carried it up to the room at the La Quinta Motor Lodge on Airways Boulevard, where many contest regulars stayed. "I just kept having this feeling: What would they think of me if I did it again?" The women laughed. It was good to be back. Dennis put his foot on a chair and hiked up his black pant leg, exposing cow-print socks and a shiny pair of new black oxfords he had just bought at the mall down the road from Graceland. "My old shoes looked too brutal," he said. "I originally started looking at low-cost shoes and then I'm thinking, What am I doing? Buy a pair of shoes that I can wear for everyday, and spend a couple more dollars." He continued, however, to skimp on Elvis footwear. He was still wearing his second pair of thrift-store boots, the brown ones he had dyed black.

As the women gossiped about who else had showed, Dennis scanned the room. Onstage, somebody sang. In their seats women jiggled and jumped. And everywhere men sailed by with big hair, tight suits, and white boots slicked with fresh coats of polish. The man with the black beehive and the glitter rash pedaled past. "Please tell me my wig doesn't look like that," Dennis said. "If it does, I'll throw it away. I'll shoot it or something. I'll never put it on again."

Gail, Shelley, Chris, and Kelly smiled. No one said anything.

Fred Wolfe sat at a table in the back of the club. The room boiled over with guys wearing oily-looking jumpsuits and hair that looked like deep-pile carpet. He held a beer by the neck and checked out the parade of impersonators. He smirked when some of the more luckless specimens staggered past. He couldn't help himself. Which, he admitted, was part of his problem.

"What drives people into doing Elvis?" he said. "Is it because of peer pressure? I don't think so! Or is it a lack—they just don't have anything better to do? I mean, that's what I kind of get the impression! Wasn't anything better to do, so they wanna be Elvis. They figure that, well, any asshole can do Elvis. And you know, people like that bring my profession down. I try to present a professional thing here. And when I get people that are nonprofessional about it, that really irritates me. You know? It's like, if you're gonna do it, do it well! It's not like you can just fall off a chair and do it, or because you're big and fat, and maybe you can sing a little, you can sing Elvis. There's more to it than that."

There was more to Fred Wolfe than the fact that he did Elvis. Like the fact that he could not believe a guy like him did Elvis. And that he made too much money to stop. He performed 150 shows a year and earned up to $200 an hour. The money nicely supplemented the income from his regular job as an assistant manager at a supermarket.

And there was above all the fact that Fred Wolfe loved Elvis too much to even think about quitting. Even though he would give up Elvis and join another rock band in a minute. Even though people always, always made fun of his hair, a situation he compared to having a mammoth growth in the middle of his head, like the Elephant Man. Even though he hadn't enjoyed a serious relationship in years. If you spent some time with Fred Wolfe it became apparent that, no matter how much he criticized other impersonators, he always came down much harder on himself.

His mother got the idea of calling some people and telling them that her son sang like Elvis. Before he knew it, he was in the newspaper and printing up business cards decorated with a picture of the Graceland gates. Before that he played in a band called Warehouse 6 that took its name from the building where they rehearsed. "I didn't like it either, but I didn't have a choice," he said. "I was outvoted." If anything, Fred's performances were more subdued when he sang rock, despite the tightness of his leather pants. Though he often roamed the stage, he tended to stand in one spot and wail out the words as guitars snarled around him. But the biggest difference between singing Kiss and Robert Plant covers and impersonating Elvis was that he no longer dyed his hair blond, and that he used to score more women.

Fred talked about sex a lot. Performing, he liked to say, is like having sex with eight hundred people. He would also explain that some of those eight hundred people, many of them middle-aged women, would like to have sex with him just because he impersonated Elvis. He said this situation didn't bother him.

"Why should it?" he asked. He looked annoyed that the subject even came up. "As long as I'm making love to them, you think I'm thinking about where they are?"

He changed the subject then returned to it, saying he seldom slept with women who loved him for reminding them of Elvis. "But I only avoid it because most of the women don't live up to my standards. I mean, I love and appreciate women as much as I can. But I'm very selective with who I decide to be with. And it takes a lot for me to even want—I mean, it doesn't take a lot for me to want to have sex with a woman, but it takes a lot for me to actually do, you know, to actually do that."

"Do you ever feel like you're losing your identity?" I asked.

"I would have to say that I don't know if I ever had one," he said. He laughed, and when he did his upper lip peeled back into a sneer. "I've always sort of looked at myself as being a chameleon. Oh, yeah. I was in a rock and roll band. It wasn't really me. I mean, you know, it was me, maybe it was me more than I know. But you know, I've never really had my own solid personal identity thing. I'm just like an actor, I'm like a character actor. You know, I just happen to be portraying somebody else.

"I just happen to look like this. Like Bela Lugosi. He used to wear the Dracula cape in public even though he wasn't Dracula. You know, that Dracula thing ruined that guy. The guy was a Shakespearean actor. From Hungary. And he could never shed that image—of the devil, of the great vampire. And as a result, it destroyed him, eventually."

Available to all who entered was a copy of judging criteria, published under the letterhead of Dr. E. O. Franklin. "Decisions of the judges are final," the form said. Franklin loped through the crowd, sometimes hanging in the back to talk to a few of the guys, sometimes moving toward the front to hug one of his female regulars. He combed his receding hair straight back, and wore a red sport shirt, white pants, and tennis shoes to match. He took the mike after the first set and said that anywhere from twenty-one to twenty-four performers would make the finals. A final list would be released Saturday morning around 2:30 A.M. He announced a table-decorating contest. He introduced three flight attendants—"flighty girls," he called them—repeating their annual ritual of wearing home-sewn glitter capes decorated with Elvis's face. As each twenty-minute break began, he would deliver a long speech about how everyone should take a bus trip down to the casinos in Tunica, or how he moved his family to Mississippi where there was less crime, while Jackie stood at the edge of the stage, a grin on her face, ready to snatch back the mike. This routine was one of the more entertaining parts of the show.

The regular competition ended Tuesday night and the open-mike sessions began. If Carol were right and Elvis were watching, he might have excused himself at this point to get some fresh air. Fred slapped his hand to his forehead and cried, "How much more of this do I have to take?"

After a couple of hours, Dennis grew restless and hungry. As much as he loved Elvis, he couldn't sit and watch this stuff all night. Most of the impersonators say the same thing. He talked Gail and Shelley into driving over to Shoney's for a late-night dinner. The service was slow, but their mood was giddy with the novelty of being in Memphis together, sharing a personal stake in the contest. Dennis teased Gail that she would have to cook more, now that he had so many female fans willing to do it. Gail replied that she cooked for one man for five and a half years and she was now officially retired. Dennis made a face of mock horror and headed for the salad bar. They returned to the Headliner at 12:15 A.M. to find Chris and Kelly furious at Dennis—Don Sims, the band-leader, had been calling his name for fifteen minutes. He had been the next open-mike Elvis for half an hour.

Dennis sprinted to the front of the room, grabbed the microphone, turned to the band and said, "Take it down guys, take it down."

He launched into "Suspicious Minds." What crowd was left—about fifty people or so—applauded heartily. He sounded strong. He whipped his arms during the drum roll at the end, then lunged to finish. Then he swung into "The Wonder of You." Kelly tilted her head, closed her eyes, and sang with him. She wore her red sundress and hat to match, a red scarf tied just above the brim. Shelley beamed. Gail ran to a table in the front, balanced her right knee on a chair, and videotaped. It was allowed after hours.

After he finished, he told the table, "You guys, I realize there's some very good guys coming up, but I'll tell you what. It seems like they got quite a few guys in the finals."

"Yeah, twenty-four, he said," Chris said.

"Shit, if it's twenty-four—I mean, guys, there'd have to be a shitload of good guys coming in order for me not to make it."

"Really? Twenty-four guys?" Gail asked. She pondered this. "Maybe you'd better save the black suit, Dennis."

"And what I'd better do is take that wig and throw a blow dryer on it before I walk out so it doesn't have that slicked, matted look on my head."

"I think maybe you'd better just dye your hair and comb it down," Chris said. She was wearing a light blue satin jacket with the name of a Milwaukee bar, Blue Suede Shoes, on the back. The jacket gave off a cool light as she told him how things should be. It lent her an air of mystical authority. The women turned to see his reaction.

"Mmmm," Dennis said. If you looked closely, you could see his molars grinding.

11

Finals

*M*emphis went about life as usual during Elvis Week. The stores were filled with displays of back-to-school clothes. Tourists proved they had the blues by buying T-shirts at B. B. King's club on Beale Street. Cars sat panting with their hoods lifted along Interstate 240, radiators steaming in the ninety-degree heat. Yet among these routines, signs of Elvis Week sprung up all over town, like an overdressed relative at a lazy backyard party. In the *Commercial Appeal,* an entire section of want ads was devoted to pieces of Elvis history, fifty-nine in all. Along with editions of Memphis newspapers from August 16, 1977, collector's plates, and a blue vinyl issue of *Moody Blue,* someone wanted to unload a copy of the Humes High School yearbook from 1953, when Elvis graduated. Condition: excellent. Price: $2,000. One ad offered a silk wreath from Elvis's grave, documented, though it didn't say by who. A man asked $1,500 for an autographed receipt and a cigar stub with a pink holder that Presley left in an ashtray. A daughter of Dr. George Nichopoulos, Elvis's personal physician, offered to sell the TLC—short for Tender Loving Care—necklace Elvis gave her for $15,000. She told the *Commercial Appeal* she was motivated by the purchase of a new house and some unpaid bills. Another ad offered notes from Vernon Presley and Ginger Alden after Elvis's death and a bottle of limited edition Golden Series Elvis wine. *Expensive, must buy all, will not separate*, the ad said. *$60,000.*

Luckily, more reasonable pleasures beckoned. *Elvis World* magazine sponsored a breakfast at Shoney's. Humes High School on Manassas held $2 tours, and the third annual Memphis Mafia Reunion convened at Alfred's on Beale, $5 a head. At the Antenna Club, El Vez was set to perform as an ambassador for what local media respectfully called the "alternative scene." He was preceded at the Antenna by Disco Elvis, who performed such modified classics as "(Shafted) in the Ghetto," "Baby Let's Play Brick House," and "That's All Right Mutha." The longer Elvis Week went on, the more alternative the celebrations got.

Temperatures began hitting the mid-nineties during the day, and the sky took on the color of a Powder Blue jumpsuit. At the Headliner, life intensified. Impersonators blurred. On Wednesday, the third day, a stocky figure in a white jumpsuit strode, arms swinging, into the women's rest room, a gray-walled chamber with waterlogged rolls of paper towels on the floor and three stalls, one of them with no door. A loose-limbed blonde in a halter stopped and hesitated before entering. She pointed to the cape swishing around the corner.

"I don't think he . . ." she began.

"I think that's a she," I replied. "I think you're OK."

"Oh," she said, starting inside. "Thank you so much."

As the contest moved into its third day, emotions and behavior accelerated. It might have been tempting to say things got weird, but that would have shown a lack of imagination. Weird is what people call a thing when they don't want to take the time to figure it out. Besides, spend time in one room for one week with 100 or so Elvis impersonators, and who's to say what qualifies as normal? Where's the precedent for that?

Still, no one could deny that from Wednesday on, the proceedings assumed a degree of cheerful hysteria. Other than the usual excitement the regulars felt returning to the midst of all this activity and reuniting with friends, three factors affected the mood of the contest. The first was sleep—nobody got nearly enough of it. The contests, after open mike and a guest set from an alumnus like Michael Hoover, wouldn't end most nights until after 3:00 A.M. And there were always the early-morning breakfasts, karaoke sessions, or Tunica casino runs to consider. That meant the faithful witnessed at least six hours of sheer, unrelenting Elvisness—the second factor—in a single night. Then they returned the next night, after a few hours sleep, if they slept at all, and did it all again. Some nights, it was typical to hear "Polk Salad Annie" or "American Trilogy" five times or more.

The third and most important important factor was that from midweek on, the quality of the performers noticeably improved. You could see the women's heads pivot as they watched the latest arrivals pass their tables or lean over to say hello. Most dressed up more as the weekend neared; shorts gave way to sundresses, which in turn made way for cocktail numbers. One recent arrival sauntered past Gail's table early in the evening, his arms stiff and held away from the sides a bit, the way Elvis used to hold his, head turning from side to side, trailing a cloud of Eternity for Men. Around the room women sprang up with cameras and programs to sign, arms flung wide, shouting: "Irv!"

Irv Cass fell into impersonating Elvis the way a lot of the other guys did—just for fun. He entered the contest at the South Bend Ramada in 1992 and in a field of twenty finished fifth. This surprised him—he had brown hair, no sideburns, a big-sleeved shirt, and a pair of black pants he got at the Goodwill.

It surprised Dottie Skwiat, too, but more than anything it intrigued her. Dottie had channeled her love for Elvis into a career in impersonator management. Seven weeks before Elvis died, she had driven down to Indianapolis to see him perform at Market Square Arena, at what ended up being the last concert of his life.

"It gave me cold chills," she said. "It was absolutely unreal. It was like when my daughter was in the Miss Teen pageant, and when she got up on stage, and she started to do her modeling steps, I hid my head between my legs and didn't look until everybody around me said, 'Raise up, she's doing fantastic!' I said, 'I don't want to!'

"He was wearing a black jumpsuit, and I remember all the sweat, and I remember thinking, Oh, my God, he's working so hard, he's gonna pass out. And then I just bowed my head and sat there. I tell you, I missed half the performance. I was in total shock."

Dottie loved Elvis so much she found it easy to overlook what others may see as shortcomings or faults or, even, sometimes, the truth. "I still don't believe he's dead," she said, and then she laughed. "I guess I don't want to. I'm sure he is—I just don't want to believe it. And I think that's the way everybody else is that thinks he's still alive: They know he's dead, but they don't want to believe it."

Her devotion allowed no room for amateurs, and so she watched Irv's first Ramada performance with interest. Though his look needed work, he had a strong voice and that mysterious mix of friendly affection and unspoken sex appeal that makes a good Elvis. Dottie would soon part ways with her first client, Doug Church, so she was looking for new talent. People at her table cackled about Irv. They called him a pretty boy. Then the music started, and Dottie turned and said, "Everybody shut up. He can sing."

"You could be good if you practiced," she told him afterward. It took him three weeks to call and tell her he would give it a try. "You think I can really do it?" he asked her. It was the hair that made him hesitate. After all, few people saw anything wrong with him the way he was. He had done some modeling. He went to the gym. He liked himself. Most people viewed impersonators, he thought, the way some people looked at kids who joined the Army: They lacked sunnier prospects, so they had to go where someone would take them in. After some thought he decided he could stomach the pompadour. But sideburns scared him. "If it weren't for the sideburns," he said, "people wouldn't mess with you."

Dottie would not be moved. To her, if you didn't have the hair and the sideburns, you were an amateur. And her own long hair, framing a round face, was as black as she wanted Irv's to be. "You gotta take it serious," Dottie told him. He did. In about two years he averaged four shows a week and charged anywhere from $300 to $1,500. And he won practically every concert he entered.

His career choice was perhaps inevitable. As a child, he was a fair mimic—he did a mean Jerry Lewis—and he dreamed of being a movie star, of seeing his name on a Las Vegas marquee. He mastered about fifteen voices, but his Elvis came naturally. In time he forgot what his singing sounded like when he was not imitating him. "Let's put it this way," he said. "Once you start impersonating somebody, it's hard to find what your real voice is."

But like the most successful impersonators, Irv combined the man he copied with the one he already was. Dottie required all of her impersonators to follow Elvis's example as much as possible. "Elvis wasn't just an entertainer," she liked to say, "he was somebody that cared about everybody." So she loved when Irv bypassed a pretty girl in the audience to sing to an older woman without her even telling him to. When she taught him that Elvis drank his water a certain way from a glass—with his hand held facing his body as he tipped the glass—he would do it, no questions asked. "Irv is just one of the neatest people I ever met in my life," Dottie said. "Not only is he good looking, he talks to everybody. He doesn't see a stranger. And the more I know Irv, the better I like him. I swore I'd never get attached to an Elvis impersonator again, because Doug Church is like one of my kids. And then after I started working with Irv, it was like, 'Let's keep this on a business level, right?' But that's just not the way it goes. Irv is so honest and so sincere that nobody can help but get attached to him."

Which might explain why his fan club exploded soon after it was founded. Its newsletter lingered on all aspects of his life. *Did You Know?* one entry asked: *Irv graduated Niles High School. Irv's birthday is November 23. Irv loves: kids, the color of blue and the cologne Eternity and favorite meat is steak.*

The attention left Irv gratified and amused. "Even though they joined my fan club, I tell them, 'I don't consider you my fans, I consider you Elvis fans," he said. "Because you're coming to see me do something that somebody's already done.' And then I say, 'I consider you my friends, not my fans.' You see what I'm saying? It makes me feel silly. If I was Garth Brooks, then I'd have fans, right?"

For a man who impersonated someone for a living, he held few illusions. He would talk at great length about continuing the legacy of Elvis Presley, about how good it felt to bring back memories for audiences. Then he would announce that anybody who says they don't do this to make money is handing you a bunch of garbage. "When you do it for a living, it becomes a job," he said. "I'm sure that even though Elvis Presley enjoyed entertaining his fans and in return they made him a very wealthy man and showered him with all kinds of gifts and let him know they appreciated it, I'm sure for him it was a job, too. You know, it was work when he was on stage. And more so for him than any of us, because there's nobody that put the energy out that Elvis did. But you know, I enjoy my job. The people who make fun of us, I bet there's ninety percent of them who don't enjoy what they do every day."

One night on the phone, Irv said, "I'll tell you a little secret. I don't know how you're going to take this. Someone might kill me, man."

"What?" I asked him.

"Careerwise."

"What?"

"I did do some modeling." He laughed, a sudden ha-HA! "You're sitting there wondering, ain't ya?"

I had to admit that I was. The news carried so much weight, Irv had to excuse himself to fetch a Pepsi.

"HA! You're gonna die."

"What?"

"I used to be a male stripper."

For thirteen years. For a while, with an ensemble called Fast Freddy and the Playboys. He went by his initials, I. C. That way nobody knew his name unless he chose to tell them. Dottie didn't like the idea of anyone knowing about Irv's previous career—she didn't think it sounded professional. But Irv didn't care who knew. This was fortunate, because everybody already did. Early on, all anyone needed to do to figure it out was watch him move. Gail dubbed his early style "pelvisy." He toned down a lot, but not so much that he could not call it forth during the arm thrashing sequence of "Polk Salad Annie." The screams that resulted drowned out the music. Other impersonators hated Irv's approach, just like they hated the busloads of fans who followed him to Memphis.

Irv disliked such criticism, but ignored it. After all, becoming a Elvis impersonator had made him a better person. When he was a male dancer, all he cared about was himself. As an Elvis, he could do charity work, meet nice people, and keep his clothes on. If he could have relived his life, he would have started his career doing Elvis.

He went to Memphis for the contest that August with some pretty strong ideas about his chances for winning but, as usual, no illusions. He looked at the field and felt confident—which he hastened to say is not the same thing as cocky. "Now I'm sure you'll agree that I'm not lying when I say this," he said. "If you see two hundred Elvis impersonators, you can probably pick maybe ten or fifteen that could do it for a living. Am I right or am I wrong in saying that? I wouldn't say that if I didn't think you'd agree with me. Because I wouldn't want you to think I think I'm a hotshot. Because I don't! I'm not that way at all. And in fact, when people call me Elvis, it upsets me. I tell them, 'You can call me Irv.'"

The mounting excitement at the Headliner in part explained Dennis's mood as he showed up for a sound check a couple of hours before the show. He set up his karaoke machine in the back near the restrooms, and soon found himself singing with Rick Lenzi, a twenty-year-old impersonator from California. Rick wore a thick gold chain around his neck and chunky rings on the last two fingers of each hand. He had a baby face and blue contacts over his brown eyes, but his voice rang so strong and true that women coming out of the restroom leaned against walls as they listened to him. Only one woman watched the scene impassively: Rick's manager, Denese Dody, a leggy woman with ice blue eyes and about fifty impersonators on her client list. She wore moccasin boots with fringes around the ankles and zippers up the back, a black-and-white jacket printed with snapshots of Elvis and tight, black bike shorts with gold rings running up the sides. Her blond hair was scooped into a ponytail.

When she talked about her job she laughed after every other sentence—partly because her business training for the job was operating a flooring business with her first husband, and partly because it became a job at all.

"The agents call me the Elvis lady," she explained between phone calls one afternoon at her Ontario, California, home. "They know basically ninety-nine percent of my work is with Elvises. So they know they can make one phone call, as opposed to calling this agent to see how many she's got in her files. Because different agents deal with different kinds of talent. But they know that they can call me and they have access to twelve different Elvises. And they know once they tell me what they're looking for that I'm going to place the guy that's going to fit their need. So they don't have to worry about it."

Denese became an Elvis fan when she saw him on Ed Sullivan. She never set out to fall for a rebel, but she got the feeling, when she heard his records, that he sang them just for her. Somebody like Rick Nelson, he just stood around and plunked a guitar. Elvis, he did everything.

When she married her first husband in 1961, he convinced her to throw away all her souvenirs—every scrapbook, every magazine, her 1956 Elvis locket. She was eighteen and in love. Once in a while, she would look through catalogs and see how much the items she threw away were worth to collectors. She said, "If that man weren't dead now, he would be." After she remarried, she started a new collection. Her second husband warned her that if she bought anything else they would be forced to hang it from the ceiling.

In 1982, she began managing an up-and-coming impersonator who worked at an asphalt company. He hired her right after he walked into her house and saw her front room. She soon opened an office in her home, and credited her immediate success to her years of loving Elvis. She grew serious when she spoke of what usually went wrong with impersonators. If they don't know what kind of Elvis they want to be, it's as if they don't have an identity themselves. "The vocals are important," she explained, "but the vocals can always be worked with to get them to where they need to be. The look—they've gotta have a halfway decent look. If they come to me with brown hair it needs to be black. You gotta do this. If they don't want to go along with the program, then it's like, 'Well, why bother?'

"I'd rather take somebody that doesn't have all that strong of a look, but he's a personality and he's got a stage presence that when he gets up there and he does his Elvis, the people get lost. They overlook the flaws."

She had a reputation among impersonators of respecting what they did without getting all goofy about it, the way some women do. That afternoon at the Headliner, she regarded Dennis with interest, chin tilted, eyes half-shut as she listened.

The show started around 6:00 P.M. The mood in the room crackled since some of the big names had hit town. More people arrived earlier, so table space became scarce. Women got bolder, not that they had ever battled shyness. They rushed the stage for scarves, and they chased impersonators, brandishing cameras.

A long look around the room revealed that not all the performers were on stage. Guys who hadn't even signed up to compete came in wearing ruffled shirts and towering pompadours. Terri Jayne showed up without her wig. The hair underneath it was platinum blond and very short. "Different, huh?" she said. And a woman floated through the room wearing a low-cut gown of bugle beads and sequins and a cloud of butter-blond hair. As she passed heads turned, and people murmured, "Hee Haw, Hee Haw."

From 1968 to 1973, Wendy Lynn will tell you, she sang and danced and emerged from a cornfield for a living as a cast member of the television show "Hee Haw." It was an interesting story, and it was also not true. The production company for "Hee Haw" has no record of anyone named Wendy Lynn ever appearing on the show. But Wendy claimed that she did, and at the contest people knew her as the lady who was on "Hee Haw." Wendy also claimed that at a reunion held several years after she left the show she met another cast member, Elvis's onetime girlfriend Linda Thompson. Wendy said this fact should explain something about her circle of friends. Before she left California this year to fly to Memphis she taped extra episodes of a variety series she was trying to sell, "Country Cousins." One show featured two bands and a roster of performers that included Andy Lee, a Roy Orbison impersonator, and a band called the Ozark Moonshiners. In another installment, her first two numbers were followed by a clog-dancing team.

She flew in every year to watch the show and celebrate her birthday, which fell on August 11. She sat at her table near the front, one curved calf peeking from the slit in her dress. Her makeup was immaculate. Her lips were ripe and full. Her chest made her lips look flat. In the valley of her considerable cleavage dangled a gold chain and a charm with the three letters TLC, like the ones Elvis gave to women in his life. Ask Wendy Lynn whether Elvis gave the necklace to her, and she would decline to answer. Then she would tell you. She said that when she died and went to heaven, the first person she wanted to see was God. The second person was Elvis.

"I have a love for Elvis that is so great," she said. "I do. The man is *love!* He shared the love. He had a special glow, a special love about him that no other entertainer will ever have. Including myself. I mean, the charisma. The *charisma*. When he touched you, you felt it. He didn't physically have to touch you—just listening to his music would touch you. You could be depressed—I could be very depressed, I could put on Elvis and all of a sudden, hey—I'm lifted up. There will never be another entertainer that anybody will ever pay tribute to as Elvis Presley. He was no god—he was not perfect, God knows that. But he loved the Lord, he showed his love. He believed in what Christ said to his apostles before he left—he said, '. . . love one another even as I loved you.' And that's what Elvis did. He loved us. And he showed his love."

I told her she must have known Elvis well for him to move her so. She looked startled, and her full lips pulled tight. Her face flushed pink. She shook her wondrous cumulous head.

"He could cry. I've seen him cry. He was not ashamed to shed a tear. I've seen him do that. And I've seen a side of him that was very tender. And I will cherish that to the day I die."

She brightened, however, just thinking about her bedroom. She prayed for Elvis there every day. "My bedroom is full of nothing but Elvis Presley," she said. "And he's on my ceiling."

"Did you say he's on your ceiling?"

"Yes."

"You have a picture of him on your ceiling."

"Yeah. And a tapestry. And my favorite one, it looks like he's going up into heaven. And he's in a suit. And that's over my bed, by the picture of my Lord. And when I want to really be alone, I pray to God—it's my special prayer place. And I do a lot of praying. And I always ask God to watch over Elvis." She looked around the room. A man on stage windmilled his arms. "I just pray that when he looks down on this that he sees that there are a lot of us that really do love him. And appreciate what he did for us. You know, we couldn't say thank you to him. Because he's gone. But *this* is a thank you. He looks down and sees this, he definitely sees 'thank you.'"

It was becoming obvious that the identity of this year's top impersonator was just one of many dramas unfolding at the contest, but it still occupied the minds of everyone here. Gail and her friends had arrived early that Wednesday to get a good seat. French fries and some kind of fried-chicken product sat in baskets on the table. The four had eaten Wisconsin cheese and sausage they had brought from home in the room earlier, but it was going to be a long night. "I'm gonna have nightmares about this place for a month," Chris said at one point, massaging her temples and trying not to look at the walls. "Those hot pink signs!"

Fred Wolfe, the impersonator from Detroit, joined the women. He had accessorized his Levi's with an Elvis belt that had an eye-bugging gold buckle. Ginger Gilmore, the female Elvis who had caused some confusion in the women's room an hour earlier, strode out in a sky blue jumpsuit and a satin-lined cape. During her rendition of "Suspicious Minds" her belt fell off, chains splashing to the floor. Fred moaned. "What kind of drugs is she doing?" he asked. "Somebody steal them and give them to me!"

He popped his gum and smirked, while the women tried to ignore him. They preferred not to insult anyone. Don Sims did a fill-in set for some absent Elvis, decked out in a black jacket with red rhinestones and black fringe on the sleeves, a white shirt, red and black boots. The tips of his sideburns reached almost to the corners of his mouth. Fred covered his face with both hands, but he sang along in spite of himself. Around the room, other men in high collars and heavy jewelry closed their eyes and joined in. The stereo effect again. By this point in the week it sounded pretty good.

"Are you girls gonna be mellow tonight?" Fred asked.

"It's only a quarter to seven," Gail replied.

Another impersonator emerged; Fred noted the absence of studs on his suit. "Jeez, Fred," Gail said, eyes raised toward the bloated tiles, "I didn't even notice." Another guy followed, with squared-off Elvis hair and a white jumpsuit. "There's no stars on the crotch," Fred reported. "No stars anywhere underneath the sleeves. Can you say: cheese? Where's Tony Grova when I need him?"

For once, Dennis showed up early. He flew into the club just after 8:00 P.M. to make arrangements for his 9:00 P.M. set and checked in at the table. He carried his black wig bag and other essential paraphernalia. Irv Cass, who also had just arrived, walked over to Dennis, crossed his arms, and leaned to speak into his ear. He wore baggy green shorts and a shirt swimming with green tropical flowers. "I wanna tell you, buddy," he said, "you've improved one hundred percent." Dennis stepped back, his forehead furrowed in surprise. He took in Irv and his amazing hair.

Gail, meanwhile, peered around tables and bodies to the door: "OhmyGodOhmyGod. There he is. Guess who just walked in?" Kelly craned her neck and smiled wryly. Ronny Craig stood framed in the doorway. "I saw that silhouette," she said. "Who else is that statuesque?"

Irv was saying to Dennis, "You sound so much more like Elvis than you used to. And you're doing the moves." He pumped his pelvis a couple of times.

"A little, yeah," Dennis said. As if he could get any worse, he almost said. His stomach felt funny. For the first time he could remember, he didn't feel hungry. He hadn't expected to be nervous. He had come here just to have fun.

"As you can see from the quality of the individuals," Doc Franklin was saying on stage, "things are picking up during the week."

Dennis came and stood behind Gail at the table on the side closest to the stage and began to run through a few dance steps. Bend, kick, twist. A few minutes earlier he had leaned over an empty table in the back, scribbling on a piece of borrowed paper and muttering, "'Just back from Las Vegas? Appearing at the Imperial Palace?' I gotta come up with something to say!" He did. Now all he had to do was wait. Bend, kick, twist. The impersonator onstage passed out blue scarves. Dennis fidgeted. His wig spiked straight up on top. A bead of glue peeked out from under one sideburn. He had remembered the wig, but forgot the tape that held on the sideburns. He improvised with wig glue. By the end of the week, his cheeks would look perpetually slapped.

He bent and kissed Gail. "Good luck," she whispered, smiling up at him.

"Good luck!" Shelley called out.

He straightened and regarded them, all smiling. They wanted so badly for him to do well. He knew that. "I won't touch the wig once, you watch," he said, and they all laughed. In his hands he clasped a wad of red and purple scarves. He stood for a long moment. He squeezed the scarves into a tight ball. He glanced around at the place, at the guy singing onstage, at Gail. "I gotta get up there," he said. Gail nodded.

Then he turned and walked along the right side of the room toward the dressing room, eyes on the impersonator on stage. The guy appeared to be wearing a pair of cowboy boots painted white, right down to the heels. Gail turned around and fixed her eyes on the pink tablecloth. "I think I hit that note," the cowboy impersonator said after one song. He thought wrong. He rambled into "Now or Never." The stereo effect soared to an all-time high.

Finally he left, and Jackie Franklin appeared. "Our next performer is just back from an appearance at the Imperial Palace in Las Vegas," she said, "home of the Legends in Concert. From Chicago, Illinois, let's welcome Dennis Stella."

Dennis burst through the curtain and ran on stage. A cluster of rainbow-colored lights rolled on the ceiling above his head. They cut through the cigarette smoke, creating a dreamy effect.

"All right, guys," he said, in a voice deeper than it was just moments before. "Take it down."

The opening guitar of "Suspicious Minds" unspooled. Dennis pumped his legs, moving in time. For a man singing about being caught in a trap, he sounded sure of himself, his voice strong. His right arm swung easily at his side. Gail turned to smile at her friends. He was really doing it.

And he didn't stop. He scaled the second verse and rocked his pelvis. He reached the bridge and he dropped to one knee, shouting "HA!" and slicing his right arm through the smoke.

He came to the part of the song where he must repeat the first verse and, like Elvis, unsheathed some arm thrashes after each line while the cymbals crashed behind him. His first flurry looked stiff, but the second time he shouted, "HA! HA! HA! HA!" as his elbow pumped and the crowd cheered. The third time he whipped his arm so easily, breathing so hard, that when he finished he smiled. Gail, who never yells during shows, yelled: "*Whooooo!*" As the song simmered to a halt Dennis fell to one knee, slashed the air with his right arm—one, two, three—leaped to his feet, swung his arm like he was pitching a softball, dropped down, sprung up and flung back his arms, and the expression on his face registered part passion and part relief.

"*Whooo!*" he shouted, and the audience shouted right back. "Let me pause to breathe just a second." He took a deep drink of water from a glass on the edge of the stage. "All right, ladies and gentlemen, we're gonna slow it down just a little bit and do a love song." He labored to catch his breath. "You know, a lot of times, I'm up here on stage, and everybody thinks that singing and all the success that comes with it is just luck. But what's really important is that you have somebody out there to care about and who cares about you. I'd like to dedicate this song to that woman." He pointed at Gail. "Take it down."

Shelley, Kelly, and Chris beamed. Gail smiled back but sat very still, her hands in the lap of her purple dress. "I'm so nervous my stomach is in knots," she said. When Gail got nervous, she twisted her fingers together and right then it looked like she was knitting. Dennis looked down at the stage and adjusted the red scarf around his neck as his karaoke tape played the piano opening of "Fame and Fortune." As he sang those two words, the audience applauded. He stepped off the stage while Doc Franklin, wearing a blue golf shirt, watched from the side, hands on his hips. Dennis approached a redhead all in white; he took her hand and sang to her. She smiled sweetly at him, and he slipped the red scarf around her neck and gently kissed her. He was working the crowd! Gail sprinted up front to snap a picture, then dashed back. Dennis weaved his way through waitresses and around restless men in plaid work shirts until he got to Gail. He gazed into her eyes and sang how just having her gave him fame and fortune, and then he kissed her cheek. The audience whistled as he finished. "All right," he said, "I made it."

He began "In the Ghetto" and the audience burst into applause. Cookie snapped a picture. Jenna ran up—she looked cute, in a poodle skirt and saddle shoes—and he put a purple scarf around Jenna's neck. Gail took another picture.

"*Dennisssss!*" Chris howled.

Kelly put down her cigarette so she could applaud. He hit the last big note while dropping on one knee, flinging his arm into the air, his face twisted in concentration. "Well, so far so good, I haven't fallen down or anything," he said. The audience laughed, and at the table Shelley shouted, "And his mama didn't die!"

He barreled through the rest of his songs. "Patch It Up": He attempted a lot of pelvic action. He did not touch the wig once. "All right," he said, "I think I'm gonna make it through this alive."

"Dennis is a great guy," Fred said. Shelley, who had somehow migrated onto Fred's lap, nodded.

"Let It Be Me," "Just Pretend": He passed men with pompadours at the tables and draped scarves around the necks of timid, giggling women. "The Wonder of You": Walking up front to Cookie, taking her hand. She raised her eyes and lifted her chin, so pretty. He kissed her and as he walked away she pointed at him, as if to say: yes.

For his finale, "Can't Help Falling in Love": Singing the concert version, repeating snatches of lines, and at the end he held the last note so long his knees buckled and he staggered backward, still singing, still hanging on. More than twenty minutes and his hair had held steady. He jogged off stage, looking toward Gail. She waited until he disappeared behind the curtain to relax.

"Oh, I have to go to the bathroom!" she said, standing up to run. Kelly and Shelley followed her.

Chris stayed behind. She lit a cigarette and craned her neck to check out the front of the club. "Look," she said, "he can't even get away from the dressing room." As Dennis emerged from behind the rust-colored curtain, a circle of sequined woman stood waiting.

Some chubby guy from New York followed Dennis to the table, asking if he could help him score some women; some blond told Dennis that she knew Cher and would give Cher his autograph if he wanted. Dennis pondered this offer. Why would Cher want his autograph? Why the hell not? He signed it, "To Cher—I wish I got you, babe."

Chris blew smoke toward the ceiling. "He'll make the finals," she said. "He'd better focus, and get his shit together, and he might even place."

As Dennis worked his way to the table, Gail and the others returned. "You know what?" Chris said to Gail. "I won't tell him, but you can tell him. Don't ever put 'Patch It Up' in the show again. It's too repetitive, it's too long. I think he felt it, too."

Gail agreed. "It goes on and on and on."

"On and on and on," Chris said. "Same words, and there's not too many. It's fun for a party, but not for a competition."

Dennis finally made his way over. He had signed about thirty-five autographs. Chris greeted him first.

"You made the finals," she said.

"You think?" he asked. Henry Newinn, father of Elvis John, the sole Vietnamese-American impersonator in this year's contest, stepped up front wearing a tuxedo with a cummerbund shining like the northern lights. He did a little boogie while he sang "Blueberry Hill." Supplemental entertainment.

"Now you can relax until Saturday," Chris said.

"Hey, the wig did not move once!" Dennis replied. "I got clips on it now, it snaps on—it don't move. It's on there. In fact, if somebody tried to pull it off me, it would actually tear out my hair. Did the wig look OK?"

"There's a little bump right here," Chris said. She pointed to the spiked crown.

"Little bump?"

"Right in the back there."

He touched it gently. He frowned. "I have tried so hard to make this damn wig work."

"Dye your hair and get it cut," Kelly said.

"Yeah, right—and walk around with those pork chops."

She shrugged. "All you gotta do is put some mousse in it and comb it back. Big fucking deal!"

Dennis's gaze settled on the tablecloth. He appeared preoccupied. "Hey, you guys," he said. "What did I do with my glasses?"

Thursday night. Three more nights of Elvis. At least eight hours a night. Stick around until 3:00 A.M. watching Elvis impersonators every night for almost a week and the brain goes kitten-soft, the eyes unreliable.

"To be honest with you," Dennis said, "as much I enjoy the performance of the other guys, after a period of time they all start to kind of half-blend together. I can only watch so much Elvis—I mean, I like performing, and I do like Elvis. But enough's enough—I mean, I love pizza, but can I eat pizza every night of the week for the next ten years?"

The most noteworthy performers that night were Toni Rae, one of the two female Elvises in this year's contest, Steve Chappell, who placed second the year before and was rumored to be this year's favorite, and Rob Hunter, a sweet-faced fifteen-year-old Young Elvis in saddle shoes and gold lamé from Michiwaka, Indiana. Little Robbie, as people called him, didn't sing like a fifteen-year-old boy and, judging from all the screaming, he didn't move like one, either.

Everyone was biding their time until the next night, when Doc and Jackie announced the finalists. Steve Chuke had just hit town and lounged at the table with Gail and the rest. He didn't sing until the next night, but he felt lucky. It had been a week since he'd bought the stereo and he still felt jazzed. Plus he looked good. The women congratulated him on the weight he had lost, all the better to fit into black leather. Steve was visibly pleased someone had noticed his makeover. He stood and modeled his tight Armani jeans and TCB belt for them, complete with sweeping arm gestures. This cracked them up.

Fred Wolfe was slated to sing next to last this night. He stood in the back, clearing his throat. He was having a nasty reaction to something he had eaten, God knows what. Butch Polston had brought down his new Peacock jumpsuit, but when Fred tried it on the flares barely skimmed his ankles. "I look like an Okie, man," he moaned. Plus he had a hangover. None of these things encouraged any Elvis inside him.

Irv Cass, meanwhile, induced craziness in the crowd. During "Polk Salad Annie" he dropped the mike during the instrumental break and spun out into karate chops and kicks with a touch of that liquid pelvis thrown in. His fan club table whooped so hard the entire front of the room turned into a whirl of permed hair.

"Does this happen to everybody that does this song?" he asked.

Noooo, the women replied.

"You get all hot and sweaty, is that what happens? Lord have mercy." He took a deep-down drink of water, a big breath.

"He looks less pelvisy," Gail said to Kelly.

A round-bellied man wearing a white mesh ball cap and sitting at the next table leaned over to the guy across from him. "Of course," he said, "Elvis could go two hours straight. He didn't have to take no break. Yessir."

The more time a person spends around impersonators, the more the consciousness expands to make room for alternative versions of reality.

For example: You can be having a typical conversation with someone about something—good catfish restaurants, the price of Graceland souvenirs—when suddenly the other person will offer a comment so interstellar that, anywhere else, you would nod politely while looking over her shoulder, searching for the nearest exit. At Images of Elvis, you nod. You beg, "Tell me more." During a break one night Denese Dody and I were making small talk about her collection of limited-edition Elvis plates when she stopped and looked at me seriously, to confirm that we understood each other. From her purse, she pulled out a snapshot she had protected with a small plastic bag. "Would you like to see my Elvis ghost picture?" she asked.

"Sure," I said.

She tipped it so the lights overhead wouldn't reflect off it and pointed out the white cuff of a jumpsuit sleeve, a hank of black hair. Misty, but visible. She took the picture on Dolan Avenue in front of Vernon Presley's old home behind Graceland, just after meeting Elvis's former backup singer, Kathy Westmoreland. All Denese wanted was a picture of the house and when she had it developed—this. Elvis's ghost was a bonus because she didn't even believe in ghosts. She weighed selling the shot to the *National Enquirer*. She even enlisted the aid of a friend, Mickey Rooney's daughter-in-law. In the end, she kept it to herself.

"This way," she said, "it's all mine. Isn't it something?" I had to admit it was.

Fred's set didn't get going until past midnight. He stood behind the rust-colored curtain in his Aloha Eagle jumpsuit, bowed his head and prayed to God almighty: "Please help me. Get me through this. Give me some light."

He ran out on stage through a cloud of smoke tinged yellow by the lights and ripped into "C.C. Rider." If Elvis had toured with Kiss and drunk a lot of coffee, he would have moved like Fred Wolfe. Fred never walked anywhere he could run. As the cymbals crashed he thrust his fist into the air. His voice shot out deep. He lunged and kicked and gave Shelley a scarf and turned "Return to Sender" into a rocker. His last song was "Polk Salad Annie." He shouted the part about the straight-razor totin' woman, then he whipped his arms so fast, flying backward, that the women had barely absorbed it all when he fell into a flurry of karate moves. The big gold ankh around his neck swung.

Afterward, he stood in the back of the room feeling that he had pulled off something surprising, considering his mood and the hour. "Just turned it on," he said. He crossed his arms across the eagle on his chest. "Once you put the costume on, it makes you transcend. It makes you feel like Superman. And you get the power from it. It's a powerful thing. It makes it so much different when you have the suit. It just drives you—it changes you."

This tied in neatly with Fred's theory that performing is like having sex with eight hundred people: "Because you're feeding on their energy. And when you have eight hundred people going 'Yeah!' and breathing in your direction, the stage gets really hot. So you know, the heat adds to the effect. And when you get the crowd clapping, hand the scarves out and you get everybody turned on, they all groove on it. You feed on it. You tap into that psychic energy. These people have so much energy in them that if I can tap into their energy, then I know that I'm doing something right. I try to give them a show that they can't see anymore. I try to put out as much as I can. Because these people, they owe you nothing.

But you owe them everything. Because they are who make you who you are." He smiled. "Or who you think you are."

We talked about his jumpsuit, his performing strategy, and his psychic connection to Elvis. "I have an interesting story that I'd kind of like to relate to you about this Elvis thing," he said. "We all believe—I believe—that my house may be haunted, and we all like to think it's Elvis. We do. Because my parents, they were at home when I was down here just the other night, and the door to my room closed all by itself. And this has happened a number of times."

Just behind him, Dennis chatted with a lifelong Memphis resident, a friendly woman with pretty eyes and a pinch of dark roots.

"Y'all gonna think I'm awful—I've never been to Graceland," she said. "You know why? When I was a kid, I'd be riding in the back of my daddy's pickup, Elvis would pull up on a motorcycle. He'd wave at us. It was just like we knew him. He'd ride on his motorcycle. We'd see him out there ridin' his horse. It was an everyday thing for us."

Dennis nodded. Two more nights of Elvis, eight hours a night.

Friday night. Tonight the judges would choose the finalists. Everyone came early. Emotions ran high. Doc Franklin got up on stage at one point to plead with the fans.

"Please don't get out of your seat to get a scarf," Franklin said. "Please don't get up. We'll ask you to leave if you do."

"He means it, too," Jackie said. "He has no pity."

Meanwhile, Wendy Lynn felt Elvis in the room.

"Last year when I left here, it was really on my heart," Wendy Lynn told me as the night began. "I wanted to write something about him. So I wrote a poem. And it's right in my heart. Would you like to hear it?"

She closed her eyes, laid her hand across her heart, and began:

> Sixteen years ago, I still remember the pain
> When the news rang out, I've never been the same.
> Elvis Presley, the king of rock and roll, was dead.
> And the world would sadly bow their head.
> He taught us how to live and love together,
> He gave us all a reason to go on.
> He showed us his love and compassion,
> And that is why our legend lives on.
> From a shack in Tupelo, to a home in Tennessee,
> He was just a country boy, he wanted to be free,

To sing and play his music, and make his dreams come true,
But little did he know what his fame on earth would do.
It's hard to believe sixteen years have gone,
'Cause we still hear his music and we still sing his song.
And every year we gather to his Graceland he loved so,
To light a special candle to the man we all love so.
We love and miss you, Elvis.

Fred Wolfe, as usual, stood in the back of the room. He was for the most part alone; the crowd appeared to have thinned a bit compared to the last two nights. He had a feeling that no one cared because everyone knew the winner. At least he did: Steve Chappell.

"I think these people don't care so much because they know that Steve is gonna be in the finals, because Steve came in second place last year. But I've seen stranger things happen—when a guy comes in, places first, second, or third and doesn't even finish in the finals. Boy, does that really irritate some people. Steve Chappell fully expects to win this show. And if he doesn't win this, he's gonna throw a real big major hissy fit. He fully expects to win this."

Steve Chappell of Augusta, Georgia, had curly brown hair, a broad face, and a bumpy nose. He was a good singer and a nice guy, but he looked nothing like Elvis. Apart from wearing a jumpsuit, he didn't even try.

"Look at Irv," Steve urged one night at the contest. Irv Cass ambled past, hair perfect, eyes blue, jumpsuit blinding white. He raised a hand in greeting. "Don't believe a word he says," said Irv, mock serious, as he walked on by. "See," Steve said, "Irv is gorgeous. He is. He's *gorgeous*. And I'm not good looking. I'm not. I'm not. And you got all these guys that just are black hair and they got the Elvis presentation—it's kind of funny."

He said people had told him he sounded like Elvis since he was six, just a boy living in Germany while his daddy served in the Army. He used to lean out of the windows of his house and sing "Wolf Call." He dreamed about someday being famous because he could sing.

But no one ever accused him of looking like Elvis. "You don't laugh at my body," he cautioned, "because ostriches run when they see me." So even as some friends egged him on to enter the contest, they suggested he make himself over. When he saw what his rivals looked like, he agreed: "And the first year, they made me wear a wig. I put that thing on, and I felt like a idiot. I put those glasses on. And I got a nose you can ski off of, OK? I don't have thick lips, I don't have high cheekbones, and I got curly hair. They always said I look like Tom Jones singing Elvis Presley. But I put the wig on, I put the glasses on, and they made me some side-burns about this big and about that wide and we glued 'em on, OK? I got pictures of it. It's hilarious. I laugh every time I see it. And I had this out-fit, you look like you could fly in it. It was, you know, big— it was *huge.* But anyway, I walked out on stage and I was so much more concerned with what people were thinking when they looked at me, because I knew I looked so stupid, that I couldn't sing. And I said, now, Steve, you're doing this backwards. So after that I never wore another wig." He had placed, sixth, then fourth, then in 1993 he finished second, behind Ray Guillemette.

That's why Fred thought Steve was a shoo-in. "He came in second last year. He thought he should have won last year. And Ray Guillemette, he won. And he was infinitely better than Steve. Infinitely better. Much better. I mean, I would pay to see him play. Really. But my money is on him to win. I think Irv Cass will come in maybe second or third—it's a tossup. I don't know if Ronny Craig's gonna place in the top three again. I really don't think he's going to. I think I'll be a finalist, but I don't think I'll get any higher than that. Unless fate comes down to it, I mean, it re-ally would take a massive shot of beyond luck. I think somebody would have to steal the score and make sure that I won it."

Luckily, the reason Fred flew to Memphis every year had little to do with winning Images of Elvis.

"The first time I came down here, I played for fifteen minutes and signed autographs for forty-five. Right then and there. And I didn't even look like Elvis—I had blond hair, you know? I sounded like Elvis, but I didn't look like Elvis. Blew me away. Absolutely blew me away. And I fig-ured, Well, hell, if this is what being Elvis is all about, damn it. I think I'll stick with it."

A few feet away Dennis listened to Ronny Craig sing "My Boy," a sappy ballad about a man's love for his son. If he made the finals, he thought he might sing it. And he hated to brag, but he thought he stood an excellent chance. He had gone out on stage and for twenty minutes played so well at being unafraid that he nearly believed it himself.

Steve Chuke performed next to last—one Elvis before the judges turned in their scores. He had shown up early in his Armani jeans, then changed into his black leather, and waited. And waited. He went outside, started his Blazer, and then couldn't turn it off. He left it in the parking lot, still running. He walked back in and the smoke hit him like a wall. Ronny Craig, who had done a fine job just three spots ahead of him, told his good buddy to calm down. He couldn't. The longer he waited, the angrier he got.

He didn't go on until long after midnight. Still, he ripped through a set of songs he chose to show off the power in his voice, starting with "Lawdy Miss Clawdy" and ending with "If I Can Dream." As he twisted across the floor, the spotlight caught the single gold bracelet he wore on each wrist.

When he finished, Dennis assured him he would make the finals. "I don't know," Steve said. Something about waiting so long had taken all the fight out of him. Still, he supposed he had done OK. When he finished, he returned to the parking lot. The Blazer still hummed. He offered a guy thirty bucks to bust the steering column and turn it off. When he refused, Steve found some pliers, disconnected the battery, and set about fixing it himself. It took him about an hour.

He walked back into the Headliner just as Jackie Franklin began to reel off the names of the finalists—twenty-four total, twelve each night, in order of the nights they performed. As she spoke the men's names—neither woman made the cut—they filed to the front: Chris Wilson. Rick Lenzi. Elvis John. Don Sims. She got to the Wednesday names and read, "Dennis Stella!" Everyone at the table screamed the entire time he ran to join the others in the front of the room. Then they cheered when Fred's name was called, and again when Irv Cass ran up front, then Rob Hunter.

"I feel like I know everybody!" Shelley said, applauding.

"I know!" Kelly said.

Jackie never called Steve Chuke's name.

The men drew numbers to determine which of the two finals nights they would perform. Jackie told them, "We appreciate your show and we all love you." Kelly checked their pick list. Counting maybes, they had correctly chosen every finalist but one.

"I'm fired up!" Dennis cried when he returned to the table. "I'm Saturday, the fourth person. Which seems a little too damn early for me, but eh, what are you gonna do? I guess it's probably better to get it over with, though, huh? That way I can have some fun tomorrow."

For once, Fred acted excited. He said, "I've got the right number—ten. You know, that's my old number from my softball days—number ten."

Wendy Lynn walked up to Dennis. "Congratulations," she said. "I come here every year. I used to be on 'Hee Haw.'"

"My God—you know what?" he said. "I kind of remember you, now that you said that."

"God bless you," she said.

Chris sunk down at the table, debating whether she should call Steve Chuke and break the bad news. She didn't know he had heard the news himself and had said to Ronny, "I'm going home, man, I'll see ya." Ronny had begged him to stick around.

"No," Steve said. "Not after that." And he climbed into his Blazer, jimmied the busted-up steering column, turned onto Brooks and headed for Kentucky. He decided right then that he would someday return to Graceland, but never again would he visit the contest. And so far, he never has.

Chris, not finding Steve, turned her attention to Dennis.

"Now you need to get down and not say 'Don't worry about it,'" she told him. "Keep concentrating."

"Aa-ahhh," Dennis said. The last thing he wanted to do right now was concentrate. "Now, I have to ask you guys: Do you think I should just repeat the last set?"

In unison, they chorused: "No."

Few of the impersonators walked around in their suits before they performed in the finals. It was a courtesy and also a superstition, like not letting the groom see the bride before the wedding.

Chris had told Dennis that all he needed to do was to relax and remember how good he felt Wednesday night. He kept telling himself that all he had to do was stay loose and he would be all right. Around 6:oo P.M., he left the contest to visit an all-you-can-eat Chinese buffet down Brooks Road. He had waited around for a sound check that never came, and he worried that he wouldn't be able to sing well if he didn't eat, and he wouldn't be able to eat later if he sang poorly. Then he returned to the motel to put on the wig. He ended up going third, after some scheduling glitch, after a twenty-minute break, after Irv Cass.

"I'm glad there's a break between Irv and Dennis," Chris told her friends at the table. "I'd hate him to follow directly behind him." Everyone agreed. Irv had done one of the strongest early sets. From the moment he emerged from behind the rust curtain the finals followed the same course. He wore the Peacock suit again—the one Fred had wanted so much—and when he turned to face the audience the turquoise bird winging across his chest shimmered like sun on water. A roar rose from the audience that was so loud some people instinctively covered their ears. His silver sunglasses hid his eyes.

"Take it home, man," he growled.

Oww! Whooooa! the women screamed.

The King's Highway Band boogied into "Polk Salad Annie." Irv leaned forward a little, as if he planned to fly straight off the stage into the crowd. He motioned for them to clap along and they complied. As he spoke the intro he shouted over the drums *"Polk!"* (bomp!) *"Salad!"* (bomp-bomp!) and pumped his pelvis each time.

Aah-whoooo! the women howled. And from then on he really laid it down.

Impersonators are supposed to look and sound and act like Elvis. But in contests, they also must impress as individuals. Come across like everybody else and you get lost. This night, Irv kept finding himself. On the second verse of the song, as he kicked through the smoke billowing from the stage, Dennis entered in baggy shorts, carrying his black suit in a garment bag.

"Hey, guys!" he called out to Gail and everyone at the table. They waved at him. All of them were dressed up. Kelly's low-cut red jacket had sheer, striped sleeves. The neckline of Gail's black cocktail dress was sprinkled with pearls and jet-black beads. A woman at the table behind them checked out his hair. "Oh, my God," she said to her friend, "that was Elvis!" Chris studied him as he passed and rolled her eyes. "He's sticking up like Alfalfa in the back," she said to Kelly. Sure enough: The part of his head Dennis couldn't see when he faced the mirror stood electrified.

Irv motored into the last verse of "Polk Salad Annie." He sang about the no-good brothers stealing watermelons out of his truck and asked everyone in the room to sock a little polk salad to him. He started into that little side shuffle again; his hand snaked up next to his head while the drums and keyboards and guitars clanged. He began to move his arm as if he were cracking a whip, then he rolled his pelvis and slid across the stage while the music surged like a truck that had lost its brakes: *Bung-bung! Bung-bung! Bung-bung!*

The women screamed as if they saw the truck coming toward them and they had lost all desire to leap out of the way. By his next song, "You've Lost That Lovin' Feelin," when he kneeled on the stage then rolled onto his back, the way Elvis did it live, laid flat on his back and crossed his left leg on his right knee, singing about lost love and tapping his right boot in time while the women wailed *eeeaah!*, everybody knew.

"He's got it," Chris said.

Even Jenna chimed in: "Top three! Top three!"

Doc Franklin materialized on the stage. A red handkerchief hung like a tongue out of his back pocket. "All right," he says, "we're ready with three more." He reminded everyone that all four bars were open. Jackie took the mike. "When you get caught up in the passion of the moment," she said, "please don't stand in front of people who are seated at the tables. Do not come up to the performers to get the scarves. Let them come to you. Don't get in front of somebody's number-one fan, because they will let you know it." The women exchanged smiles and turned forward. Then Jackie read the introduction Gail had written in the car on the way over:

"Our next performer just came back from a trip to the Imperial Palace in Las Vegas, home of the Legends in Concert. From Chicago, Illinois, Mister Dennis Stella!"

He kicked out from behind the curtain, spread his arms, and did a few side shuffles across the stage, the kind Elvis did so that he always faced the audience, then removed his sunglasses and gently placed them at the front of the stage. The gold studs crackled on the black jumpsuit; he had accessorized its emerald stones with a green scarf. The whole table applauded and exchanged glances. So far, so good. He hopped into "Suspicious Minds." They exchanged glances again. Something was wrong. His vocal sounded faded. The King's Highway Band roared right over him like a monster truck, cymbals skidding across his vocals. He motioned for somebody to turn up his mike; he motioned again. No one did anything. Gail looked at Chris; her mouth formed a straight line.

"They're way off, they're way off," Chris said of the band. Don Sims, the impersonator and bandleader, had a reputation among the other Elvises for burying their vocals. And Dennis sounded six feet under.

The break and Irv's electric set seemed to have exhausted the audience, especially the women at the front tables. They applauded, but few of them cheered. Gail's table clapped and whooped, and Chris called her usual "Denniiisss!" Then the room fell strangely quiet. While Dennis sang, they talked. And Dennis, unlike Irv, failed to build intensity as his set went on. The lack of volume was dragging him down. "I'd like to sing a pretty song," he said, "and uh . . ." And before he could finish, the opening of "Fame and Fortune" began. Then "My Boy." His voice rang out a little clearer, but the mike still sounded weak, and the volume on the tape he had switched to needed to be higher. He motioned to Sims to turn it up. Sims did not appear to see. Dennis knew he had to plow forward, even as the increasing chatter of the crowd washed over him. He waded into the audience and let a woman dressed in orange with hair to match wipe the sweat off his face. He tried joking with the crowd. "Before I put you people to sleep tonight, we're gonna pick it up a little bit. Maybe sweat off some calories."

"Patch It Up" kicked in, and Gail's eyes filled with tears. Jenna came over and sat in her lap for a while, then slid into a chair. Gail knit her fingers in her lap again and again. As Dennis sang, Irv emerged from behind the brown curtain, wearing a blue jumpsuit and sunglasses with silver frames. Chris stared straight ahead and sighed. She had been right—too many ballads would drag down his set. People sprang up and approached Irv for autographs. "You know, this is getting to be kind of fun," Dennis said, smiling at the front row. "Let's do this again." No one responded.

Dennis turned his attention to Sims at the sound board. "Ladies and gentlemen," he said, "your idea is as good as mine; I have no idea what I'm going to sing next." Gail looked at Jenna, shaking her head. She frowned and turned her head away from her friends and toward the stage. Then she clasped her hands in her lap, leaning her wrists on her thighs. Chris and Kelly pulled at the two tiny brown straws in their Zimas and drank deeply. Shelley didn't even turn around. Sims said later that he didn't turn down the volume on Dennis or anyone else, and hoped that he or anyone else wasn't angry at him. He sounded sincere. Still, Dennis didn't buy it. Sim's performance, separated from his own by one Elvis, boomed loud and clear all the way to the back of the club.

It was a long twenty minutes. After the set ended, Gail glanced at her legs and noticed that while she was knitting her fingers in her lap she had raked her rhinestone bracelet against her black pantyhose and shredded them. She looked like she'd joined a punk band. Things had unraveled enough; she couldn't walk around like that. In a few minutes Dennis walked over, still sweating in the black jumpsuit. He had suspected he wouldn't win. Now he knew it. He couldn't be sure, but he thought he felt hungry.

"Well, I did what I could," he said. Gail held him tightly for a long moment. Then she pointed to her legs and said, "I have to go to the drugstore. You have to take me."

The temperature still hovered in the low eighties but compared to the club, the muggy air felt fresh. They drove about three miles, down Brooks Road, left onto Elvis Presley Boulevard, past the car dealerships and fast-food joints and the pawn shop, past Graceland. It was lit up like a welcome home, the trees shining blue-green and yellow and red. The twenty-four-hour Walgreen's at the corner of Elvis Presley and Raines was lit up almost as brightly. They parked the Corvette and crossed the parking lot. A thought crossed Dennis's mind just then—in seconds he would stroll into an all-night drugstore down the road from Elvis Presley's house to help his girlfriend shop for pantyhose while wearing a black jumpsuit jammed full of fake emeralds. He considered this. Then he remembered the difference between himself and the other Elvises: They had fun. He took all of this too seriously. Who did he think he was, anyway? On his way to copying another man, he had forgotten. Now he remembered how hard he had danced, how long he had driven, how far he had come. It felt like he was almost there. He opened the door and crossed the threshold.

The store shone like a dime in the sun. Emerald cabochons catch fluorescent light in ways the average drugstore shopper cannot comprehend. The pantyhose were in the back. You pass a lot of people walking to the back of a drugstore.

"Hey Elvis!" a guy yelled. "How's it going?"

"Hey, man," Dennis said. He couldn't remember the last time he felt so good.

12

Losing and Winning

*W*ith the finals behind him, Dennis decided to score some other action. Sunday night, he and Gail drove east up I-240 over to Lamar, to a contest he'd signed up for at the Americana Eagle's Nest.

The nightclub billed itself as the site of Elvis's first paid performance forty years before. The original club no longer stood. But then, neither did the original Elvis. It seemed a logical place for an impersonator contest.

Dennis was grateful for a change of scene. He wore his Pinwheel to the club and entered a party in progress. The tiny bar contained small tables, stained-glass Tiffany-style lamps, knotty pine walls and practically everyone Ray Guillemette knew in Memphis, including his parents and members of his fan club, all wearing hot pink A-Ray of Elvis T-shirts. Because he was—as usual—late, Dennis took the stage just a few minutes after he arrived.

"He sells insurance, ladies and gentlemen," said the announcer, a man in painfully tight jeans and cowboy boots. "Watch out! From Chicago, Illinois, let's give it up for Dennis Stella!"

Dennis jumped out onto the dance floor that served as a stage and bounded into "Suspicious Minds." The crowd applauded, and you could see his shoulders relax. The stage was about the size of his patio at home, and the club's size made every cheer sound loud. Next came "Welcome to My World." Ray's family cheered him on. "All right," Dennis said, "OK. Y'all having a good time? Look at that—one week in Memphis, and I'm already saying 'y'all.'" After "Walk a Mile in My Shoes" he said, "I hate to go, but all good things must come to an end." Then he sang "Can't Help Falling in Love." Gail, who was serving as scarf girl, sighed with relief.

Dennis did well enough to let himself believe he stood a chance of placing in the top three. He leaned against a wooden banister near the door, watching the last performers. As he relaxed, two women approached and congratulated him on doing so well. Dennis, being Dennis, asked the women, both Memphians, how they were enjoying Elvis Week. The first, a pretty woman with wavy brown hair and a drink in her hand, leaned in close and told Dennis she had no idea whether Elvis was really dead.

"There's too many tales," she said. "I mean, he may be. And God bless his soul if he is. But there are too many things happening. Too many things—it's too much. If he was—I mean, I'm not knockin' you, I'm not knockin' any of the performers, anybody—why don't you let him lie. If he is dead, then let him lie. Just let him rest. Rest in peace, you know? Why don't they let him rest in peace? I have no offense—I'm not knockin' him or whoever."

"Yeah, you are," Dennis said.

"No, I'm not," the woman replied, a little louder. She leaned in closer. "Let him rest in peace if he is dead. This is my opinion."

"OK," he said, "now you have to understand something: I'm not trying to take his place. We just enjoy his music."

"Well, everybody does, but why, why? He's a legend, but let him rest."

"Y'all think he's dead?" another voice asked. It was the second woman, a petite, sturdy blonde.

"No, I don't think he is, no I don't. That's my opinion," the first woman said.

"I think he's dead," Dennis said.

"I waited up there all day and all night to see him," the blonde said. "You know, to see him when he died? And the man just looked like a wax dummy."

"Oh," Dennis said, eyebrows lifting, "you saw him? You were there?"

She nodded. "Yes. I saw him. I live here in Memphis and I went—stayed all day and all night. And the only thing that really bothered me about it was that his *head*—see, I used to work in a nursing home, so I've seen dead people all the time, and his head was just so out of proportion with his body. Have you ever seen a water-head baby? You know, when their head is so big? His head just seemed so out of proportion with his body and then the whiteness and the pastiness of him just looked more like wax."

Dennis reminded her that Elvis had been prescribed many drugs before his death and had been rather ill.

"Yeah, that's true," she said. "He'd laid there so long and all. I mean, I don't know. If you want to think that he's dead—and then you really don't know, you know?" Dennis began to answer her, but the man in the tight jeans had returned.

"What are we waiting for?" the man asked. "Oh, the winners!" The audience cheered. "It was very close, ladies and gentlemen—about one point between each individual that performed tonight for first, second, and third place."

"Oh, boy," Dennis said.

"Third place goes to Mr. Tommy Becker!"

"I think there goes my chance," Dennis said with a shrug. "I was thinking maybe I had a chance at third." He wasn't too upset.

"I guess now you want me to announce second place, right?" the announcer asked. He leaned forward. You could see the seams of his jeans warp and wince. Jumpsuit or not, everybody wears a costume. "Let me tell you a story—nah. Ha ha ha! Second place, ladies and gentlemen—drum roll, please . . . second place, Mr. Steve Sogura!" Steve, a janitor from Washington state, walked up front.

"Ray," Dennis said.

He was right. As Ray ran up to accept the prize, his contingent leaped to their feet shouting, "Ray! Ray! Ray!" Dennis's mind had already relocated to Brooks Road. "What do you think I should do—should I go back to the awards presentation over there dressed up?" he mused. "Or do you think I should go back and take my stuff off?"

Jenna appeared at his elbow. "I think you should keep your suit on!"

"Hey, Mouse," Dennis said, putting his arm around her.

"Moose!" They had been teasing each other with these nicknames all week.

Gail appeared at his other side. "You ready?" she asked. After shaking Ray's hand and hugging him, the three of them piled into the red Corvette and headed west toward Memphis.

Fred Wolfe stood in the back of the Headliner Club wearing shorts, a wildly printed silk shirt, and his big gold belt, nursing a Zima. Dennis,

Gail, and Jenna walked in from the Americana and told him hello. Somewhere in the club, the judges' scores were being tabulated. The process was kept secret, even from the judges. The night before, Fred had cut his set short because he thought he had done poorly, even though he had worn his lucky blue Owl jumpsuit and rearranged his rings. He placed the blue ring on the index finger rather than his usual red, so that when he pointed at the audience they would see a color that matched the suit. "Blue is a very vibrational color," he said. After talking with some fans and meditating over a few beers, he permitted himself to consider possibilities other than total failure. He thought maybe he could win. "I mean, realistically, yeah," he shouted over the music. "Who knows? You never know—sometimes you just might get lucky. I mean, I have to maintain that optimism. The pessimistic side of me would say, 'Well no, Fred, you're not gonna make it.' But I mean, I'm optimistic. But the thing is, is that I temper that and say, well, if I don't make it, I don't make it. Big deal, I don't care. I come here to have fun, drink and party, and meet a lot of new people, and that's what it's all about for me. But like I said, we all know the winner. And I will prove to you that I was right all along. And that the entire thing is a charade."

He drank and smiled while Ronny Craig emoted through "It's Over." Fred thought a moment. "But I'm not really wanting to go home so much as I really want to party tonight. I want to get naked somewhere in a room, you know? Other than the room I'm gonna sleep in, you know? That would be nice. What I'm hoping for is that somebody will just come and take me away from all this and I can just forget about it and just have—just have a really great experience with somebody. Of course, it's not gonna happen, but while I'm wishing . . ."

While he was wishing, Ray Guillemette walked in. Word had already hit the Headliner and the other guys beelined over to shake his hand. "Worked out well," he said. "The only thing I need right now is a big, fluffy bed."

Doc Franklin walked up to Dennis. "How was it?" he asked. Dennis looked at him. He knew Doc knew about the Americana. He knew Doc hated Elvises in his contest to compete anywhere else. He didn't really care. "OK," he replied. Doc smiled slyly and walked on. He did the same thing to Ray Guillemette. After the show, Ray said Doc took him into a back room and told him it was "morally wrong" to compete in other contests while he was in Memphis. Ray was infuriated—didn't he have the right to make money if he could? He got even angrier when he found out Doc had bought Ray's father a drink and scolded him about letting his son perform elsewhere. After his father told him that, Ray left the Headliner that night with a lot less respect for Doc.

In the front of the room, Jackie began announcing the winners. She called Dennis's name about halfway through. He flashed a smile and headed for the stage. She called more names. Then she hesitated a moment to study her list. "Come on, girl!" a woman cried.

"OK," Jackie continued, "that's all we've got. And our third place winner is: Irv Cass." The screams made the ears roar. "And we have two left and that means our second place winner is . . . Robert Caballa and . . . Steve Chappell!"

The place tore in two. Fred shook his head and walked to the back of the room. The three winners shared the stage.

"I didn't realize how it would feel," Steve was saying. "I thought I did. But I didn't realize how it would feel to win first place. And I just can't say enough. Thank you for my family. Thank you for all of the friends I met the last four years and guess what—I guess I will see you again next year." The crowd crowded closer to the stage. "Thank you very much and God bless you all."

"I've had one heck of a good time coming down," Irv said. "Last year was my first time to Memphis, and there are truly some very beautiful people down South here. And I love you, man, you're great people. Thanks for the good time. Thanks, Doc, and everybody in charge here, and thank God for Elvis Presley. Thank you—I'll see you next year. And I'm gonna be on this guy's toes if he shows up, I'm gonna be right behind him, man."

"You're already on my toes, buddy," Robert Caballa said.

In the thick of the crowd, Wendy Lyn stood wearing a black gown with a plunging off-the-shoulder gold neckline that matched her TLC necklace. She was crying. Over to the right Carol Henry and her sister, Joan, compared notes. Both were judges. Neither of them had voted for Steve Chappell. He had won anyway. Carol became upset. She felt that if Elvis had seen some of the winners he would turn over in his grave. It disgusted her to feel this way. She was taking all of this much too seriously.

"I probably shouldn't comment too much on Steve," she said some time later. "I like Steve very well as a person, and an entertainer, but I found that for you to be the winner, I kind of felt that hey, you needed to look something like Elvis, whether it be a natural look like Elvis, putting on all the garb, you know. And I just really felt that Steve Chappell did not fit that bill at all. There was maybe a panel of, let's see, six judges. But then I think they had the idea that it'd be better to spread out and not know who the judges were. And that's probably good too. So that's when we really kinda lost . . ." She stopped herself. "I guess what I'm trying to say is, we really became unhappy with the decision. And so I said, 'No. I want to enjoy this, and just had the attitude, I can have my favorite but come out with the attitude that hey, so my guy didn't win.'"

Despite her doubts, she denied smelling a conspiracy: "Oh, no, I really didn't. To me, I didn't want to do that, because that would take all the fun out of it. And hey, if you think about it, it's just like I said—it's not like Doc and Jackie are begging people to come.

"I appreciate Doc and Jackie because no matter what I've heard around me, I've always tried to just always focus on how they've treated us. And they have treated us girls just great."

Rumbling had started in the audience even before the applause had died down. It was the usual stuff—Doc had chosen Robert Caballa to get in good with the casino where he sang, that it had to be fixed because Steve Chappell didn't even look like Elvis. A couple of people walked up to Irv and insisted he should have won. "Hey," he told them, "there's always next year." Despite the crowd's reaction he thought his finals set wasn't his personal best—his voice went weak on him, and Caballa beat him fairly. He wasn't crazy about a curly-headed guy taking first, but he figured he could settle that score that next August. "I don't get mad about stuff like that. But I tell you what—there's some guys that do. I don't think it's got a lot to do with politics, I really don't. There might be some involved, maybe."

In the front of the room the three winners started the traditional jam session. In the back by the doors, everybody else got on with their lives. Carol, in a gold lamé skirt and black halter with gold beads dangling on the breasts, and Cookie, in a white studded halter and a black leather skirt, had their picture taken with Ronny Craig. Rick Lenzi, the twenty-year-old Elvis, sidled up to Dennis. "You gonna buy me a drink?" he asked. "Come on, man! My manager don't care!"

"Party! Party!" Chris yelled.

Doc mingled, telling people next year's show would be a real classy affair, and that Zima was on sale for ten dollars a case. Fred went to his car with a box of it slung over his shoulder. In a half hour he would be sitting at the foot of one of the beds in Dennis's room, guitar in his arms, singing the Doors's "Roadhouse Blues." And Dennis would get on the microphone and beg him to sing some Elvis already. And for the first time that night, Fred would smile like he meant it.

Dennis and Gail walked into the muggy night, arms circled around each other's waists. He leaned against the Corvette and whirled her around to face him as she laughed. They stood whispering under a sliver of cool white moon. Their faces drew very close. They stayed that way for a long time.

Steve Chappell learned to deal with the burden of being judged the best Elvis in the world. He had overheard a lot of people who saw the contest in Memphis saying that he didn't deserve the honor because he had committed the sin of not looking like Elvis. At all. But he could sing. And he wanted to win so bad. And he understood his own limitations. Chappell thought it even funnier that people believed he did something to throw the contest. It made him giggle to think about it, and when he did, his round face got shiny and he reached his hand back and rubbed his curly-haired head.

"Well, if something was going on, it didn't have nothin' with my doin's. I can promise you that," he said. "None whatsoever. If I coulda bought it, I'd have done it two years ago. Three years ago. You know what I mean?" He leaned forward. "I'm not saying the contest—not this contest. I'm not saying." He shook the thought out of his head. "It had nothing to do with me if it was. And I don't have any political influence in this place, this town. I don't do it where I *do* have political influence. Because it always comes back on you. Somewhere. It hurts my feelings that people think that. 'Cause I ain't never did nothing to these people up here."

If he hadn't won when he did, he doubted if he would ever have returned. The contest made him strange. He had become obsessed with the idea of winning. He felt as if some disease bubbled in his blood. Before he competed he dieted for weeks. Before he performed he would throw up two, three times. He understood a little about how Elvis must have felt, all that pressure. Still, he didn't want it bad enough to cheat.

Back in the real world, life was a comfort. He sang country at a club in Augusta called the Honky Tonk and to the folks there, he was famous no matter what he did to his hair. He owned a flooring business and had a girlfriend who was studying to be a CPA. His two daughters were world-champion cloggers. The rest he could handle.

He realized some of the impersonators resented him. It hurt him terribly, but he had to laugh. He couldn't help himself. "They were furious!" he said of the night Jackie Franklin called his name. He leaned back in his chair and wheezed happily at the memory. "Very furious. They still may be. But they'll get over it. Or die with it." He propped his elbows on the table and laughed again. "I don't hold it against them for being mad at me, I really don't. They're the ones that's got to deal with it, not me. I sleep good every night."

13

Changes

*W*hile Steve Chappell grew more comfortable with being himself, Dennis Stella came to accept the idea of becoming somebody else.

It all started in a Denny's restaurant in Hickory Hills, Illinois, down the road from the Sabre Room. Dennis and his friends were having a late-night snack after a combination bridal show and Elvis revue. It was around 2:00 A.M. on an unusually warm October morning, and no one wanted to go home.

Irv Cass walked in with a friend. He wore a sport shirt and shorts and, of course, his Elvis Head. He ambled over to the booth by the front door where Dennis sat eating a grilled shrimp platter, with not nearly enough shrimp to his liking, and they discussed the set list that night. Then, without warning, Irv said, "Hey. I want to show you something." He whipped out his keys. They dangled from a plastic-laminated picture of a handsome man with white teeth, high cheekbones, and brown hair streaked with blond. Gail, Chris, Kelly, Shelley, and Dennis leaned over the picture. Their eyes locked on the man holding it.

"Is that . . . you?" Dennis said.

"Yeah, that was me before," Irv said. He straightened and jerked his shoulder, waiting for a reaction.

They all stared at the picture. Dennis, visibly moved, put down his fork. "I gotta tell you, Irv," he said, "you're one heck of a good-looking guy without the black hair."

"Yeah," Irv said with a sigh, "but I think I'll keep this, see how it goes."

They moved on to talking about who got to sing the best songs that night, while in the next booth two beer-bellied men eating sandwiches smothered in cheese took turns doing double takes.

A few months earlier, that scene might have convinced Dennis he was right not to grow a pompadour. That fall, it made him question his own appearance and the person behind it. Although he had seen what Elvis had done to Irv, Dennis couldn't stop thinking about what he had done to himself. Although he hated to admit it, he knew what everyone said about his wig made sense. He believed it himself, but for months he had told himself he was only playing at Elvis.

But the summer changed him. He had delved deep enough into the Elvis life to see that if he wanted to excel, to compete with guys like Irv, he had to give up thinking of himself as just one man. In Vegas, he had gained faith in his ability to improve; in Memphis, he had learned to have fun whether he soared or failed. As he merged these parts of his personality, his dislike of himself as Elvis took on tangible form: the shape and color of a woefully altered woman's wig. It wasn't just glimpsing Irv's past, hanging from a set of keys, that moved him. After all, Irv did Elvis full time—he needed a pompadour. He had received another, stronger sign that night after the bridal show. While a crew packed up the Hawaiian wedding set, Mario, Dennis's older brother, came over to him and marveled at how much Dennis had improved since the first time he'd seen him perform. Only one thing spoiled the illusion for him, Mario said. That wig. It looked terrible.

The critique hit Dennis hard. For months, he had clung to that wig. Although Gail bugged him about it, and Chris urged him to dump it, he had discounted what they said. Gail, he liked to joke, tried on seventeen outfits before she settled on one—how could he trust her opinion? Besides, she and her friends hung out with impersonators. And they knew him for who he was, not how he looked. He couldn't count on anyone to defend him when he sat in his office trying to look businesslike while clients ogled his head. As long as he wore that wig, he could believe that Elvis hadn't totally taken over his life. But when Mario criticized the wig, Dennis had to consider the situation in a different light. Mario was his older brother. He was the one Dennis viewed as the family philosopher. And he knew next to nothing about Elvis. Dennis felt a strange liberation. Elvis had made him feel more sure of himself. Impersonating had unearthed strengths and talents he'd never suspected he had. Blurring his identity had actually made him feel more confident about it. The idea of changing no longer frightened him. A week or so after that October night, he called Gail and told her not to tell anyone, but he had made a decision about his hair.

The first time he saw himself in the hairdresser's mirror with hair the color of a starless night, he cringed. Like the time he had caught his reflection in the mirror near the elevators at the Imperial Palace, he didn't recognize the man staring back. He had finally decided to lose the wig, only to make his real hair resemble one. Gail was so delighted Dennis had finally committed to an Elvis Head she would support him no matter what. The first time she saw him, she threw her arms around him and shouted, "Oh, my God, it's really dark!"

He had to admit that the hair did lend more authenticity to his act—he could whip his head from side to side without fear, and his sideburns moved when he smiled. He grew more used to the way he looked, and when he returned to the hairdresser he asked her to replace the blue-black dye with a black-brown combination. The result looked more natural. People at shows complimented him on his new look, and the respect and surprise showed on their faces. Many impersonators had privately wondered how a nice guy like Dennis could wear that wig and those stick-on sideburns. Now he was one of them.

But as good as he felt, Dennis could not escape the feeling that the quality of his day-to-day life had darkened along with his hair. One afternoon he ducked into a Burger King for lunch and he heard another customer laughing—at him. Dennis was not a vain man, but no one had ever laughed at him to his face just because of the way he looked. It hurt him so much. He wanted to snap at this stranger that he ran a successful business, that he owned a home, that he had a life. But he didn't say anything. He knew the guy was right.

Gail, too, noticed people staring at them. Not always, but often enough, when they went to the beach or to a restaurant. She joked to her friends that she wondered if people decided Dennis was strange or if they were just thinking, "Hey—cool burns."

Dennis had always thought idolizing a dead man had its weirder aspects, and he still did. For a long time he thought he could sidestep the worst. He had hoped he could stay unchanged. But he had come to accept that, even if you impersonated Elvis for all the right reasons, you always went through life a little bit wrong.

Gail knew this, but her reaction surprised her anyway. She hadn't anticipated how it would affect her when she saw this change she had accepted on so many of her friends happen to the man she loved. She had rejoiced when Dennis decided to dye his hair. She hadn't counted on her happiness mingling with a sense of regret.

"I don't think I really realized what it's like to be him and try to have two looks," she said. "I mean, it's almost impossible. I want him to have a good look when he's got to perform, but I want him to be my regular Dennis when he's not."

Once in a while she would take out the first photo album she had filled with pictures of her early days with Dennis. She always smiled looking at the pictures she had taken at that party the night before Greene's West that cool June night—Chris and Dennis mugging, she in her light blue satin jacket, he in a jumpsuit and that goofy wig. And there was another picture of Dennis next to the grill, wearing a beige sweater and shorts that set off his light brown hair. Her regular Dennis. In five months, she had found someone to love. But in a way she had lost him, too. She would look at that album and say, her voice carrying traces of sadness and pride, "That's the Dennis I met."

He showed off his new identity at some shows and a few paid gigs that had begun to come his way. But it looked like the 1995 Memphis contest would be his next major proving ground. Ron and Sandy Bessette had received word from the Imperial Palace that the hotel was terminating its contract with the organization. "They felt it was too, I guess, in competition with their Legends in Concert," said Sandy Bessette.

Actually, the official reason was just the opposite. The EPIIA never stood a chance in the big time. What the group considered its greatest asset—being able to boast its members performed on a popular Las Vegas stage—John Stuart of Legends in Concert saw as a threat to his reputation.

"The Elvises would take pictures of themselves on stage," he said, "they would take pictures of them in front of the hotel. And on all their brochures, a week after they went out, it would say, 'Directly from the Legends in Concert stage.' And they would pirate the notoriety and the ability, and all at once it would be a conflict of interest."

In the impersonator world, whoever makes the most money can usually claim to be the most genuine imitation. And Stuart decided that it eroded the image his show had worked hard to create if he allowed a band of pretenders he considered inferior to take over the stage at the Imperial Palace, his show's headquarters. It wasn't that he wished failure upon the EPIIA members. He just didn't want to be the engine behind their success.

"All at once," he complained, "they became big megastars overnight."

Although the Bessettes had nearly a year to look for a new location, none they scouted had enough available space, the proper acoustics and lighting, or an affordable price. They decided against returning to Chicago. After making it to Vegas, going east again felt like a step backward. Ron decided to abandon his impersonator and karaoke businesses in favor of a new venture, a package and mailing service. Sandy quit her job to help him.

They had no choice but to inform the membership that they would not hold a convention. Sandy brooded over what had happened. They charged fair ticket prices; they held the shows in the center of the Strip. She had worked hard. She thought the impersonators supported the association and what it stood for. What went wrong?

When word got out, most people weren't surprised. Some of the members always suspected the EPIIA of being on shaky ground, financial or otherwise, even though they attended the conventions. Though Ron had said they had identified anywhere from 2,500 to 3,500 impersonators worldwide, membership had topped off at about 300. Even though representatives of the retarded citizens' charity attended the conventions and told the impersonators how they spent EPIIA donations, even though credible sources like Jerome Marion vouched for them, many impersonators thought the Bessettes had their own interests at heart more than they did the brotherhood of Elvis.

"Let's put it this way," said Ronny Craig, who liked the Bessettes. "It's not happening anymore, is it? So let's just take it for face value."

Others considered the convention an idea conceived for all the right reasons but executed poorly. Robert Lopez, better known as El Vez, said he visited the convention and was shocked at the Bessette's lack of marketing savvy. To him, they took themselves so seriously they eliminated a large part of their potential audience. They catered so much to the diehard Elvis fans that they ignored tourists who might be curious about a room full of people dressed up like Elvis.

"I think lots of times they fear people are gonna say, 'Oh, let's go see the freak Elvises,'" he said. "And of course, that's gonna happen. That's just the nature of the beast. I mean, the whole idea of impersonating a dead rock star is curiosity's sake for anybody." He envisioned ways EPIIA members could have exploited themselves, from standing on the Strip handing out flyers to playing videos in the lobby. "People want a show in any kind of sense," he said, "so you have to give them entertainment."

He worked on some early conventions with the Bessettes, but soon realized that they didn't welcome his kind of act, which celebrates the Elvis mystique by gently warping it. He got the idea only certain performers who fit the Bessette's standards of quality were welcomed. "At first they were real nice to me, and then they got big headed. 'Oh, no, we don't want you and that thing.' I said, 'OK, that's your prerogative.'"

Dave Carlson had the opposite view: Too many Elvises spoiled the mix. He had helped the Bessettes start the group but bailed out because he grew disillusioned with the caliber of some of the people who joined. He had worked as an impersonator for more than twenty years, and as a businessman he had hoped the EPIIA would encourage professionalism. It used to be that not just anyone could impersonate Elvis. Now anyone with some gumption and a plane ticket to Vegas could horn in on the action.

"I can't really say for sure if they've created a good or bad image," he said. "They've certainly opened the floodgates for getting a lot of exposure for impersonators, and creating a lot of wannabes—opening the door for them. In other words, if you didn't know how to go about it, you would now, because they would tell you where to get a jumpsuit, where to buy boots, everything down to black hair dye, what kind you use, how you market yourself or establish yourself—everything you need to know to be an impersonator. So if there were, let's say, a thousand people who wanted to be an impersonator, and maybe only one or two would be able to make it out of that, I think probably with the association coming into being, I would say, probably, seven hundred fifty out of that thousand could be impersonators. Because you don't have to figure out anything on your own anymore."

The Bessettes considered this one of their greatest successes, that anyone with the drive and skill could visit Las Vegas and learn from the masters. And they thought their work had been appreciated. But Sandy was surprised to find that impersonators, people used to being set apart in the world, regained that attitude when they left Las Vegas. With all the joy the last convention had created, only three members called to thank her. And she became bitter when members were surprised that things ended so fast. Hadn't they read the warnings in the newsletters? Didn't they hear Jerome and Ron at the convention? She had stayed up all night some nights writing those newsletters. She had poured five years of her life into the association. And now she realized she had done it all for nothing. When she talked about it—and she didn't like to talk about it—her voice had edges like shattered glass. She said if she had to do it over again, she would never have started the association.

"It's a lot of work," she said. "A lot of work. And really no reward." She paused. "It's kind of sad to leave it like that, but that's the impression it left on me. To work, to work all year long, to give these guys something to look forward to, and get no reward out of it. We couldn't even get the guys to give us information for the newsletter to let the fans know where they were performing. They wouldn't even send in their schedules. They wanted us to do all the work, and they wanted to be on the stage and get highlighted."

The only two who kept in touch were Rick Marino and Jerome Marion. Rick had some ideas about salvaging the showcase, but he had other commitments. He and his wife, Susie, had a baby boy—conceived, he believed, on Elvis's birthday. Plus he was building an addition on the house and maintaining his own career. Jerome decided to see what he could do to keep at least part of the group going. It had helped to boost his career five years earlier, and he hated to see it die.

So, after after seeking written permission from Ron and Sandy to use the association's name, he scheduled a one-night convention at the Sabre Room in July, almost one year after the Las Vegas blowout. He put up about $1,000 out of his own pocket for tickets and worked out a deal where the club would make money on a two-drink minimum and ticket sales. It wasn't Las Vegas, but Hickory Hills was better than oblivion. He put out the call for performers, and a lot of the usual suspects showed, especially ones from the Chicago area like Dennis. That night, as the Exspence Account tore down their equipment, Jerome stood near the stage hugging people like he had just won the lottery. In a way he had: The show cleared $2,500. If he could keep the guys interested, make money—and spend no money out of his own pocket—the EPIIA would continue. He put the money in an account, for the next year. The rest of the Elvises set their sights on Memphis.

Irv Cass headed south that August on a chartered bus with forty-two of his most serious fans. Another twenty-two drove down, a convoy coming from Indiana and Michigan just to hear him sing—and, they hoped, take first prize in the Images of Elvis contest. It was quite a ride. Irv sang to the fans, and they watched Elvis videos like *Aloha from Hawaii.* This is the only video that Louise Rozek can remember seeing. She claimed she could not remember most of the trip, and blamed it on the failing memory of a sixty-seven-year-old. More likely it had something to do with another memory of the ride down. Halfway to Memphis, Louise walked up to Irv and handed him a small, neatly wrapped package.

"Here, Irv," she said, "this is for you."

Louise worked as a social worker for the elderly. She shared a house in South Bend with her youngest daughter, Lorrie, that they filled with impersonator pictures and at least eighteen Elvis collectors' plates. Sometimes at Irv's shows Louise would jump on stage, run her hands up and down his body and look into his eyes while he played along with the joke. People would tell her they wish they had her nerve. She told them nerve had nothing to do with it. If she felt like doing something, she just did it. Life had taught her that. "That's why I act so crazy and I have fun," she said. "Every day of my life. Because I never know when that curtain's gonna come down. And everybody can say, 'Well, Louise enjoyed herself.'"

Her life wasn't always so sweet. She divorced her husband of twenty-seven years after she went to the Prayer Tower at Oral Roberts University and asked God what she should do.

"I now look back on my married life and think, 'Why did you put up with this?'" she said. "Mine was not with hitting and all that. It was verbal. And I did not like myself. I would look in the mirror, and I hated what I saw. Until I got the courage to change it."

She then met a wonderful man who took her to Hawaii nine times. They spent twelve years together. After he died of a heart attack, she said, "I kind of put myself within." But her older daughter knew how much she loved Elvis and in 1990 convinced Louise to come hear Doug Church sing. After Doug left town for bigger things, she began following Irv. She came to consider his fan club an extended family and Irv a special friend. "He's just so genuine," she said. "He's not cheap. He lets everybody know he doesn't think he's Elvis. He makes sure sometime in the evening, he will get back to the farthest person in the back and he'll shake hands. He'll just make you feel like you're a very important person. And not all of 'em do that. I mean, it's like this—he's just a nice guy!"

She especially liked the way Irv hit it off with her youngest daughter. Lorrie, who was thirty, had Down's syndrome and a deep affection for all things Elvis. "Teddy Bear" was her favorite song, and her favorite impersonator was Irv. At Elvis shows she worked the room, visiting with friends and showing off her collection of scarves. "I was blessed with Lorrie," Louise said. "And I was blessed with her for a reason, I always say, because God knew that I would have a lonely life without her. I really feel that. People say they send special children for special people." She laughed. "Well, they sent a special child to me and I'm not special!"

One of the joys in her life was watching how Irv and Lorrie got along. He would clown with her during shows and hang out with her after he was done. It thrilled Louise when people asked, "Is that your son? Is that his sister?"

"To see the love," she said, "it's nothing fake."

Louise wondered if she could ever thank Irv for the ways he enriched their lives. Before Memphis that year, she hit upon an idea.

She had gotten an idea to surprise him after she inherited a ring from a dear friend. It was a woman's ring with three diamonds, two small and one large—a beautiful piece of jewelry, but too gaudy and elaborate for her taste. She was a sturdily built woman who combed her thick silver hair straight back, wore hardly any makeup, lived in pants. Louise also owned a more simple ring with rubies, her birthstone. It once had held five stones, but two had fallen out. She studied the rings and hatched a plan to do something special for Irv. He had treated Lorrie so well since they had met. He bought her teddy bears, in honor of her favorite Elvis song. He paid attention to her. He treated her like a sister, a friend. She shared her idea with her four other children first. Did they approve, or did they need anything for the kids? No, they told her, do whatever you want. It never occurred to her to keep the ring for herself, or to make money from the deal. "Value don't mean nothing," she said. Then she laughed. "Sorry—I sound crazy when I say that. But the value of it *doesn't* mean anything—it was just a gift."

She took the rings to a jeweler. When she returned she picked up two rings that used the same stones in new settings. One was a simple woman's ring set with two small diamonds and three rubies. It would be her ring, a keepsake for her daughters after she died. The other was a man's ring, fourteen-karat gold, with a half-karat diamond in the center and four smaller diamonds in the band, sized to wear on a little finger. This ring would belong to Irv. The jeweler gave her papers on it. It was worth nearly $5,000.

Irv stared at the ring, and Louise heard a couple of the women behind her grumbling about the gift. It saddened her, but she brushed it off.

"Are you sure you want to give this to me?" he asked her.

"No, I want it back," Louise said, teasing him. Then she told him, "Yes, I want you to have it. I want you to have it, I want you to wear it, I want you always to remember Lorrie and her mother, and always remember that we love you dearly, and this is what we can do for you."

Irv barely knew what to say, and he didn't know what to think. He was touched and uneasy all at once. Gifts from family were one thing, but sometimes it felt funny getting presents from fans. If he tried to repay them all, he would go broke. At that moment, he had one hundred teddy bears in his attic. And now this ring—he hadn't done anything to deserve it. Women who were sitting nearby leaned over their seats for a look.

"Why don't you take me to Red Lobster for a shrimp dinner?" he asked Louise. "That's *nice*, you know? Don't give me no diamond rings." But then Louise told Irv the whole story: how the diamonds had come to her, how they hadn't really ever belonged to her. How now, if he so chose, they belonged to him.

He accepted the gift, to Louise and Lorrie's delight. It was an emotional moment for him, too. But it also was one of those times when Irv realized that though he may impersonate Elvis Presley, the love he received and the problems he faced belonged to nobody but him.

"And then the funny thing about it is somebody else on the bus got jealous," he said. "She says to me, 'Well, we don't have a lot of money, we don't give you a lot of gifts, but we're your fans too.'

"And for this lady to say this to me—I told her, I said, 'Look.' I said, 'Trust me.' I said, 'That diamond ring—I didn't want that diamond ring. I treat Lorrie the way I treat her because she's special. You're special in a different way. But she has got Down syndrome, she's special to a lot of people.' And I said, 'Don't think for one minute that I treat her extra special to get a ring!' It made me mad! I told her, 'You got me all wrong if you think I'm in this for the gifts. I'm not.'"

More and more Irv had begun to see how success must have weighed on Elvis. No matter what he did, someone would love it and someone else would slink off hurt or offended. By becoming an Elvis impersonator he had made real friends and inherited real problems.

"I'm a simple guy," he said. "I like real stuff, you know. Don't buy me a car, or a ring, or nothing—take me to dinner, you know? Get me a card, take me to dinner for thirty bucks. To McDonald's. I don't care."

The first full day they spent in Memphis, Gail and the rest of the gang lounged by the pool at the La Quinta, their traditional haunt. The night before the show had ended early, and they had used the time to get some sleep. By the end of the week they would forget what feeling rested felt like. And they couldn't wait. As he had promised, Doc Franklin had moved the contest to the Best Western near the airport. Not only was it a cleaner, classier venue, but it was a two-minute walk across the road from their motel. Just about everyone was coming to town—Rick Lenzi, of legal drinking age and performing this year on Denese's advice as Ricky Aaron; Ronny Craig, driving in from Branson; Carol Henry and Cookie Mignogno, who was staying in a room just off the pool; and Steve Chappell, last year's winner, starring as one of Doc Franklin's featured performers. The only person not coming was Ray Guillemette, who had decided, after his talk with Franklin at the 1994 contest, to sit out a year.

Forecasts predicted that every day that week, the temperature would climb into at least the mid-nineties. By the next weekend the temperature would hit 100. But nobody came all the way from Milwaukee to complain about the heat. The women lounged on chairs around a table with an umbrella and rubbed ice cubes from the vending room all over their arms and throats. Empty bags of potato chips and empty soda cans chased around them in a breeze that felt like hot breath. Jenna frisked in the pool with a group of new friends. Some might call them foolish for sitting out in such heat, but then they were used to having their motives questioned.

"That's like our family," Shelley was saying. "They think we're all like the craziest people: 'Oh, traveling around? What's the matter with you?'"

"'Aren't you ever going to quit that?'" Gail chimed in, laughing.

"They think it's like a stage or something," Shelley said.

"They say, 'Don't you know he's dead? What are you going there for?'" Chris said. "I say, 'I'm not going to look for Elvis—I'm going there to see the Elvis impersonators.'

'What do you do there?'

'Party. Eat.'"

"Relax," Gail added, and the others leaned back and moaned in agreement.

"What do you *do* on vacation?" Kelly said, and everybody laughed.

"You could go to Florida," Chris said, then shook her head. "There's more to do here than there is in Florida."

"A couple times in the beginning when we first came," Gail said, "we went hard. We'd stay up late and we'd get up after three, four hours and hit it all day. But I mean, how many times can you walk through those shops?"

"The main thing I tell people is that when we go there, we've met a lot of people through the years," Chris explained. "And everybody's there for the same reason. Everybody's here for the Elvis music, or that type of music. Everybody. You have that in common. And even if you went to Florida, every year, how many times would you actually run into the same people?"

"Right," Gail said.

"It's just like a big reunion." She nodded at Gail and Shelley. "I mean, you guys have been coming here longer than us, but just between Indiana and Illinois and here, we've probably met like a hundred people and we see them at least twice a year."

From the parking lot Fred Wolfe and his younger sister, Sonja, came loping in, carrying shopping bags.

"Evvis! Evvis! Evvis!" Chris cried when she saw him.

"Oh, Fred Nugent, hey!" Gail said. They all liked to kid him about his hard-rock take on Elvis.

He nodded, mock solemn. "We're here," he said, sounding as businesslike as possible for a man wearing baggy shorts and a half-combed pompadour longer than it had been the year before. "Let's get some music on," he said. He passed out cans of beer that turned instantly sweaty from the heat.

He was in good spirits. The night before he performed in the semifinals. He wore his lucky Blue Owl suit and, except for a few moments during the slower songs, never stood still. He churned into a small tornado during "Suspicious Minds," lunged and touched his right big toe, made a woman in the audience bury her face in her hands when he sang to her. "Don't be shy," he pleaded. The audience loved it.

"What do you wanna hear?" Chris asked.

"What you got here besides Elvis?" he asked. The women laughed—Elvis was all they had been playing all day. "Come on, this is Memphis. All you hear is Elvis!" They kept laughing until Fred joined in. "Kind of ironic, isn't it?"

"I got some Yanni up in the room," Gail said, teasing him.

"Don't you have any Zamfir or anything as equally good?" He fiddled with the antenna and settled on some Tom Petty. "I've already programmed all the stations in the car," he said. He told the women he had decided to base one of his Elvis shows on a Jimmy Page-Robert Plant concert he had just seen.

"See, Elvis is rock and roll, but too many people tend to dwell on the past of Elvis," he said. "I am the fired-up, charged-up Elvis, man."

Gail mentioned that Dennis had torn his house apart and still could not find his white Pinwheel jumpsuit with the ruby jewels. He finally decided he must have left it at the EPIIA convention at the Sabre Room just a few weeks earlier. "He called there and they said that there's a backstage," she said. "They probably figured that whose ever it is would know that it's missing. Who would not notice that?"

"Dennis," Kelly said, and everybody laughed.

Fred slouched in his chair and studied his beer can. "I find it really silly when people wear those suits out in public and shit."

"You can tell the goofs from the professionals," Chris said. "You go to Graceland, and the ones that are walking around in their jumpsuits at Graceland, don't even talk to them. The more professional ones have regular street clothes on."

"I know," Fred said. "You can't wear your gig all the time. Kinda takes all the fun out of it."

A plane roared overhead. The motel was minutes from the airport. Everyone tipped their heads back for a look; Kelly and Chris, who live near the airport in Milwaukee, didn't even flinch. Time dragged. Everyone talked about nothing in particular. They moved only to lift their drinks.

"This is about the most fun I've had all year long," Fred said. "It's so good to be back home, you know? It's so good to be back where all of us have such good times. We all really do, no matter what, we all come out of this having a good time, and that's what's more important than anything else." The women all nodded. "Elvis brings us together. I mean, the poor guy croaks, and we're all having a great time!" The women laughed.

No one moved. Jenna splashed in the pool.

"You know, Kiss is my favorite band," Fred said. "And those guys were a very visual band, you know, putting on a very visual kind of show. If I had the money to do what I wanted to in an Elvis show, I'd do it in a Kiss vein. I'm serious. I would have risers, I would have the stage that would go up and down and stuff like that, I'd have smoke, fire, fireworks—I mean, people would be walking out of my concert going, 'What the hell was that?' And you know what? I would be able to carry it off. 'Wow, what was it? I think it was the Elvis show.' But I would make it into more my own show than just an Elvis thing. You know, get us some really wild costumes. I've got some ideas for costumes already that would be really wild. Something with a really huge cape. A pleated kind of cape that would come up and you could go all the way up with it, and it would fan out like a real fan. Then it would look like a big sun or something like that. I'd have a spectacle where people would come and see me and go, 'Wow, that was something just to see.' You can't dazzle 'em with brilliance, baffle 'em with bullshit! That's my motto. You know, people are very susceptible to a visual thing."

They all listened, closed their eyes, and smiled. It did feel good to be back home.

The performing at the 1995 contest stacked up the same as always—unknown Elvises the first two nights, with abilities building as the week wore on. For those with a hankering to see impersonators, few places were as comforting that summer as the ballroom at the Best Western. Dozens of impersonators had entered. And four past winners—Steve Chappell, Michael Hoover, Mori Yasumasa, and Kevin Mills—would perform as special guests through the week.

"Many fans assume that Memphis is a hotbed of Elvis talent all year round. Wrong!!" June's Images of Elvis newsletter said. "Either familiarity breeds contempt, or the Memphis fans would rather hear the real thing on their CDs and tapes, because you can't find an Elvis tribute show around here except in January or August. But these shows make the wait worthwhile. And the charismatic personalities of these winners make us all feel as if they are performing for each of us alone. How many of us don't return, in our minds, to days gone by, when we hear those . . . voices?"

On stage that second night, Kevin Mills, the 1990 Images of Elvis winner, performed a special show. The contest had helped him build a life beyond his pizza restaurant; this summer, he was singing at the Hollywood Casino in Tunica, Mississippi, not far from Memphis.

The mood in the room was hungry and happy. The women seemed fully prepared to return to days gone by while they had some fun right this minute. It was early in the week, they were fresh, and they screamed a lot. Most of the impersonators looked nothing like Elvis, even with all the trappings. But what they managed to suggest told the audience everything it needed to know and craved to understand. The hair sloshed across the forehead, the shoes flashed, the clothes agitated around dancing legs. Then an expression, or a shout—*rock it!*—and for an instant the impersonator actually looked like Elvis. But as soon it it happened, the illusion vanished. Maybe that's one reason why everyone screams when a man shakes his body or twists his face into something so strange and familiar: Illusion is fleeting, and when one appears you hold on as long as you can.

One person in the room holding no illusions whatsoever was Fred Wolfe. He stood near the back of the ballroom watching Kevin Mills sing, wearing shorts, a silk shirt, and a sour-lemon expression.

"Maybe I'm just me," he said, "I'm just a cynic and I'm just very fussy about my Elvis. If that's Elvis, I'm Schmelvis. If that's Elvis, I'm the pope."

"Are you as hard on yourself as you are on other people?"

"Yes," he said. "I am." Fred did 200 performances a year, and if he was lucky he liked maybe two of them. It is not that he aspired to mimic Elvis exactly, but he wanted to conjure in the people who watched him the exact essence of hysteria and passion audiences got from Elvis. "I mean, how can you be satisfied with your performance if the whole audience doesn't get up, rip their clothes off, and go into a frenzy and rip everything off of you?" he asked. "Obviously you're not getting that kind of response that Elvis did, so how good can you be?" He laughed. "How good can you be?" He retained the attitude he'd displayed at last year's contest, but there was something else this year. His attitude was not only self-critical, but also self-reflective. Seeing his friends had cheered him earlier that day, but being among the other Elvises and the crowds darkened his mood.

After midnight the ballroom bar shut down. The screaming intensified to the point that Fred's philosophies became inaudible, and he grew bored. We decided to leave the contest in search of beer. We walked through the lobby to the back parking lot and climbed into Fred's rental car, a four-door Pontiac roughly the same purple as the 1956 El Dorado convertible Elvis once owned, the one whose color he chose by smashing a fistful of grapes on the fender. On Brooks Road we passed the former Bad Bob's, still a strip club. We looked but didn't say anything. We went by a fast-food chicken joint, and Fred expressed his affection for fried foods and macaroni and cheese.

"It's really funny," he said, "because Elvis never got to appreciate fine cuisine, but I like both ends of the spectrum. I can eat fine cuisine anywhere, anytime and appreciate it for what it is. And most people—well, they see only a certain dimension. That's really sad. It's the first impression thing that everybody has. And that seems to be what sticks with most people."

About two miles from the hotel we turned left into a convenience store called Mapco Express. Two young guys, maybe eighteen years old, gaped as Fred and his pompadour emerged from a car the color of smashed grapes. His silk shirt glowed under the humming parking-lot lights. I wondered why they were staring. Then, suddenly, I remembered why. I realized with a start that I had spent the last hour talking to Fred, and I had totally forgotten what he looked like.

"Elvis!" one of the boys, a skinny blond, yelled, though we stood maybe five feet away. "Hey, man, I thought you were dead!"

Sometimes, when people harassed him, Fred pretended he didn't speak English. Or he played dumb. His logic was that people would leave him alone if they thought he was just stupid, as opposed to crazy. But that night he wasn't playing. "How's it goin', guys," he said, a little wearily, and we ducked into the air conditioning. Fred steered straight for the beer cases against the back wall and fished out a six of something called Gold Crest. At the counter he asked the cashier, a pretty African-American woman with tall hair twisted like an ice-cream cone, if they stocked something else. She told him no. The entire time she rang up the beer she never took her eyes off Fred's hair.

We returned to the car as the young guys left in a white Camaro turned gray with age and southern sun. The skinny blond guy leaned out of the driver's side window. "Elvis is not dead!" he shouted. "Elvis has left the Mapco!"

Fred chuckled, in spite of his mood. "That's pretty funny," he said. To the boys he shouted back, "Hey, you guys, have a good night. Take it easy." They waved and roared off.

Back in the car, Fred opened a beer. "Nice and smooth," he sighed, fiddling with the radio. "I like to buy craft beers if I can find them," he said, and he tipped back his head and drank. "Oh," he said, "this is just not bad at all." He stumbled onto the song "Without You."

"Oh, this is my favorite Mötley Crüe of all time!" he cried, cranking the volume. He sang a line. He sounded fine, raspy but not too rough. "I'm a very good singer. I just happen to do Elvis, you know? Like I always say, I'm an actor. I happen to be portraying Elvis at this point. I'm not Elvis, I'm just portraying Elvis."

"Do you feel like a rocker trapped in an Elvis's body?" I asked.

"Elvis *was* a rocker," he said. "Do I feel stifled? I don't know. I don't think so. I don't really feel stifled, other than the fact I can't grow my hair long. If I had my druthers, I'd rather have my hair a little longer. It's just the way I am, you know? It's just me." He sang: *"Without you* . . . I should be in the top rock and roll band in the world!" He pointed at the radio: "I should be that guy! That's the way things should be—I'm tellin' ya. I could be the number one guy out there. I'm serious. I could do it and I could keep the audience with me and not just let them go. Not like a one-hit wonder kind of thing. I could be the next big entertainer. I could make it happen. There's no reason why it could not happen to me." We passed the Headliner Club, squatting in the dark. Fred shrugged. "I don't have that image. But fate has conspired to deal me that. I don't know—I guess I'm continually experiencing a endless search for recognition."

"Really?"

"Oh, yeah. If nothing else, it's a search for recognition. It's hard to get recognition and acceptance because of what I do. And that bugs me to no end." The song ended. "Great song. Oh, man, it's too classic. I really wish that I got recognized for what I did in rock and roll. I mean, the Elvis thing is cool, but as an artist, it's ultimately unsatisfying, because you're imitating somebody else. I mean, you're mining territory that's already been mined. You're picking through the tailings of a diamond mine, looking for another diamond that somebody else overlooked." He laughed, pleased with his own analogy. "That's exactly how I feel about it. It's a drag, I'll tell you that. And all you're going to pull out of this is little tiny diamonds—you're not going to get anything big."

The night turned purple where the streetlights shone. We made a right into the Best Western parking lot. There was no one singing inside that Fred wanted to hear, so we sat in the car, drinking Gold Crest and listening to the radio. We spoke of many things—the lack of Frank Sinatra impersonators, the way that after all these years Fred still looked up to Elvis. Moths whispered at the windows.

"I don't consider myself an impersonator," he said. "Everybody else does. I don't." He caught me looking at him, and he laughed. "I'm not an impersonator, man. I'm a rock and roller. I mean, maybe I really have not come to fully accept what the hell I'm doing. That could be it, too. I don't really accept what I'm doing. I refuse to be pigeonholed as just an Elvis impersonator." He aimed the neck of his beer bottle toward some imaginary enemy in the parking lot. "I say, listen, dammit, I'm a good entertainer. I'm not just an Elvis impersonator. You asshole. Look past the immediate of what you see and take a good look. Don't dismiss me. You can't dismiss me. Oh, what do you say? You just lump me in with the rest of those fucks? That is not me. And when you lump me in, that will piss me off. Because that is not me. I am not like the rest of them. I am not. I am not." He grinned. "But I guess by virtue of what I do, there you are. You're as good as the lowest common denominator."

The air outside the car was so thick you began to think you could hear it pass by. In the bushes, cicadas. "Oh, this is beer," Fred said.

About an hour had passed since we left. Inside, Michael Hoover, or maybe now it was Steve Chappell, sang and shook inside the ballroom. Certainly, women were screaming. On the car radio, Judas Priest ground into "Breaking the Law." Fred paused from talking long enough to sing the refrain while thrashing his head about an inch from the steering wheel. He looked genuinely happy, more so than he ever did at the contest. "I love this shit," he said. "If I were to say anything about myself, I just love rock and roll. The music is my life. Sad but true. Sad but true."

We spoke of many other things. Fred described the biggest triumph and shame of his career. Both were rolled into the same event, a baseball game at Tiger Stadium. He sang "Take Me Out to the Ball Game" to his biggest crowd ever. Unfortunately, he got past the first verse and forgot the words. The fans booed Elvis.

We also discussed the fact that Fred has not had a serious relationship in two years. He said this, then slammed the dashboard with both hands. "It's his fuckin' fault," he said. "Rotten prick. It's Elvis's fault." He thought for a moment. "Actually, it's my own fault. It's my own fault for looking like him." He laughed. "It's my own fault for doin' this shit. Because I choose to make the money for looking like Elvis, and doing the Elvis thing, is the only reason I'm not getting anything on the other end." If he didn't impersonate Elvis, girls could see him for who he really was. But he loved what he did too much to stop. And he couldn't imagine another way to get people to pay him $250 an hour.

Fred cursed how society seemed to embrace the lowest common denominator of cultural endeavor. He said this trait complicated his life; too many lame impersonators made things difficult for rockers like himself. He complained that people depend so much on television for entertainment that they have stopped forming opinions on their own. "Unfortunately, the real sad thing about it is that people nowadays don't have concrete opinions about anything, because they want to be politically correct," he said. "That's the biggest fuckin' crock of shit there is. It is, I'm telling ya, it's the biggest crock of shit of all time. But I guess unfortunately, that's the way things are gonna be. Because of this political correctness crap, we're all forced to do things that do not necessarily make us a better group of people living in this time. But you know what? We're the only sentient beings in the universe, so why don't we get our shit together? We're the only sentient beings in the universe! Act as if you are. That's the thing. Act as if you are! Act your age! Doesn't that mean anything to anybody anymore?"

He smiled. "I tell ya, though—somebody's gonna tell it like it is one day. And things are gonna change. And that's cool. I can appreciate it. There's hope yet. I have hope. Like Pandora's box—the only thing that was left was what?"

"Hope," I said.

"Hope," he said right back. "Hope is the only thing we have left in Pandora's box. We left all the evil out in the world. Now all we have left is hope. And hope is the only thing that can get us by. Because we have that hope that maybe things are gonna be different, and maybe, if not in our own lives, things are gonna be different on the other side."

On Monday most of the gang—Shelley, Kelly, Chris, Fred, and Sonja, plus Steve Chappell and his brother, Ronnie—piled into a chartered van and headed for the casinos in Tunica, Mississippi, about thirty miles south. Gail stayed behind with Jenna at La Quinta to wait for Dennis, who was driving down in the red Corvette. On the trip, Chris dreamed aloud of what she would buy with all the money she planned to win. Fred engaged the driver in a discussion about kudzu.

The casinos, arranged in a sort of strip-mall complex, sat in the middle of a green field. There was nothing else. It looked as if a tornado had picked up a piece of Las Vegas, gave it a few gyrations, then let it all drop into the soybean fields.

Inside the Hollywood Casino, it was sweepstakes bright, and the buffet featured unlimited prime rib. At the door everyone got an ID card to collect bonus points from the machines. Fred told the woman at the registration desk that his name was Gene Simmons, who is the lead singer of Kiss. Every time he inserted his card into a slot machine its readout greeted him with: "Welcome to Hollywood, Gene." Fred and Sonja played mostly nickel slots, then Fred racked up 562 million points in two games on a *Stargate* pinball machine. They wandered on jungle-print carpet through rows of slots and tables, pointing out all the show business memorabilia displayed everywhere. There was a jumpsuit Elvis wore in 1974, and a car he used in *Spinout*. Sonja pulled out her camera as Fred examined the tiny racer, and when he saw her he scowled.

"Don't you want a picture?" she asked.

"It's just a car," he said, walking away.

Chris enjoyed a more memorable trip, winning $618 playing dollar slots and video poker. The money would come in handy, she decided on the way back to Memphis, for snow tires. By the time the group returned, via Elvis Presley Boulevard, Dennis was sleeping at the hotel.

14

Vigil

*D*ennis entered the contest in 1995 with hopes of making the finals. "And it's not even with the thought of going down there to win or whatever," he said after he signed up. "Because I think you and I both know that winning that thing has a lot more to do with just being there for a while and people liking you. It's a political thing, I think, more than actually who's the most talented or the best Elvis impersonator. But the way I look at it, I'm nowhere near the best anyway, but I think that I do a fair enough job that I'll probably be a finalist. Maybe." He laughed. "But that's not saying a lot—I mean, there are a lot of finalists!"

But his chances had improved because he had. Since the contest the previous year, he had swung a few paid gigs at parties and bars, enough to earn about $1,500 from January to June—money he considered outside investment in his dream. He had unleashed enough foolish mistakes upon unsuspecting audiences to learn how to better conduct himself onstage. Whenever he attended a gathering of impersonators, he seized the chance to ask for tips on movement and voice from local guys like Rick Saucedo and Joe Tirrito. He won $600 singing karaoke at a Milwaukee bar called, fittingly, the Red Corvette. He strayed from safer ballads in favor of more demanding songs like "American Trilogy" or "Polk Salad Annie." More often he nailed the risky notes, like the final reach in "Trilogy."

Nobody said much about his hair in the months since he'd dyed it. Shelley joked that they needed to give his retired wig a name, it had

been so much a part of their lives. Once she sneaked into Dennis's bathroom with it and tried it on, just to see how it felt to look like Elvis. Not
to be outdone, Gail wore it with one of Dennis's jumpsuits and sang a
little karaoke one night. Both of them quit their Elvis careers after seeing
themselves in the wig. As for Dennis, he had grown accustomed to his
pompadour, though he cheated a little by growing long sideburns only
for major shows.

The technical problem that dogged him most—still—was movement.
Overall he had improved; he danced more out of purpose than panic.
But he still looked stiff on stage, a little afraid he might fly apart if he let
go. His good friend and fellow impersonator Bob West bugged him to
move more when they held practice sessions at Dennis's house. He had
a good voice, Bob told him, why not put some moves with it? But cutting
loose when no one was around to see it struck Dennis as silly. Every
time he had tried it he felt like a goofy son of a gun.

His stage patter still needed work. At a Sabre Room show a couple of
months before Memphis, he took a drink of water after a strenuous song
and told the ladies he could always go for something warm and wet. The
ladies didn't quite know what to make of that. Dennis didn't blame them.

But his biggest problem continued to be internal. In Memphis the
year before, Dennis had achieved his dream of performing at the contest, and he had reached the finals besides. He had finally rid himself of
the wig and learned to have some fun. He wasn't the same person he
was fourteen months earlier—which was of course the point.

Now he needed to learn something more precious and difficult because it sprung not from natural talent but from faith—a belief that he
could shake free the feeling that he had not only stopped looking foolish
but also admit that he had gotten good. This was hard because, like Fred
Wolfe and a lot of the other Elvises, he struggled with how mastering the
art of being someone else had endangered, even erased, parts of his
own personality. It surprised him how easily everyone had adapted to
him with black hair and sideburns. He had refined the surface, but a
piece of him resisted the total transformation that claimed his face and
hair. He wanted more than anything to be serious, but he feared being
overtaken.

Having fun came easier, though not without a fight. After checking out
the contest Monday night Dennis slept until noon, then woke and set
up his karaoke machine by the pool. One of the reasons the group

stayed at La Quinta was because no one seemed to mind if the impersonators sang around the pool, as long as they kept it quiet at night. This didn't always happen. Dennis had a way of forgetting it was 4:00 in the morning when he started to sing. Police officers have sometimes been surprise guests at his parties.

Around 1:00 P.M. people started to trickle in, carrying coolers and towels: Fred, Sonja, Rick Lenzi, Chris Wilson from Cincinnati, and Chris T. Young from South Bend. Everyone was talking about how much weight Chris Young had lost since last year's contest—about eighty pounds—and the buzz was that he stood a good chance of placing this year. He had improved enough that a slight rivalry had grown between him and his fellow South Bend area Elvis, Irv Cass. With young Rob Hunter from nearby Mishawaka, and each with a busload of fans to support them, speculation was that Indiana could pull off a clean sweep of the contest's top three slots.

But that kind of talk had no place at Dennis's karaoke parties. These poolside sessions were Gail's favorite part of the week. Without an audience around, without any competition or gossip to goad them, the guys could relax and act like themselves. After all these years it still fascinated her to see how intense some of them could become when they sunk into the spirit of a song. At those times it was easy to see why they loved doing Elvis.

Dennis started things off, singing some movie songs from a tape he had made himself. Chris Young had taken over when a heavy woman emerged from the manager's office and leaned on the metal fence around the pool. "I don't think you should be doing that there," she said.

Dennis explained to her that they had sung freely last August. Besides, it had taken him an hour to set up the equipment, and they had been singing less than ten minutes. Chris Young tried to joke with the woman, pointing to Dennis and saying, "I know he's not that good of a singer, but we can get somebody else to sing." Her face registered no expression.

"Can we possibly turn it down?" Dennis asked. "It's Elvis Week."

"No," she said.

"How about if we wait to see if somebody complains?"

"We can't have that," she said, and walked away.

As she left Fred bellowed, "We don't want your *Elvis kind* up here. Makin' fun of our homeboy."

Dennis scratched his neck and stared at his tennis shoes, deep in thought. With Gail and Chris Wilson in tow, he headed for the manager's office. After a few moments the manager, a stocky fellow in a sports shirt, walked out with them and leaned across the fence, resting his chin on his forearms. He asked how long they planned to continue. "Until about two or three," Dennis said, using his best wide-eyed, niceguy face.

The manager squinted at the scene. Five impersonators in sloppy shorts and swim trunks squinted back. A very Memphis standoff. "Well, the way I see it, if it's daylight . . ." the manager said. Everyone thanked him. Three women in tight perms at the opposite end of the pool, one in a T-shirt bearing the message "Elvis Fan," applauded him as he walked away.

Relieved, Dennis handed Fred the mike. "I know you're shy," he said. "Oh, yeah, I'm Mr. Shy," Fred said.

He urged Dennis to go first. As he cued up the machine, the others marveled over how mean that woman had been. Fred said, "If I'd stopped doing it when people gave me shit, I'd have stopped doing it a long time ago." After Dennis, Chris Wilson and Chris Young did a duet. Then Fred, who had stripped to a pair of black bikini swim trunks, took the mike and performed a gospel tune a cappella. A hush fell over the group; everyone in the pool stopped splashing. While he sang he closed his eyes and reached his hand up to his face, the gold bracelets on each wrist catching the sun. When he finished he shook his head as if he were shaking off a dream and barreled into "Jailhouse Rock." The women clapped and snapped some pictures.

Rick, his wet hair sculpted into a black mohawk, started "For the Good Times," then Chris Young grabbed the mike and Fred stepped in to finish. All of the guys smiled and told each other how great they sounded. Cookie arrived—her room was on the opposite side—and took a table in what little shade was left. She wore a low-cut lilac shirt, tight white capri pants, and sandals with beads jangling across the toe straps. This year her hair was a cool blond. She leaned back and listened, a little smile playing on her lips. On the other side of the karaoke machine, Kelly alternated between applying sunscreen and rubbing herself with ice cubes out of a beer cooler. The guys talked among themselves, dragging the wet mike cord across the wet cement. "Isn't that dangerous?" Gail asked them. They just shrugged.

It was well over ninety degrees, and after a couple of hours the heat finally got to them. Fred fell face first into the pool, and when his sideburns got wet blond hair showed through the tips of his sideburns. Rick plunged in after him, then Chris Wilson. It was a scene: all those slick dark pompadours bobbing in the bright blue water, their owners singing in unison. Fred climbed out to sing "My Way" and when he stuck the note at the end Chris Hottinger called to him, "You got it, boyfriend." She had just returned from a brewery tour with Steve Chappell and his brother, Ronnie. Chris Wilson soloed on "Sweet Caroline," known for the swinging one-arm move Elvis did in concert to its refrain. When Chris got to that part, Sonja, Shelley, Gail, Chris, and Jenna, all in the pool, did it along with him, laughing. Steve and Ronnie Chappell eventually showed up, drawn by the music. Dennis asked him to sing and the women in the pool egged him on, so he crooned "Love Me" and Garth Brooks's "The Dance."

"All right, do it up, Steve!" Fred yelled. Steve tossed him a towel as he finished as if it were a scarf. Fred clutched it like it was a million-dollar check and staggered across the hot cement, impersonating an impersonator fan.

It is hard enough to be different in this world. You could argue that impersonators are brave because they assume a new burden along with their original identity. It is as if they are saying: It is not enough to be me, for me or for anyone else. I also must become somebody else, no matter what happens.

But there are, it turns out, different kinds of different. After the death of Elvis and the resulting rise of impersonators, it was inevitable that men and women of all races, sexes, and ethnic backgrounds would want to reshape themselves in his image. More than ever his image has become a global commodity, a universal symbol of all things hopeful and attainable and American. It was not enough to follow that dream, as Elvis once sang. They wanted to own it, too. As El Vez, the Mexican Elvis, has said, Elvis is too important a job to be done by just a white man.

Some in the impersonator world agree. Irv Cass thought that Elvis would have flattered by the number and variety of impersonators. "He would have been more flattered that a black man, a Japanese, somebody of a different race, was trying to impersonate him—to know that that person from that race admired him that much," he said. "Elvis grew up around black people. Black people taught him everything he knew.

So I think he would have been more flattered if a Robert Washington impersonated him than he would have a white guy.

"People don't think about Elvis when they come to these contests. They think about what they think about—what *they* think Elvis was about. They don't know anything about him, you know?"

A few, however, preferred their impersonators white and male, just like Elvis. Just like them. They regarded these hybrids of cultures as disrespectful and dangerous to the image of what was right—ironically, the same complaint made about Elvis when he started out. The fact that most white male impersonators look nothing like Elvis seemed to be irrelevant. These were small criticisms circling a larger, more complex point: Elvis has become a figure upon which people project their own fantasies and dreams. When the results interpret more than they reproduce, it unsettles some people on a more intense level than do the guys with full-term beer bellies and home-sewn suits. It challenges the idea of what Elvis really means and who he really is. Racism and sexism are not dead in society at large, so it is naive to think that they would not appear in a population that, despite some sizeable quirks, is basically like everyone else. When a person expands his own definition of normal, it doesn't require him to accept anyone else's as true.

Some impersonators claim that nonwhite Elvises dilute the positive image of Elvis they try to put forth. Some even say they are not against impersonators of different races, but they worry it will give people who are racist more fuel for their beliefs.

"There's a couple black Elvises," said one impersonator, who did not want his name linked with these sentiments. "I have nothing against them—as a matter of fact, I think that they're probably better than a lot of the white Elvises. I mean that sincerely. But why are they doing Elvis? I don't understand that part, you know what I mean? It's like me going out and doing Michael Jackson."

"I'm not knocking Japanese people!" another said. "Japanese people are Japanese people. Americans are Americans, you know? It's just not right."

Most fans don't care. As long as an Elvis can sing and shake, they are satisfied. After a heated discussion on a 1992 segment of "Geraldo" about whether African-Americans should impersonate Elvis, the audience voted Clarence Giddens, the program's sole black guest, best of the Elvises assembled. Mori Yasumasa, the Japanese Elvis who won

Franklin's contest in 1992, has complained about a shortage of gigs. But he cannot return for special-guest sets at Franklin's contest without being mobbed.

"Mori was excellent," said Cookie Mignogno. "I have nothing against the foreigners. Some of them are quite good. I give them credit, I do, for doing it, because a lot of people are against, especially, like Robert Washington. You know, they said, 'Elvis wouldn't want a black person impersonating him.' But he's got a voice, he's got a terrific voice. To me, that's immaterial. When you think of it, Elvis, that's really what got him started—he had that black and white voice combined."

Cookie's friend and fellow impersonator expert Carol Henry also enjoyed watching unconventional performers. She was strict on one point—impersonators must look and sound like Elvis or they have no business calling themselves an impersonator. "I guess what I'm saying is a lot of people do not think any black people or Orientals, any other but just Caucasians should be in that contest," she said. "Now I can't say that I feel that strongly against it. But I do say that they need to sound and look like Elvis, if they want to be in the contest."

There was one variation Cookie and Carol refuse to accept and can barely stand to consider: women impersonators. "We never felt comfortable with those females," Carol said, "because we couldn't identify. Just couldn't identify. A lot of it being that I could think, hey, Elvis was a man. And I don't think Elvis would have liked a woman that was trying to be him."

Female Elvises stirred the sharpest disapproval among most women who attend the shows. Watching Toni Rae, a female Elvis with a gravelly Texas drawl, sing her way through an audience was a study in sexual politics and downright squeamishness. Cookie and Carol fixed their eyes on the ceiling when Toni paced nearby, searching for someone to sing to. She came right up in Gail's face once and Gail froze; it unsettled her, having this woman with the angular face, baggy fifties-style suit, and blond pompadour gaze into her eyes and sing. Others would laugh and hide their faces, but some accepted a hand and some deep eye contact. Then they sat with their mouths slightly unhinged, trying to figure out what had just happened.

Child impersonators were viewed as cute diversions, at worst vehicles of their parents' ambitions. But to these women, Elvis—and by association, impersonators—called to mind sex, but they didn't appreciate someone switching genders on their fantasy.

The girl who grew up in Texas as Toni Belinda Jernigan sometimes found it hard to be both a woman and an Elvis impersonator.

"Some people—true Elvis lovers—don't have a problem with it," she said. She leaned back in a chair outside the Best Western ballroom and unbuttoned her jacket, puffed out her chest. "But then you have your outside crowd that are not necessarily Elvis lovers and they all kinda make fun of me. But it doesn't bother me because they laughed Elvis off the stage at the Grand Ole Opry. And look what happened to him."

Toni knew from the first time she saw Elvis on TV she wanted to be a singer like him. Which is not the same, she stressed, as saying she wanted to *be* him. By sharing her own interpretation of how he moved and sounded, she could pay tribute to Elvis and maybe carve out a life in music for herself. So she moved to Memphis and got a job as a cook in a Waffle House off I-40. Sometimes, when somebody played an Elvis song on the jukebox, she would drop a couple of moves right there behind the counter, then keep on with her cooking.

"To me, Elvis represents rhythm," she said. "We all have a showman in us, whether we're writers, or whether we're artists with paintings, or singers. We all have a showman in us. And we like to excel."

In fact, Toni Rae believed that being a woman made her a better Elvis than many men. "I can move better than a lot of the guys," she said. "I have the shimmy in the chest that Elvis did that I use a lot. And I've had other guys come up to me and say, 'How do you do that shake thing?' Well, I have breasts to do it. Now I just tell 'em it's big clothes. I'm not gonna give away the secrets, you know—tricks of the trade."

Robert Washington, who spent his childhood listening to Elvis, said no one ever treated him differently because he was a black impersonator—along with Clarence Giddens, one of just two of any fame in the entire United States. When Robert advertised his shows he never mentioned that he was black. Often the first time the audience learned he was not the typical Elvis was when he walked out on stage. "And that's the way I like it," he said. "And out of twelve years that I've done it, I haven't had anything bad, racially. I've had guys come up to me after a show, they shake my hand—'You did a great job,' and it means a lot to me. They accept you for being a good Elvis entertainer. Regardless of your color—which is good, which is great."

He knew that some people found it unusual that an African-American would want to imitate a man many accuse of stealing black music, gospel, and rhythm and blues. After reading criticism and interviews with black musicians on the subject—and examining his own conscience—Robert decided that Elvis opened more doors than he barricaded for black musicians. "Some of the books coming out, and some of the artists who were around when Elvis started out, said that he stole from them and stuff," he said. "There's going to be hard feelings, I think, but if they would just take a minute and think about what Elvis did for black musicians of that time—how segregrated the United States was back then, and the South—especially the South. Any musician of that time would have to thank Elvis for opening doors by doing their music. It's sad, but you couldn't have been a black artist and probably got any further than those guys did. And I think a little bit is owed to Elvis for covering some of their songs."

Alice Dickey, Robert Washington's manager, considered herself a serious Elvis fan. Ten years after Elvis died the *New York Times* ran a picture of her in Memphis standing alongside a cardboard cutout of him from the sixties, one hand resting on his shoulder, the other on his arm. To her Robert was different from most impersonators only because he was more like Elvis. Alice, a small-boned, blunt-speaking, heavy-smoking woman, raised four children, three of them older than her sole client.

She met Robert through a fan club they both belong to in Maine called True Fans for Elvis. After she saw him perform, she suggested that if she could come up with fifteen reasons why she should be his manager, he should consider her for the job. "You're hired," he told her. "I don't need any reasons at all." Widowed and retired from an office job at Sears, she had time. So she booked his gigs, made his travel plans, and sent out his press packets—white folders with color photocopies of Robert cradling a guitar and lunging in his black leather suit in a grassy yard, in front of a bed of fuschia impatiens. When he was not at his shipbuilding job or at home with his own family he often hung out at her house—so much so that Alice considered him her fifth child.

She thought Robert made a superior impersonator because he wasn't white. "I think it makes him more recognizable," she said. "I don't know about the prejudice. I really don't. I've had suspicions, but there's nothing you can say for sure. I feel that him being African-American is an advantage. I think that's why he sounds so much like Elvis. Both of them were raised in the South, and they were both raised with the music, the rhythm and blues and the gospel. All the same things. Actually, the only difference between Robert and Elvis in their early years of growing up— there isn't any, except the color of their skin."

The impersonator who relied most on his differences as a selling point was El Vez. After doing Elvis as a lark, he began to realize he could take people's expectations of who Elvis was and who they thought he should be and use them to advance his own ideas about race, ethnicity, and identity. The results may not make him Elvis, he reasoned, but they made him more Elvis than you.

"I'm taking the icon, the history, and the expectations," he said. "And then I say, OK, we all know this. Now let's go beyond that. Or what if? An idea, if you will, of: OK, we have this as our basis, this part of Americana, this part of American heritage, this part of the American dream. Can this American dream be transposed with the Latino story?

"The American dream can be for anyone—black, white, man, woman, Jewish, straight, gay. It's the whole idea of self-empowerment. It's the whole idea of king, King Elvis—you can be king, too, if you want. And the idea of greatness can be for everybody. And it's a thing of pride. I think lots of people can walk out of an El Vez show proud to be Mexican. Even if they're not."

When it came to competition, few shared his sentiment for the new. In 1993, Toni Rae became the only woman ever to make the finals at Images of Elvis. Since then she had been unable to duplicate her success, a failure she blamed on herself. The year after she made the finals, she bound her chest to conceal her breasts. The elastic squeezed her like a snake every time she breathed, literally choking the song out of her. In 1995, she wore a sports bra but then found herself battling a fever, lying in bed the night before she performed sweating and freezing and unable to get the music out of her head. But she had to go on. She had moved to Memphis to pursue a dream. Until then, she planned to work at the Waffle House. "Until," she said, "I get famous."

Because their relationship was equal parts business and friendship, it hurt Alice when Robert delivered a performance so strong—running across the stage and giving a flying leap, falling flat on his back and still singing, so wild that she had to put down her cigarette, stand and applaud with the rest of the crowd, feel as proud of him as if he were one of her own kids—and then watch him lose to impersonators even strangers told her were inferior. At times she felt angry enough to challenge judges in contests, but resisted because she feared it would demean them both and ruin Robert's future prospects. "But he doesn't complain," she said. She shook her head. "He really doesn't."

They came to Memphis in 1995 hoping he could recapture the momentum he had when he finished second in 1992. "This one happens to have a history," she said of the contest, "if you can say you were an international champion in Memphis, Tennessee." She leaned her head forward for emphasis, and smoke scrolled around her pale sliver of a face. "But: I would hope it's worthy of being the winner of."

In the early evening after their pool party Dennis, Gail, Shelley, Jenna, and Rick got cleaned up and headed for Graceland. In the heat everyone wore shorts, except for Rick. He dressed in a copy of the two-piece black prison suit Elvis wore in "Jailhouse Rock," right down to the white stitching down the legs.

A lot of people asked him to pose for pictures, but that didn't exactly mean he stood out from the crowd. The atmosphere across the road from Graceland—at a strip of shops called Graceland Crossing and a small mall run by Elvis Presley Enterprises itself—attracts people who would attract attention themselves, if there weren't so many of them. Men, women, and children wore jumpsuits and mingled with the tourists. Knots of kids with blond spiked hair and German accents emerged from souvenir stores, giggling. Where else in the world could you buy Love Me Tender shampoo, or a stamped-metal reproduction of the movie poster from *Viva Las Vegas,* or a jewelry box with a lid depicting Elvis shaking hands with Richard Nixon in the Oval Office? A woman with cat's-eye glasses and a tattoo of a nurse on her right shoulder traipsed past a bald man wearing a Hawaiian shirt and gold-rimmed Elvis sunglasses, who stood near a hefty woman with a blond beehive and elastic bandages around her puffy ankles. She sat in front of the souvenir store Loose Ends, feet elevated on a chair, not even looking up when someone wearing a T-shirt from the Ray Guillemette Fan Club passed a man in a Kurt Cobain T-shirt, just to the left of a impersonator in need of full-body dry cleaning who danced with two women, then offered them business cards redeemable for one free hug. "If I can't have it all the way, I don't want it," one of them said.

Dennis and the rest weaved through this mix, window shopping and greeting people they knew. At a faux fifties diner called Rockabilly's, at the Graceland shops, they crammed into a booth and ate cheeseburgers and hot dogs beneath a picture of Weird Al Yankovic dressed like Michael Jackson. After that Dennis wanted to visit the record store, Good Rockin' Tonight, but Gail pressed him toward Elvis Presley Boulevard, which had been closed to traffic from Bluebird to Dolan. The candlelight service was starting.

From the first anniversary of Elvis's death people have stood in the street outside his house, held candles, and paid their respects. As Dennis and the group filtered into the crowd they saw Todd Morgan, director of communications for Graceland, standing behind a dais to the right of the mansion's gates. "How many Elvis fans we got on the boulevard tonight?" he asked.

Whoooo! the crowd said.

"The vast majority of the people here are very avid and devoted Elvis fans," Morgan said. "Those of you who are here for curiosity, or for whatever reason that brought you here—we'd like to remind you that the nature of this evening is a respectful tribute, and like I warn everybody every year, you cut up, the fans will tear you apart before we can get there to save you."

Whoooo! the crowd replied.

Morgan then explained how things would unfold that night and on into morning. After a brief service featuring songs by Elvis, the crowd would form a line, light their candles at the gates, and proceed quietly and reverently through the gates and past the Presley grave in its landscaped oasis in the side yard called the Meditation Garden, just off the kidney-shaped pool. Vernon Presley had Elvis moved there from the mausoleum at Forest Hill on October 2, 1977, after unfounded rumors of a plot to kidnap the body and hold it for ransom. His immediate family also lies there.

"Even though you light your candles at the gate for the procession," Morgan said, "if you could do it now for a few minutes, and hold it high—we've got TV cameras from all over the world, and this is your chance to send a message to the world that Elvis Presley is the greatest entertainer who ever lived." The people lit their candles and raised them above their heads. The night sky rippled with light. Hardly anyone spoke. It was an emotional moment, suitable for beaming via satellite around the world.

Dennis stood next to Gail in the center southbound lane. The air smelled of melting wax and sweaty bodies jammed shoulder to shoulder on six lanes of road still sizzling from the sun. The temperature was in the low eighties, and with the humidity and crush of people clutching hundreds of tiny flames it easily felt ten degrees warmer. Morgan turned the program over to the Elvis Country Fan Club, which advanced a theme of everlasting love. A woman spoke, and then over speakers Elvis eased into "If I Can Dream." In front of the fieldstone wall a traffic signal flashed: WALK. DON'T WALK. Two men approached wearing red windbreakers, the left side on each accented with two white vertical stripes from shoulder to waist, just like the one Elvis wore in his movie *Speedway*. Rick checked them out as they passed. They eyed his prison suit. Two Japanese women, their candles glowing in paper lanterns, stood silently nearby. Elvis sang about how he knew there must be a better world somewhere. Two women held each other tight and softly cried.

A man from the fan club moved up to the microphone.

"Our love for you, Elvis," he said, "goes on and on. It is an everlasting part of who we are, an endless ocean of love upon which we are set adrift together tonight, as we again come together to share in a solemn tribute to a man of great power and spiritual beauty."

Dennis looked around him. People had their heads bowed. Many were crying. Strong emotion stuck in the thick air like a lump in the throat, a palpable sadness. He sucked in his lower lip and shook his head. He had given in to the hair, but he couldn't buy into all of this.

The man said, "We realize that after all these years, our respect and appreciation are undying. The love we share with Elvis and with one another is a never-ending circle. A circle of never-ending love."

"I think it's nice that people come out here," Dennis said, "and remember what the singing was all about and the man and all that, but you know what? I think that perhaps I lack some of this reverence that some of the other people have."

The man said, "We know like a candle, your light shines eternally . . ."

"Now don't get me wrong," Dennis said, "I have respect for the dead and all that. But see, some of the people, they act like he passed away yesterday, and they cry and they . . . I don't know."

"Just as heaven has no boundaries," the man said, "neither does our love for you. Words cannot explain the gratitude we feel for having lived in your lifetime, or the love that we will forever possess. All because of you, your life, and your music. For this we bring you never-ending, never-ending love."

The crowd fell silent. Dennis did too. The candles cast flashes of heat. He lowered his eyes and gazed into the light.

"I tell you what," he said finally. "This thing is a good insect repellent, if nothing else."

After about an hour they headed for the contest because Gail knew from experience that if they got in line right away it would take them hours to reach Elvis's grave. No competition that night, just Mike Albert wearing a cape covered with three leaping orange tigers, and Michael Hoover, who spoke of an empty feeling that filled him every year on this night. At the table Chris mumbled, "Are you gonna talk all night?" There also was Steve Chappell, who walked past as Hoover sang and said to Chris, "I wore that long hair and sideburns one time. I felt like an idiot."

For the open mike session that followed, Dennis changed into a gold lamé jacket he had received as a gift for singing at a friend's wedding, plus a black shirt and pants. Around 2:00 A.M., everyone returned to Graceland to get in line for the vigil.

Sweet, sweet quiet. Cicadas. The sound of Elvis coming from the trees. He was singing "Any Way You Want Me." Dennis, Gail, Jenna, Shelley, and Rick filed up the driveway through oaks and elms washed with spotlights colored blue-green and red and yellow. About 10,000 people take part in the candlelight vigil every August, and this year the five of them were among the last in line. Dozens waited ahead of them. Gail spoke in a whisper, as if she were in church. "Isn't it something," she said, taking in the grounds, the fieldstone mansion bathed in white light. "You could have all of this and it still wouldn't make any difference, when it's your time."

Behind the group a man with a neck brace and a beer belly stretching his Elvis Week T-shirt started talking to Dennis. He said he had been coming to Graceland since 1974. "That's when I was *born*," said Rick, eyes wide. The man scratched his head with the same hand he held his candle with and said that sometimes Elvis came down, just to say hello. Dennis nodded sagely.

The line moved slowly, a trail of swimming light. Jenna squirmed in her pink overalls. "I'm tired and my feet hurt," she said.

"I wish I could sing," Gail whispered. Everyone fell silent, and they moved closer to the garden. In front of Gail a little boy wearing a white satin jumpsuit sprinkled with tiny jewels and stars and a pair of clean white sneakers hugged his mother's hip.

On the black driveway wax droplets from the candles shone like a sky full of stars.

Dennis said little. He palmed his candle from hand to hand. He had taken off his gold jacket so that he wore nothing but black. Rick still wore his Jailhouse suit. At this time of night, in this place, no one even looked.

An hour passed, maybe more. As the line snaked, Dennis wondered aloud if he should save his black jumpsuit for the finals and his black leather for when he performed tomorrow. Gail shushed him. They approached the house. The path veered gently right.

Along the path, crickets sang. Elvis sang "I Want You, I Need You, I Love You." Nearer the house, on the path to the grave stood flower arrangements on wire easels sent by fan clubs to mark the week. Belgium, France, England. Illinois, New York, Florida. Elaborate tributes, with glitter and pictures and poems. The perfume of flowers mingled with the smell of wax. Gail wondered aloud if people paid this kind of tribute to their own relatives and friends. Dennis said he was thinking the same thing.

At the entrance to the Meditation Garden, two steps led to the pergola, the trellised walkway that surrounded the graves, from left to right, those of Minnie Mae Presley, Elvis's grandmother; Elvis himself; and his parents, Vernon and Gladys. A smaller plaque remembered Elvis's stillborn identical twin, Jesse Garon, still buried in Tupelo. Dennis leaned on the railing at the foot of Elvis's grave. At his back was a brick wall containing four Spanish stained-glass panels. Before him stood the house, the pool where Elvis had played. Around him bloomed the Meditation Garden, the place Elvis had come when he needed to think. Dennis had his own thoughts as he stood regarding the dark plaque with Elvis Aaron Presley written in gold. No jokes now, no talk of black leather. Who could imagine anyone's life would turn out this way, in this place? A teddy bear sat on the grave. The roses piled on top of it reached to Dennis's hips. He stood there a long while, and his face was soft and sad. The garden was quiet, except for Elvis's voice, the brush of whispers, and a few quiet sobs. Dennis bowed his head, made the sign of the cross. He moved on to the Presley family monument, Jesus with his arms raised in blessing. He paused there. Then he followed the walkway around the fountain that would lead him back the way he came, and for a moment he stopped to study the house. In just two hours the sun would rise.

"I don't know about you," he said, "but I sure could use a dip in that pool."

Rick Lenzi sat at the table with the Milwaukee girls on Wednesday, drinking hot water with lemon, which he had carried around with him in a brown paper bag that also contained a bottle of hair dye in Natural Black. Impersonators tend to develop sore throats during Elvis Week—too little sleep, too much fun. They were all feeling a little sad because Fred and Sonja were flying back to Detroit early, before the finals that weekend. Fred had a gig at an outdoor festival and he wasn't about to turn $1,000 down at home when he assumed he wouldn't win in Memphis. Anyway, he felt relieved to be getting out. His mood had steadily worsened over the last few days. By Sunday he had become sick of hearing people sing like Elvis. The women worried that it would hurt his standing with Doc if he made the finals and didn't stick around. But nothing they said could change his mind. "If I live my life sucking up to Doc—I mean, I might as well quit now," he said. "If I hadn't been able to win the contest yet, why is it gonna magically happen now?" Safe at home, he sang and danced before of a crowd filled with dancing children and a truck selling a delicacy called elephant ears. An American flag flew over the whole scene, and a TV crew taped it all for the evening news.

Irv Cass passed by the table and pointed at Kelly, all in black and wearing a large flat hat. "She looks good in a hat," he said to the table. Kelly smiled up at him. Gail stood next to the sound equipment on the opposite side of the room. She had complained to Dennis about how the volume always sounded too low during his Memphis sets, and he jokingly said, "Well, why don't you do something about it?"

"That's it," she said. "I'm taking matters into my own hands."

A moment later Dennis marched out in the leather suit for his semi-finals set. In the audience women whooped and clapped with their hands above their heads. Leather always worked this effect, especially when the suit fit as tightly as Dennis's did. He cut the air with his left hand to silence the band. This year a local rock group was backing the impersonators. Don Sims said he was taking some music classes to further his career, so he and his King's Highway Band couldn't come. Elvis songs were not the new band's specialty, though they did a mean cover of Grand Funk Railroad's "Some Kind of Wonderful."

"Whenever you're ready," he said. Then, with a nod to his past, he added, "Before I rip my pants."

The women went *ooooh* to let him know they could accept such an accident. On the tape a drum thudded, and on stage Dennis leaned hard on his right leg and lit into a medley from the '68 Comeback Special. He started with "Trouble," his voice building strength as he sidled into "Guitar Man." Just as he was singing about getting a room at the YMCA, the tape died. A year ago, when the sound system buried his vocals, he faltered and failed. This time he ambled to the end of the catwalk.

"Wanna try it over?" he asked. "That was a rehearsal." He laughed and the audience did, too. "Well, these things happen."

He struck a pose so the women could admire his suit.

"Well, how you all doin' tonight?" he asked.

Whaaa-ooooooh! the women replied.

"Boy, there sure is a whole lot of pretty women out there tonight," he said. The music began again, and so did he. He acted as if nothing had gone wrong, so nothing did. The audience applauded warmly when he finished with his back to them, right arm raised.

"Thank you," he said. "Gotta keep goin'. We gonna play 'em one after another, baby, one after another."

A female voice squealed, "You need help gettin' out of your costume?"

Dennis laughed, and so did everyone who heard. A year earlier that comment would have paralyzed his tongue. Not anymore. "Anytime, honey, anytime," he said. "I'm comin' to get ya right now, baby."

And as he opened "Trying to Get to You" he walked down the stairs, his voice growing stronger with each step. When he hit the floor he shouted "HAH!" and convulsed his body in time to the screams. At their table, Chris watched and muttered between puffs of her cigarettes. "He needs one powerful song," she said, "that's all he needs."

Dennis acted as if he had no worries at all. He kissed women, then picked up lyrics where he'd left off—something he had once found so hard to do. At the bridge of the song, he crouched near Louise's table and shouted the words to her. She reached over and grabbed his thigh with both hands and while he sang she hung on, reared back her head, and howled. When she let go, he kissed her goodbye. She dropped her head down on the table while her friends laughed, then sat up and raised both thumbs in the air. It was a sign of not only how tightly Dennis's suit fit but of how far he had come, for an Irv Cass fan to go that crazy about another Elvis.

He jumped into "Big Boss Man"—lots of lunging and kissing there—and "It Hurts Me." Denese Dody came up to snap a picture. He kissed Sonja during "Any Way You Want Me" then worked his way over to Cookie, who sat at her usual table in the front with a jacket of silver lamé draped over her shoulders. Then "Let Yourself Go."

"He's come a long way," said Chris Young, who was standing behind the table watching. Rick Lenzi, standing next to him, agreed.

In front of them a chubby woman with her hair set in finger waves grabbed Dennis around the waist and wouldn't let him go. When he finally freed himself, a blond with puffy bangs clamped on tight, encircling his waist with her right hand and rubbing his bare chest with her left. Chris Young and Rick Lenzi, enjoying this, sang along with him. The music stopped a moment, and everybody groaned because they thought the tape player had died again.

"Come on!" Shelley said, more to herself than anyone, leaning forward, "I'm nervous."

But it was just a pause into "Big Boss Man." A red-haired woman wearing a suit just like his sneaked up to him. He kissed her too. The audience cheered. "I'm havin' too much fun to leave," he said, and he sounded like he meant it.

Chris and Kelly called, "Denniiiissss!"

When he finished "Can't Help Falling in Love" he told the audience, "You guys are great." They kept on applauding. They may have liked his illusion, but they had also warmed to him. Chris clenched her fist and muttered, "If he gets a standing ovation . . ." And as if on cue, people began to stand. Ten, twenty, thirty . . . Their cheers rocked the room.

Everyone at the table sat back and sighed. He would make the finals. But they still worried.

"I think he spent too much time off stage," said Chris.

"He can't go up and down in those pants," Kelly said.

Dennis came straight to the table. He was grinning like a kid. He wanted to make the finals, partly because he didn't want to lose, and partly because he didn't want this feeling to end. "Well?" he asked.

"Nice, nice!" Shelley said.

"Now," he said, "I can eat."

Then he turned around. He was surrounded by women with cameras and programs to sign. Food would have to wait.

Meanwhile, Terri Jayne, the part-time Jayne Mansfield impersonator, was still recovering from the effects of a visitation. She had taken her four-year-old son Joshua to Graceland early Tuesday morning—the estate holds two hours of free visitation each morning before the mansion opens for tours—when she saw a man in a red shirt who looked the spitting image of Elvis wandering out where the horses graze.

"He was wearing a big-sleeved shirt with some lace on the front, and black baggies, and he looked like he had a gold belt on—not like this," she said, pointing to her belt, "but it had the chains on it. And I looked *everywhere* for him. And I even told a guy at the gate there was a loose Elvis impersonator, because he was over in the fence where the horses used to be. And my little boy said, 'Mommy, let's find him, let's find out who he is.' My little boy's a huge Elvis fan. And he said, 'What if it was Elvis?' And I said, 'Boy, don't talk like that—that's scary up here this early in the morning!'"

During the excitement, she noticed one of Joshua's shoelaces had come undone. She bent down to tie it, and when she looked up, the Elvis was gone. They searched everywhere. Joshua even combed the restroom. "He said, 'We're gonna find him,'" Terri Jayne said. "He said, 'We need to tell security that he is at Graceland.' I said, 'Fool, they'll think we lost our minds.'"

Here is the difference between an unusual life and a crazy one: A Jayne Mansfield impersonator has a chance to march up to a security guard at Graceland soon after sunrise and announce she and her four-year-old son have just seen Elvis roaming among the horses, and now they couldn't find him, and they didn't think he was hiding in the bathroom. But she does not. Instead she takes her son home before too many people arrive. Her baby gets so wound up around people, and he tends to catch upper respiratory infections. Best to be safe.

Thursday night Chris asked Irv to sign her program. He picked up a pen and wrote quickly and with a big flourish at the end. She looked at the entry and screwed up her face.

"You just scribbled," she said. "You didn't say anything."

He put his arm around her. "It says everything," he said, voice low. "You just don't know it." That cracked both of them up.

He went on stage soon after, and did a fine job. Even Doc Franklin paused on his rounds to stand to the right of the stage, watching—never a bad sign. Irv did flub a line in "Suspicious Minds." But the busload he brought down with him cheered anyway, Lorrie the loudest of them all. After all, he was wearing her ring.

Despite the kind reception, after he finished he retreated to the back of the room and leaned against the wall. A few feet away Ronny Craig, Kelly, and Shelley were carrying on, but he stood stone-faced. He stood there for ten minutes, which for Irv counts as two eternities. Because ten minutes earlier, as he left the stage after his set, something had happened.

"I happen to be critical of myself, and like I said, I can tell when I've done good and when I haven't," he began. "And I walked off the stage, and she says to me, 'You know, even though you're very arrogant, you did do a very good show.' And I said to her—I kinda chuckled—'Well, you don't know very well. Why would you think I'm arrogant?' I said, 'Did I do something to you to make you . . .' and then she didn't answer me. And I said, 'What did I do to make you feel that way?'

"She says, 'Oh, you got an air about you.'"

He leaned his head and right shoulder against the wall. "And I didn't know what to say. I just said, 'Well, if you get to know me—I'm gonna be here for a couple more days. You gonna be here the end of the week?' She says, 'Yeah.' I said, 'You get to know me, and you talk to me, you're gonna find out that I'm not what you think at all. I don't know—maybe on stage, I came across, you know, a little cocky or whatever, I don't know what I did to make you feel that way.'"

He gestured with both hands. "Treat Me Nice" played in the front of the room. "Three and a half years, when I started out, to be honest with you, I was terrible. Terrible Elvis impersonator. It takes a lot of practice, and maybe because in those two or three years everything's been going my way, as far as the business end of it, and working and getting jobs—because I do do it for living—maybe she thinks I'm a hotshot. If people think you're a hotshot, even if they don't know you, and never talk to you, they're not gonna like you."

Irv had to wonder: If performing could feel so good and hurt so bad for him, a guy from Niles, Michigan, what must it have been like for Elvis?

"Even though he had problems toward the end and he was lonely, that man had more pressure on him than anybody in the world," he said. "As far as being an entertainer. We'll never know. Even being an

Elvis impersonator, there's pressures on you, just being an Elvis impersonator. Because all the people expect a lot, you know? You do a good
show, the word goes like fire—a wildfire—and everybody knows, and the
next time you go back, it's packed. So if you don't do a good show, you
might as well forget it."

A few feet away, next to the bar, Ronny Craig was talking about God and
Elvis and how it annoyed him when people confused the two.

"We're not talking Grammy-nominated stars like Billy Ray Cyrus or
Vince Gill," he said. He underlined his point by gesturing with the neck
of his beer bottle. "We're talking guys that put jumpsuits on and paint
their hair black with paint, and sing. I mean, let's give a tribute, but let's
try not to emulate a guy—no one can walk in that man's shoes." Shelley
and Kelly, his audience, nodded. "Nobody can touch him. And this
world does need Elvis impersonators, to carry on the memory. But the
impersonator has to remember: That's all you're doing. So when you put
your head on the pillow at night, and you pray to God at night, I mean—
it's almost a joke. It's comical."

He started picking up steam. Shelley and Kelly leaned in to hear over
the music. "OK, suppose I was born Joe Smith. That's who I am. That's
the name my mother and daddy gave me. Now whatever profession I
do choose, if it's a prostitute or president of the United States—I'm
using one extreme to the next—that's who I am. I am nobody else. And
if you're an actor—his job should be an actor. And not to carry it on
every day. I mean, to walk around and emulate a guy—come on, people, what do you mean? Is it something that you lacked in childhood,
you didn't get enough attention in class, maybe your mother and daddy
didn't love you enough. You know, what niche do you have to walk
around in, for someone to say, 'You know what—you look like Elvis
Presley,' Or why? Because you have black hair and sideburns? You see
what I'm saying? You follow me in my degree? I'm not talking about talent or anything, I'm talking about the personality of a person. A hundred percent of these Elvises that are here—I don't know how many
there are, eighty to a hundred and twenty-five, whatever block—I
would say seventy-five percent of them have psychological problems.
Seventy-five percent. I mean it. Seventy-five percent." Shelley and Kelly
laughed as if they couldn't believe what they were hearing. He laughed,
too. "Hey, I mean, I'm having a good time, too. For God's sake, let's draw
the line."

Kelly brought up the guys at Graceland parading around in their jumpsuits. Ronny nodded. "We all love Elvis, and I love Elvis. It's not the thing of the love, I respect him so much as an entertainer, but people. I was born Craig Plueger. Craig—C-R-A-I-G. I mean, we're all individuals. A lot of these Elvis guys are my friends. A lot of them are my close friends. But they're still ate up." He laughed. "'Well, why won't you do this?' 'Well, Elvis wouldn't have done that.' '*Oh*.' Here's the biggest charge I get—the guys that are having the plastic surgery done. These guys. Oh, *God*."

"That's when I think they take it a step too far," Shelley said, "when they start doing surgery."

"Well, how far can you take it? Who is around—who are the Elvis police? Where are the Elvis police? Listen: Elvis is an icon, we love him. Nobody will let go of him. That's America. It's like a call to Jesus Christ. There are Jesus Christ followers, which we all should be following. They follow Elvis like Jesus Christ. It's the same kind of thing, like the Grateful Dead—same kind of a clan. It's the need to be loved, to be accepted. If they can have just one whispering memory, they'll take it, and they'll pay top dollar. Because Elvis is gone. And they've seen all his tapes a thousand times."

He was still talking when, up on stage, Jackie announced that she was ready to announce the finalists who would perform Friday and Saturday nights. The women hushed him, and Jackie began reeling off the names: Jamie Turner. Travis Morris—his voice was still raw, but no impersonator had eyes bluer or an Elvis head more lustrous. ("You can just stand right here if you want to, so everybody can look at you," Jackie told him.) Irv Cass. Fred Wolfe (the Milwaukee gang let out a huge groan). Ricky Aaron. Tony Ciaglia. Rob Hunter. Dennis Stella. Darren Lee. Ronny Craig. The impersonators ran to the stage to pick up their plaques.

Toni Rae stormed out. "I know why I didn't make it," she said. "I'm a woman." Rick Lenzi, who was standing near the door, gaped at her. His mouth hung open a little bit. He was getting an education.

"Oh, I just love this part," said Chris, standing near the back bar. Once more, all of their friends had made the finals. Rick came over and she grabbed his hand. She had been squeezing it for luck all night. "We did it!" she said.

Jackie Franklin came off the stage and a woman—the wife of one of the impersonators who didn't make the finals—walked up to her. She said she knew exactly why her husband didn't make it. She said her husband wasn't for sale. "I don't know what you're talking about," Jackie told her.

"It hurts my feelings," she said the next night. "But you know, I can't take it personally, because they don't know me. It's not like a friend being mad at me." She cleared her throat. "It does hurt my feelings, though, because we really do try to be fair in selecting the winners."

In the back of the room, Dennis joked about this business getting to be old hat. Someone onstage was singing "Polk Salad Annie."

"You ready?" Chris asked everyone. When the song came to the part with the arm thrashes, she and the whole gang did the move together while the music roared: *Bam-bam! Bam-bam!* They formed a crazy arm-flailing chorus line, half Elvis, half female, all laughing.

Dennis stood off to the side, not saying a word. He had already begun to think: What could he do to top his night in black leather? He couldn't have dreamed that when he performed in the finals he would top anything he had ever done onstage, without even trying.

15

"Oh Dennis, Not Every Time . . ."

*H*is white-and-red Pinwheel missing, Dennis decided to wear his black Spanish Flower, the same suit he had worn during finals the year before. In the motel room before the contest a minor drama erupted when Gail decided to iron out a few creases and instead melted the lining to the suit. She managed to separate the mess without coming unglued herself, and they headed for the show across the road under a mango-colored sunset.

Dennis didn't even mention the incident as he prepared to sing that night. He had more pressing concerns. He gargled with white vinegar and water in the bathroom in the men's dressing area, making the tiny room smell like a salad. He studied his reflection in the mirror over the sink, turned his head to check his sideburns. "I definitely know I'm not as nervous as I used to be," he said. "Do I look nervous? I am." He laughed. "I'm a better liar than I used to be."

Then again, he had reason to be nervous. He was doing "American Trilogy," a song that he had never before sung in competition. Before that he would sing "Polk Salad Annie," which contained more movement than he usually put forth in an entire set. He left the bathroom and walked out in the hall to stretch his legs. A skinny guy with sun-browned skin approached him.

"Hey, you got a nice-lookin' suit there," he said from behind his camera. Dennis posed—put one foot in front of the other, leaned his torso back, tilted his head and shot the man half a sneer. No wasted movement. Then he excused himself.

"I gotta go take a walk," he said. "Nerves are starting to kick in."

Jackie Franklin, wearing a long brown dress with a white collar, announced Dennis right after Yaniv Rosen, the only Israeli impersonator in the contest and one of the Elvises Dennis had befriended this year. The band broke into the "C.C. Rider" theme. Outside in the hall Dennis hiked up his belt. He paced around the corner. He did a couple of arm chops. "All right," said Chris Cave, another Elvis who was standing near the door. "Do it, Dennis."

Dennis bolted through the side door, ran up the three carpeted steps to the stage and dived into "A Big Hunk o' Love." Either he wasn't nervous, or he really had become a better liar. As he danced on the catwalk, Jackie darted to the front of the stage to snap his picture. Everyone at the table whistled and called his name, except for Gail, who stood by the sound board to ward off technical glitches like the ones in last year's finals. During the second instrumental break he played a little air guitar; a blonde snapped his picture, then took a drag on her cigarette, tipping her head back to blow the smoke. To finish he flung out his arms and reared back his right leg. As he scraped his foot on the stage a small hoof-shaped black object fell to the floor. He glanced down with a puzzled look and picked it up.

It was the heel to his right boot.

"Oh, Dennis, not every time!" Kelly cried.

Shelley sat very still. Chris blurted something unintelligible. Rick's mouth dropped open. Gail stood near the sound board, frozen, eyes wide.

He stamped his foot a couple of times. "Well," he said. He picked up the heel. "Thank you very much, ladies and gentlemen. This is what you call Murphy's Law. I walked around all day, shoe was fine. I walk out on stage . . ." He held up the heel. The audience burst out laughing. "So don't feel sorry for me, I'm not crippled." He dropped the heel at the end of the catwalk. The tape started up as he walked back toward the drum kit and whirled into his next song. In Dennis's world it could be only one song—"Walk a Mile in My Shoes."

"Walk a Mile in My Shoes" is a song about understanding people, one of those songs about brotherhood and common ground that would sound corny if anyone but Elvis had sung it. Except maybe for someone impersonating Elvis who had something to prove. And as Dennis sang the words—about seeing people as they are and not as they look, about not ridiculing them because of how they wear their hair—the crowd forgot he was limping because of his blown-out, hangdog, thrift-store boots. Because Dennis was dancing. He chugged across the stage, swinging his arms, smiling as if the whole thing had never happened. A year ago a disaster this big would have flattened him. This year, he danced. He had to. He had fallen flat on his back, he had nearly lost his wig, and his life didn't stop. He had always gotten up and tried again. So not only would he keep going, but he'd enjoy himself. Kelly leaned back and relaxed a little. He was going to be all right. Maybe even good.

"All right, thank you. You guys are great," he said. Before he could step into the crowd, "What Now My Love" began. He handed out scarves, favoring his foot so little you could barely notice. He even nailed the last note. And then he just kept going. During "Way Down" he even flexed his pelvis.

"OK," he said when the clapping eased up, "before I start this number here, I just want to say to all you people it's the end of the week, almost. And we came from all over the country, and I've met a lot of nice people, and I hope I never forget you. So this next song, I dedicate to you, the fans. Thank you for coming tonight." When people heard the song, "I'll Remember You," they cheered their approval.

"Thank you. Thanks a lot," he said. "OK, now I'm gonna really have to work—I'm going back on the stage, one shoe on, one shoe off." He brightened. "Hey, now I've got an excuse. If I don't look too right up there, it's my shoe." The audience laughed, and he walked up the steps. The pulse of "Polk Salad Annie" hummed; people clapped in time. "Now I know you all haven't heard this song tonight," he said, knowing they had already heard it enough. "That's OK. I was in the back—I didn't hear it." His nerves had left him now. He had gone from wanting to be Elvis to fighting for his own identity to reshaping Elvis into another version of himself. His transformation was complete.

When he started into the first big arm thrash he joked, "Let's see if I do this right." He did the final thrashes sliding across the stage, chains bouncing on his belt, cheeks puffing in and out, a big howl tearing out of the crowd, and then he jumped up and dropped down on his knee, flinging his arms to finish. "I'm gettin' too old for this," he said when the music stopped.

He took a drink of water. "Before I go on any further, there's a nice little lady in the green dress who had to put up with me all week. Give a big round of applause to Gail. Come on up here, honey. I got somethin' for ya."

Whoooo, the audience said.

Gail, standing against the wall, rolled her eyes. As she maneuvered through the tables in her sequined dress—aqua, with matching high heels—she willed herself not to fall on her face. "Now be nice to me, baby, don't hit me," he said. "Can you dry me off just a little bit, honey?" He handed her a scarf, and she smiled up at him on the stage and swiped at his face and chest. He kissed her, and as she ran off he said, "OK, I think I'm alive. All right. Forgive me if this song doesn't go over too good, ladies and gentlemen. I've been doing my impression for about three and a half years, and I've been scared to death of this song ever since I started. But tonight I decided I'm gonna try it. So if it comes off good, good. But if it doesn't, forgive me. Go ahead."

The guitarist played the opening notes of "Dixie"— the first of the three songs in "American Trilogy." And Dennis sang it the way he would in his den with the karaoke machine, with his face folded a thousand ways, his eyes closed, stabbing the air with his hand as he sang. He sailed through "All My Trials," and he nailed the last note in "Battle Hymn of the Republic" and hung onto it, his left hand tensed in the air.

"So great, that last note," Chris said, rising out of her seat to cheer. The rest of the table did the same. So did everyone around them. He was focusing so hard on hitting the note he didn't notice until he finished. He thought maybe the audience was being kind because he had tried, but that wasn't true. Dennis had seldom had worse luck, and he had never performed better. He picked up his heel, took a bow, and left the stage, the crowd still standing.

All week long people predicted that Irv would take first place. On Saturday, the last day of the contest, he said he hoped to finish in the top three. He didn't want anyone to get the impression he was a hotshot. People continued to speculate about his fellow South Bend area Elvises, Chris T. Young, who had begun seriously pursuing Elvis after his marriage broke up, and Rob Hunter, who was only sixteen, but one of the youngest working Elvises. Word on all three was positive. And they had each brought down busloads of fans to cheer them on.

On Friday, Chris Young had served up a set that started with "I Got My Mojo Working," a seventies number impersonators seldom perform. He unwound a chain of kicks, lunges, and drop spins, and when he stressed a lyric he wagged his pelvis or his butt. After he finished the first song, he rested his hand on his belt and said, "My name is Irv Cass and I hope you enjoy the show tonight." This annoyed a lot of Irv Cass fans. They knew there was a rivalry between the two, but they wondered why he would say a thing like that.

Darren Lee followed him. His set was an elaborate tribute that featured a costume change and ended with him standing on the stage in Comeback black leather, holding a single white candle and singing "The King Is Gone." Rob Hunter came next, wearing a baggy sport coat and a pair of two-tone shoes and warbling "Blue Moon of Kentucky" and "You're So Square (Baby I Don't Care)." All three got strong applause. Audience participation counted for just a small percentage of the final scores, but the audience saw it differently. The audience always did.

Before he sang on Saturday, Irv kept telling friends his throat felt sore. He did sound raw on some of the rougher notes, and afterward even Dottie admitted it wasn't one of his strongest performances. He opened with the speeded-up seventies take on "Blue Suede Shoes," then "Love Me" and "Until It's Time for You to Go."

Dennis, kicking back in a tank top decorated with a picture of the Italian flag, was puzzled by his friend's song selection—not a "Polk Salad Annie" in the bunch—and even in the back of the room he could detect a loud hissing on his karaoke tape. Chris Hottinger, who had brought in her dinner from Burger King, kept shaking her head over her fries. Still, what Irv's set lacked in fire it made up for in emotion. His Tiger jumpsuit had a blinding orange tiger across the front with crystals for claws and black-and-orange stripes down the legs. "Look at his scarves," Gail told her friends, "they all match his outfit—orange, black, and white." The women lined three deep at the edge of the stage looking for a scarf, or something more. They gave him a standing ovation for every song.

"I hope he picks some better songs for the last ones," Dennis said to Chris.

"You know what?" Chris said as Irv polished off a frenetic "Suspicious Minds." "I think no matter what, it's his turn. It's his turn to win."

"Is it warm in here," Irv was asking the women, "or is it just me?" After "Let It Be Me" he asked the audience to indulge him a moment while he introduced his father, Irv Cass Sr. Irv Sr., who wore a shirt decorated with a leaping tiger identical to the one on his son's suit, stood and slicked back his thinning white hair, which got a big hand. "And ladies and gentlemen, somebody who's also very dear to me. She is a very special person. She's the one who gave me the flowers here. She gave me a little gold medal a while back. I've won many plaques and trophies and contests. But I gotta tell ya—I got this little thing from her, about that big, it's gold-plated. Had a ribbon on it. And it means more to me than anything in the world. It's a Special Olympics medal, and I just want to say, I carry it with me everywhere for luck, and I got it with me tonight. Where's Lorrie? Stand up, Lorrie—I love you, sweetheart. She's a beautiful person—trust me, I would not lie to you about that."

Louise looked at her daughter as she stood to wave to Irv and acknowledge the cheers of the crowd. He pointed at Lorrie and smiled and she beamed at him. Louise was the first to admit that she took her daughter's talents for granted. But tonight she felt such pride in her, and such love for Irv for showing he felt the same in front of so many. The crowd did, too. After "Hurt" he walked off waving to yet another standing ovation.

Things were winding down. Ronny Craig sang his usual power ballads like "My Boy" and the women screamed every time he smiled. Elvis John, the Vietnamese-American Elvis, had improved his voice and movement from the year before, and he stood on stage and announced, "I'm living proof that Elvis's music crosses all boundaries and borders." The audience offered him a big round of applause.

Rick Lenzi had chosen to recreate the Comeback Special, and Gail told him, "I'm not just saying this because I know you. You were really good."

"Thank you," he said, slurring his voice. "Thankyouverymuch."

Now that the show was almost over, everybody loosened up. Dottie sat at a back table, sharing a pizza with some friends. As somebody on stage sang "Polk Salad Annie," Rick Lenzi and Chris Wilson, the Young Elvis from Cincinnati, stood in the back of the room imitating the arm movements. The longer the night went on, the more guys gathered in the back to join them.

The last performer of the night was Robert Washington, back after a year off. Like Irv, he complained of a sore throat. He entered the room from the back to "Peter Gunn," passing Wendy Lynn, who sat alone in the back drinking coffee from a paper cup. She looked at him, nodded and smiled. From the beginning he turned it on, the macramé fringe on his jumpsuit banging on his chest as he did "Suspicious Minds." To finish he fell on the floor, kicking his left leg high in the air and the crowd, mellow in this midnight hour, woke up and began to scream. He swung into "Johnny B. Goode" then a slower one, "Just Pretend." Dennis stood with his arm around Gail's shoulders. "He's so good," she said. Then Robert speeded it up again with "Mystery Train" and "Tiger Man." He aced a note and Rick Lenzi yelled, "Fuckin' A! He sang that with no voice? No fuckin' way! You can tell that came from deep down in his belly."

Dennis nodded. He was obviously impressed. "Hey, he got through it. He did a great job." From the noise in the room, a lot of other people agreed. Gail set down her drink so she could applaud.

When Robert left the stage, the room relaxed. No matter what happened, no one could control it now. Nothing to do but dance and grab a last drink before Jackie appeared on that stage. Michael Hoover came out to do a show while the judges' scores were being totaled. Doc stood talking to a guy in the back. Robert said hello to Cookie, who stood in the back shimmying to the music. Elvis John and Robert posed for pictures with Phyllis Collas, a woman who lives in a house on Dolan Avenue behind Graceland that she claims is haunted by Elvis's ghost. She keeps a Christmas tree in her living room all year round and a picture of Elvis propped on her toilet tank. Rick did an all-over body twitch in the background, then staggered over to Robert. "I swear to God, man," he said, "you have a voice!" Robert smiled, showing his deep dimples.

"I'll have a twenty-eight-inch waist next year at this time," Chris Wilson was telling someone. "Just like Elvis. You wait." He draped his arm around Carol, who had wandered back from her ringside seat. Irv walked in and gave a guy a mock karate chop, headed straight for Robert and gave him a hug. Then Irv started to pace. Gail teased him to calm him down. "You gotta teach me those moves," she said. Dennis wandered from group to group, having his picture taken, complimenting people on their suits. No one could stand still, they were so excited about what would happen next.

Suddenly Jackie stood on the stage, holding a piece of paper with the names they had been waiting all week to hear. She told them that this show had been full of wonderful talent. "There has not been a low spot anywhere—and we have had a hundred people tell me, 'I don't know how you pick the winner, there are just all these good entertainers.' It was hard, but we do have winners."

Gail stood in back, hugging herself. "I am so nervous," she said, "and I don't know why."

"We have a plaque for finalist Prentice Chaffin," Jackie began. "Ain't he got beautiful eyes? Jamie Kelley. We've all seen Jamie grow up, haven't we? Tim Bunn. Tony Ciaglia. Bill Cherry has already gone home. Janiv Rosen. Dennis Stella."

"Ooooh," Gail said. She sighed and then smiled, clapping as Dennis trotted up front for his plaque. "Chris Cave," Jackie said. "Ricky Aaron. Robert Washington." Gail frowned. Too low—he deserved better. "William Toulson. Jack Curtis. Irv Cass."

A groan rose from the Cass contingent. "What?" Gail said, now truly surprised. "I don't know. I truly don't know."

"Chris Wilson. Elvis John. Ronny Craig. Kevin Curtis. Fifth place winner, Travis Morris." The audience started to wind up. "Fourth place winner, Ron Friel." Gail started to count who was left. Jackie beat her to it: "Our third place winner of the evening, of the week, of the year— Darren Lee." The audience let out a long *eeeeeee* for the Young Elvis. "Our second place winner is Rob Hunter, and the winner is—Chris Young!" As it always does, the room erupted in screaming. Chris picked up Rob Hunter and lifted him off the ground, sending his black-and-white oxfords kicking. Chris would offer this moment later as proof that the contest wasn't fixed—he couldn't have faked that reaction. Besides, he joked, he was about the only person left who hadn't ticked off Doc. A woman at a table near the door snubbed out a cigarette and shouted, "Come on, get a clue." She picked up her purse and stormed out. Gail looked at her. Every year the same thing happened— somebody won, and somebody got angry about it. It always surprised her how people didn't understand that their favorite couldn't always win.

"I'm happy for him," Gail said of Chris Young. "I didn't see his finals performance, but I'm happy for him. It's kind of odd, though, that every year whoever brings a bus wins. I don't know about that." She thought about that. "But Irv's here, he's got a lot of people here."

The winners took turns thanking the audience. "For you guys that were riding home on the bus with us—let's party," Rob Hunter said.

"I've been saying all week there was gonna be a surprise," Chris Hottinger said. She had thought maybe Darren Lee would take first. "Everybody was saying Irv, Chris, and Rob—it's like, do you know what scuttlebutt there would be? They brought in two buses of people, then they finish first, second, and third? You know, I didn't think it would be all three of them. I didn't think they'd pick even two of them. I think

Robert Washington's performance was a lot stronger." The year before Steve Chappell had fueled gossip. Irv and Robert Washington took his place.

Irv's manager Dottie Skwiat sat against the wall in a tall chair, hugging her purse. She was having her caricature drawn by Cliff Hewlett, an artist who had sketched pictures of people at the contest for six years. "I'm fine," she said. That was all she would say. Cliff drew a little smile on her face anyway.

It was about 1:30 A.M., and the party was ending for another year. Doc and Jackie packed up and walked out. The winners sang on stage. Wendy Lyn went up to duet with Chris Young. Gail, Dennis, and the rest wandered out into the hall, where Dennis said his usual long goodbyes to everyone. He was talking to Robert Washington when Irv walked over in shorts and a polo shirt. He looked pale. "I don't know what I did to piss them off," he said, "but the judges did not like me." Gail complimented him again and assured him he had looked and sounded great.

"Oh, you guys are all friends of mine, though," he replied. "I thought I would have come in the top five. But the thing is, maybe they think I was a hotshot, I don't know. I'm not mad at Doc. I like Doc. He picks the judges and the judges do whatever they think—but you know, the best thing for me is probably to not to be in this stuff anymore, just to leave it alone. Because I'm doing real well, and I don't need to. My manager told me I shouldn't be in the contest to begin with. Maybe I should take her advice, I don't know." At least he was leaving at 7:00 A.M. that morning for Las Vegas. He was booked to sing a private engagement at the Las Vegas Hilton, where Elvis himself once performed.

His fan club had been sitting by the pool waiting for him. When they saw him they began to clap and chant: *Vegas! Vegas! Vegas!* As he walked out among them, their applause echoed through every floor of the hotel.

Once and for all, Dennis had learned where not to buy his boots. And he discovered that he had more nerve and foolishness inside him than he had ever expected. The next morning, his last day in Memphis that year, he woke and went to Graceland. Gail took a lot of pictures—in front of the house and in the kitchen, which had just opened to tour groups that year. She shot a picture of Dennis standing in front of the Jungle Room, the tape recorder that served as a self-paced guide hanging from the belt of his shorts. He looked exactly like what he was: a visitor to another man's house and another man's life, to a time long gone, judging by the avocado shag carpet on the floor and ceiling. He definitely didn't belong here with the tiki furniture and fur lampshades and leaky waterfall. Yet Dennis couldn't have smiled any wider. He couldn't have looked any more at home.

16

Rock! Rock! Rock! Rock!

*F*ive days before he performed in the finals at the 1996 Images of Elvis contest, Dennis dyed his hair in a motel room. These days he dyed his hair only when he had a show. He had done some thinking and a little math and decided that resembling Elvis all month long when he needed to for maybe two or three days made little sense, from a business or personal perspective. He felt comfortable with his Elvisness now; if he needed it, he knew where to find it.

One thing he couldn't locate was a hairdresser in Memphis. A woman in Calumet City usually dyed his hair, but he had been running late the previous weekend, with a friend's wedding and a gig back to back, and never called her. So he bought a bottle of brown-black dye and ducked into the bathroom of his room at La Quinta. It took him a long time. He did a very thorough job. "Oh, no," Shelley said, "you dyed your forehead!" Gail grabbed her camera.

The rest of the week oozed by the way Elvis Week did every year—days by the pool, nights at the contest, dawn in a circle, jamming and laughing. The weather was cooler than it had been the year before; the temperature barely broke ninety, with cloud-streaked skies and little chance of rain. It rained only once—Saturday, the night Dennis performed in the finals.

Over the past year he had turned more and more to Elvis's movie tunes—songs of love and girls and paradise—that had thrilled him as a child. When he had begun his impersonator career two years earlier, he would never have dared to sing these songs. He had to become somebody else before he could realize that what he was in the beginning was enough. "Because, see, then I was more interested in blending rather than sticking out," he said. "Now I'm more interested in sticking out than blending." The Best Western had been converted to a Sheraton, and Dennis sat in its ballroom, next to a table Gail had set up of Dennis Stella souvenirs—key chains, cassettes, and pictures from his various Elvis eras. Inspecting the selection was like seeing the last two years of his life pass before your eyes. He found it kind of silly, like much of the Elvis business, but liked it in spite of himself. Kelly, her hair platinum and frothed like Marilyn Monroe's, tended to customers.

He said, "I thought, I can put a jumpsuit on like everybody else and get all serious"—he gripped his hand into a claw, contorted his face— *"Aaah!* And I said, no, I always used to do that. I want to do something where I have fun."

In the semifinals, he wowed the crowd with his brand-new routine inspired by the movie *G.I. Blues.* The same set had impressed them at the EPIIA convention the month before, held once again at the Sabre Room by Jerome Marion. Jerome was now considered the president and leader of the organization, with the blessings of the Bessettes. Dennis wore khaki-colored fatigues and a matching black-billed cap, and he saluted the crowd before he surged into a version of "G.I. Blues" capped by a funky shuffle that coaxed from the women a long happy *Whooo!* After he did the number in Memphis, Jackie Franklin came on stage and said she didn't know how the judges were going to choose finalists, everyone had so many original ideas.

Still, Dennis doubted he would win in Memphis, and his hunch turned out to be right. (The Milwaukee girls guessed correctly that Mike Albert, the popular impersonator from Columbus, Ohio, would win. He had come down, they had heard, and entered the contest on the spur of the moment. His a cappella rendering of "Unchained Melody," delivered in his Sundial jumpsuit, moved the crowd to silence. Two young Elvises placed second and third. Neither Irv Cass nor Robert Washington, the newest addition to Dennis's circle of friends around the pool, placed as high as their fans had hoped. Both of them complained of sore throats; Irv joked that at least he sounded like Elvis with a sore throat.

One thing did change that year: The Franklins introduced the judges to the audience, no doubt spurred by complaints from people like Louise Rozek, who wrote Doc a long letter telling him she thought the previous year's results were unfair. And Dottie Skwiat called Doc about three weeks after the 1995 contest to tell him that something had happened with the judging and he needed to straighten it out. Still, the tallying of final scores was done out of sight of the judges, according to one of them; another reported for duty more than an hour late to one of the shows, a dereliction of duty that made the woman at the ticket table stare at him as though he'd lost his mind.

Doc made another noticeable change, one that riled Dennis. On the entry form, impersonators had to agree that if they competed in Images of Elvis, they would not compete in any other Elvis Week event. Dennis didn't embrace the idea of agreeing to have his freedom taken away, but he signed. The contest had become a place to be with friends and measure his own progress, whether he won or not. But even though Dennis considered his own contest prospects dubious—and perhaps because of that—he decided to try something different. He had another movie in mind. The day after he arrived, he went shopping.

The finals fell on Friday and Saturday; he performed the second night. That morning he planned an elaborate set, with two costume changes and a big finale: He would disappear, then return in a jumpsuit and proclaim that becoming an impersonator had been a dream come true. Then he would launch into "The Impossible Dream." It would be a time capsule of his life since he started on the Elvis circuit. He hoped it would impress the judges. But around 6:30 that night he vetoed that idea as too complicated. Gail was disappointed because she had been waiting to hear him sing "The Impossible Dream." But she respected his decision.

Instead, the night of the finals he arrived in a cranberry red sport jacket, the one Gail and Jenna had bought for his birthday in June, over a black shirt and pants—sort of a *Girl Happy* lounge-act look. His hair was short and tapered in back; he wore no sideburns. He sported a tan from those days singing by the pool. He looked almost exactly the way he did before he got started doing Elvis—his hair was blacker, that was all. In the dressing room backstage, he studied his reflection in a full-length mirror propped against the pale rose wallpaper and with his palms smoothed the sides of his hair. He turned his head from side to side. "Hey," he said, "at least it's not a wig." Gail turned to laugh. She looked beautiful. Her hair was piled on top of her head, and she wore a gold and black beaded evening dress, and black patent leather pumps with four-inch heels.

Dennis fidgeted. He picked up a thirty-two-ounce bottle of white vinegar, poured some in a glass with water and gargled. He fell backward into a chair, pumped his knees up and down. "Boy, this sitting really sucks," he said. He went over to the mirror and popped a few swivels. Then it was time.

Outside the stage door, Gail handed him a cordless mike she had just borrowed. "I hope you know how to use this," she said. Jackie told the crowd, "Please welcome Mister Dennis Stella." Dennis took the mike without a word and ran through the side door, down the steps, and to the stage. Gail leaned as far as she could through the door without following him. "Oh, please, God," she whispered, "let it go OK." He bounced up the stage stairs, raised the mike to his lips. Nothing. "He's got no mike!" Gail cried. Then Dennis looked into the audience and said, loud and clear, "Hello. Hello. How are you? We're gonna do a song from *Kid Galahad.*" Gail leaned against the wall and closed her eyes.

The music started, and Dennis moved into "King of the Whole Wide World," snapping his fingers. During the saxophone bridge, he slapped his thigh. He looked like he didn't have a care. When he finished he took a sip of water, leaped off the stage, and started into "I Got Lucky," also from *Kid Galahad.* In the back of the room Kelly closed her eyes and Chris swayed and they both sang along—*"Yes, I got lucky . . ."* Then Dennis said, "I'd like to try a new one tonight, from the movie *Loving You.* He bounced into "Got a Lot of Living to Do." "Oh, wow," Chris said. He had goofed with this one around the pool but said nothing about doing it here. This wasn't like him. Cookie suddenly appeared in a silver lamé dress. Over her right breast she wore an Elvis temporary tattoo, and she offered one to Chris. Dennis fumbled a couple of lines, cuffed himself in the forehead for forgetting, but kept on smiling. The audience, grateful for a different Elvis act, didn't lose interest. He snapped his fingers, popped his heels, and whipped his arms to finish. As the applause died down, he ran through the side door without a word. On the tape Dennis had made a couple hours earlier in his motel room, Elvis himself began to sing "Paradise Hawaiian Style."

Always the critic, Chris was miffed. "This was not in the plan," she said. "That red jacket was not in the plan all day. Neither was that 'Got a Lot of Living to Do,' and he forgot half the words."

Fifty seconds later, in the hallway outside the right side of the ballroom, steaming as fast as a woman in an evening dress possibly could while wearing black patent leather pumps with four-inch heels, Gail ran. On her heels huffed Dennis, wearing a Hawaiian shirt, white shorts, tennis shoes with no socks. Around his neck—and up past his chin, he was trying so hard to catch up—flopped six plastic leis. He pulled ahead of Gail, turned right at the pay phones, pistoned down the steps, and barreled toward the ballroom. "Pull those leis forward!" Gail shouted. She tried to catch up to clear the doorway of freeloaders too cheap to pay the $20 cover, but Dennis had already pushed past. He paused to catch his breath, then strolled through the doors just as Elvis finished. He put the mike to his lips again and began to sing "Ku-U-I-Po," the luau song from *Blue Hawaii*. He moved between the round tables, touching women as he passed by.

At first, most of the crowd sat murmuring and looking around. For all they knew, this song was just more Elvis. But eight seconds into it, when he had worked about a third of the way into the room singing of love, a woman with barrettes pinching the flips in her hair stood, pointed, and screamed. Then all the women turned. Then all the women screamed. The room burst into applause. People began to stand. Thirty women, forty, maybe more, jumped from their tables and ran to the right side of the room where he moved through the crowd, slipping leis gently over hair. Some got close, and some just stood there and stared. Cameras flashed like summer lightning.

After they all stopped applauding, he slipped, gently, into "Can't Help Falling In Love," still walking among the women, stopping to hold them while he sang tender words about rivers flowing to the sea, about surrender and destiny. He sounded softer and surer than he did the first time he sang this song at the semifinals two years earlier or in the finals the year before. Gail stood watching him in just about the same spot where she had been when he broke his heel the year before, along the opposite wall near the sound board. Her brown eyes were opened wide.

"Thank you very much, ladies and gentlemen," he said, climbing the stage. "OK, we're gonna speed it up a little bit. Too many slow songs—my bones are starting to get tight." On the tape, drums. An electric guitar twanged—"Rock-a-Hula-Baby." A fast one! At the tables women swayed and men nodded their heads in time. Everybody clapped along. Dennis smoothed through the first verses, bouncing as if he didn't have a care. He could have been on his patio. Then, at the song's break, he strutted across the stage. The guitars laid down a steady rhythm, and once in a while squealed as if in surprise. The backup singers on the tape shouted "Rock! Rock! Rock! Rock!" And Dennis cut loose. He did almost the same dance Elvis did at this exact point in *Blue Hawaii*. And he did it right.

His legs looked like liquid. His toes barely touched the floor. He swung his head from side to side and he pumped his arms.

"He always tells me he can't move!" Gail cried to a man standing next to her. "Look at him!"

All through the room, the women at their tables, the impersonators standing in the back, they all shouted it: *Rock! Rock! Rock! Rock!* And he did. He really did.

When he slowed down, he bent to kiss Jenna, who stood on her toes near the stage wearing a black dress covered in daisies. Elvis had slowed down the finish and so did Dennis, spinning his arms and making the women scream so much that his voice barely rose above them. And as they applauded and whooped he stood center stage and addressed the audience one more time: "Thank you, Memphis. God bless you." He saluted and ran down the steps to the stage door. "Dennis Stella!" Jackie said. And the crowd surrendered a loud *whooooooooo* that lasted until after he disappeared through the side door.

In the lull that followed, Chris asked Gail what had happened to "The Impossible Dream."

"He said it was just way too much," Gail said.

"But that really would have showed his . . ."

"Vocal quality, I know," Gail said. "We didn't know how to fit it in." She had wanted him to sing it, too, but he had to make a choice. Singing a song from Elvis's jumpsuit era while dressed in movie-era clothes would have been wrong and probably redundant. When Dennis was a boy, he had watched Elvis and wished he could be like him. That night he had lived a small piece of that dream. Maybe singing about it would have been beside the point.

Gail ducked through the crowd to the back of the room to watch for him. A woman caught up to her, breathing hard. "That was so different, so unique," she said. "Nobody has done that." If Gail noticed the irony of that remark, she didn't say. She smiled and nodded but kept her eyes on the door. Just then Dennis strolled in, one pink-and-white lei still framing his face. He shone with sweat, and he was smiling. People swarmed to greet him. The other Elvises shook his hand—Rob Hunter, Robert Washington, Irv Cass. Women swooped in with more cameras, and flashes strobed over him. He stood in the middle of the flashing lights and the fans and his friends, and they told him he was special, and they told him he was different. And over and over, they called his name.